COMMUNICATION: CONCEPTS AND PROCESSES

Joseph A. DeVito
*Herbert H. Lehman College
of the City University of New York*

PRENTICE-HALL, INC., Englewood Cliffs, New Jersey

To Boo

Library of Congress Catalog Card Number: 76-138382
Printed in the United States of America

Current Printing *(last number)*:
10 9 8 7 6 5 4 3 2 1

PRENTICE-HALL INTERNATIONAL INC.   London
PRENTICE-HALL OF AUSTRALIA, PTY. LTD.   Sydney
PRENTICE-HALL OF CANADA, LTD.   Toronto
PRENTICE-HALL OF INDIA PRIVATE LIMITED   New Delhi
PRENTICE-HALL OF JAPAN, INC.   Tokyo

Contents

iii

To the Student

I assembled the articles in this collection in the hope that they would provide you with greater insight into and understanding of communication and at the same time increase your own ability to communicate more meaningfully and more effectively. For the purposes of this reader to be achieved it does not matter whether you are sitting in a course entitled "Communication" or "Fundamentals of Speech," "Principles of Rhetoric," "Public Speaking," "Persuasion," "Group Discussion," "English Composition," "Argumentation," or whatever. All of these courses are—or at least should be—concerned with communication and it is communication that these readings deal with.

The emphasis or point of view which pervades the entire collection should be stated at the outset. As viewed here communication is not a device or bag of tricks for winning an argument or for selling a product. Rather, it is a means for breaking down the barriers to interaction, a means for achieving mutual understanding, a means for relating to each other on a more meaningful level, a means for communion. These are the significant ends of communication. In some of the articles these functions of communication are explicit; in others they are only implicit. Each, however, contributes substantially—whether directly or indirectly— to the total scheme. If the insights provided by these articles help us to achieve these goals, they and this reader will have served a most important purpose.

In selecting the articles to be included I used a number of different guidelines and these should be made explicit since they will give you a clearer idea of what to expect in the pages that follow. First, I included only those articles which required no prior understanding of communication theories and principles.

Second, I attempted to achieve a balance between those articles which are currently regarded as "classics" in the literature of communication and those which represent new and different approaches. Thus, Wendell Johnson's "The Fateful Process of Mr. A Talking to Mr. B" and Daniel Katz's "Psychological Barriers to Communication" have been reprinted in a number of collections and have reached the status of near classics. Their influence has been considerable and their importance verified by their endurance. Perhaps their popularity is due to their being as "contemporary" and as relevant today as they were when they were first published. Other articles, such as Albert Mehrabian's "Communication Without Words" and Jack Gibb's "Defensive Communication" are more recent contributions and consequently have not yet achieved wide recognition. Yet, they too pose highly significant questions which demand thoughtful consideration.

Third, I tried to maintain a balance between those articles which deal with general and abstract formulations and those which offer specific and concrete principles. A judicious mixture of the abstract and the concrete, the general and the specific, is essential if the structure and function of communication are to be understood in any meaningful sense and if the resources of communication are to be mastered.

Fourth, I selected only those articles which I felt to be well written and interesting to read. Nothing is worse than creating a text which contains all the right information but never gets read because it puts you to sleep. The readings contained here are all written in a lively and penetrating manner and will easily hold your interest and attention.

The readings are divided into three major sections. The first section, "Communication Processes," contains four papers, each of which explains the nature of communication from a distinctly different point of view. These articles should serve to introduce you to communication-as-a-whole before you tackle articles dealing with specific elements and processes. Ideally, these articles will provide a framework into which the remaining articles may be fit.

The second section, "Communication Messages and Channels," contains eight articles. Each of these deals with a different approach to the nature and function of messages and to the channels by which information may be communicated.

The third section, "Communication Sources and Receivers," contains eight articles dealing with the problems of eliminating communication barriers and of increasing our abilities for meaningful communication.

Each article is prefaced by a brief introductory statement which attempts to provide some general orientation. Following each article is a brief list of questions for discussion. These questions are designed to provide you with the opportunity to work actively with the concepts and processes discussed in the article and to relate these insights to your own experiences and interests.

At the end of the reader is a bibliography of general works in communication with brief annotations designed to guide your further reading. Ideally, the references included here will be consulted, read, and most importantly, questioned.

These articles will introduce you to a subject matter which I personally find challenging, fascinating, and most meaningful. Hopefully, you will find it equally so.

To the Instructor

Communication: *Concepts and Processes* was designed for the undergraduate college course in communication, regardless of its specific orientation—whether theory or practice, whether oral or written. Common to courses in rhetoric, oral communication, public speaking, persuasion, group discussion, English composition, argumentation and the like are certain fundamental and universal principles of communication. It is to these principles that the authors represented in this volume have addressed themselves.

This collection was prepared to serve either of two basic functions. As a supplement it may be used with any of the standard textbooks on speech fundamentals, rhetoric, persuasion, group discussion, public speaking, argumentation, and composition. Since each article can be understood and appreciated as a separate unit, there is complete flexibility; articles may be rearranged to suit any number of purposes and can be easily coordinated with specific texts to serve the needs of particular courses and syllabi.

Since the articles included here cover most of the topics normally included in introductory courses, this collection may also be used as the principal text in which case it may be supplemented by one or more of the numerous paperbacks now available or by lectures.

The question following each article should provide the basis for stimulating and lively classroom discussion and debate and may also serve as topics for oral and/or written assignments. Primary emphasis is placed on encouraging the student to relate the content of the readings to his own everyday experiences. Only when he does this will he be able to really understand and internalize the principles of communication.

The bibliography should provide the student with additional avenues for exploring communication. The number of works is specifically limited so as to provide more effective guidelines to further reading. Additional references can be found in all of the works listed in the bibliography.

Acknowledgments

It is a pleasure to thank those persons who provided me with the motivation and the guidance for writing this book. As with all teachers, my first debt is to my students who stimulated and challenged my thinking on communication. I especially wish to thank Jean Civikly, Cynthia Roth, and Diane Shore, now graduate students in communication at Florida State University, Temple University, and the University of Illinois, Chicago Circle, respectively, for the many insights into communication they shared with me.

To all my colleagues at Herbert H. Lehman College and particularly to our Chairman, Cj Stevens, I owe a great deal. They have consistently provided the stimulating atmosphere necessary for such a task. Special thanks goes to Professors Helen Fleshler and Norman Isaacson. Together we had the pleasure of team-teaching an undergraduate seminar in communication theory, from which many of the ideas in this book evolved. From them I have learned much.

Professor James C. McCroskey, Illinois State University, Professor Larry L. Barker, Florida State University, and Professor Robert J. Kibler, Florida State University, who read earlier versions of the manuscript, offered many helpful suggestions which were incorporated into the finished product. For these suggestions and for their reinforcing commentaries I am very thankful.

I am most pleased to acknowledge all the help given by the people at Prentice-Hall, especially Charles Durang for providing the initial encouragement to write this book, Arthur M. Rittenberg for allowing me the freedom to develop this reader in the way I wanted and for his helpful guidance, and Ellen Traul for making the transition from manuscript to book a most easy and enjoyable one.

Most importantly, I would like to thank the authors and the copyright holders for granting me permission to reprint the articles. Without them, of course, the book would not be.

J. A. D.

COMMUNICATION PROCESSES

The
Speech
Chain

PETER B. DENES
ELLIOT N. PINSON

Denes and Pinson here introduce the concept of the
"speech chain" by which they mean "the events linking the
speaker's brain with the listener's brain" and provide
us with a schematic diagram of the speech communication
process. Viewing speech communication primarily from a
physical and physiological perspective, the authors provide
an essential foundation for examining the more complex
and abstract dimensions of communication which are
treated in later articles.

We usually take for granted our ability to produce and understand speech and give little thought to its nature and function, just as we are not particularly aware of the action of our hearts, brains, or other essential organs. It is not surprising, therefore, that many people overlook the great influence of speech on the development and normal functioning of human society.

Wherever human beings live together, they develop a system of talking to each other; even people in the most primitive societies use speech. Speech, in fact, is one of those few, basic abilities—tool making is another—that set us apart from animals and are closely connected with our ability to think abstractly.

Why is speech so important? One reason is that the development of human civilization is made possible—to a great extent—by man's ability to share experiences, to exchange ideas and to transmit knowledge from one generation to another; in other words, his ability to communicate with other men. We can communicate with each other in many ways. The smoke signals of the Apache Indian, the starter's pistol in a 100-yard dash, the finger signing language used by deaf people, the Morse Code, and various systems of writing are just a few examples of the many different systems of communication developed by man. Unquestionably, however, speech is the system that man found to be far more efficient and convenient than any other.

You may think that writing is a more important means of communication. After all, the development of civilization and the output of printing presses seem to parallel each other, and the written word appears to be a more efficient and more durable means of transmitting intelligence. It must be remembered, however, that no matter how many books and newspapers are printed, the amount of intelligence exchanged

"The Speech Chain." From Peter B. Denes and Elliot N. Pinson, The Speech Chain: The Physics and Biology of Spoken Language (*Murray Hill, New Jersey: Bell Telephone Laboratories, 1963*), *pp. 1–8. Reprinted by permission of Bell Telephone Laboratories.*

by speech is still vastly greater. The widespread use of books and printed matter may very well be an indication of a highly developed civilization, but so is the greater use of telephone systems. Those areas of the world where civilization is most highly developed are also the areas with the greatest density of telephones; and countries bound by social and political ties are usually connected by a well developed telephone system.

We can further bolster our argument that speech has a more fundamental influence than writing on the development of civilization by citing the many human societies that have developed and flourished without evolving a system of reading and writing. We know of no civilization, however, where speech was not available.

Perhaps the best example of the overwhelming importance of speech in human society is a comparison of the social attitudes of the blind to those of the deaf. Generally, blind people tend to get along with their fellow human beings despite their handicap. But the deaf, who can still read and write, often feel cut off from society. A deaf person, deprived of his primary means of communication, tends to withdraw from the world and live within himself.

In short, human society relies heavily on the free and easy interchange of ideas among its members and, for one reason or another, man has found speech to be his most convenient form of communication.

Through its constant use as a tool essential to daily living, speech has developed into a highly efficient system for the exchange of even our most complex ideas. It is a system particularly suitable for widespread use under the constantly changing and varied conditions of life. It is suitable because it remains functionally unaffected by the many different voices, speaking habits, dialects, and accents of the millions who use a common language. And it is suitable for widespread use because speech —to a surprising extent—is invulnerable to severe noise, distortion, and interference.

Speech is well worth careful study. It is worthwhile because the study of speech provides useful insights into the nature and history of human civilization. It is worthwhile for the communications engineer because a better understanding of the speech mechanism enables him to exploit its built-in features in developing better and more efficient communications systems. It is worthwhile for all of us because we depend on speech so heavily for communicating with others.

The study of speech is also important in the just-emerging field of man-to-machine communication. We all use automatons, like the dial telephone and automatic elevator, which either get their instructions from us or report back to us on their operations. Frequently they do both, like the highly complex digital computers used in scientific laboratories. In designing communication systems or "languages" to link man and machine, it may prove especially worthwhile to have a firm understanding of speech, that system of man-to-man communication whose development is based on the experience of many generations.

When most people stop to consider speech, they think only in terms of moving lips and tongue. A few others who have found out about sound waves, perhaps in the course of building hi-fi sets, will also associate certain kinds of sound waves with speech. In reality, speech is a far more complex process, involving many more levels of human activity, than such a simple approach would suggest.

A convenient way of examining what happens during speech is to take the simple situation of two people talking to each other; one of them, the speaker, transmits information to the other, the listener. The first thing the speaker has to do is arrange his thoughts, decide what he wants to say, and put what he wants to say into *linguistic form*. The message is put into linguistic form by selecting the right words and phrases to express its meaning, and by placing these words in the correct order required by the grammatical rules of the language. This process is associated with activity in the speaker's brain, and it is in the brain that appropriate instructions, in the form of impulses along the motor nerves, are sent to the muscles of the vocal organs, the tongue, the lips, and the vocal cords. The nerve impulses set the vocal muscles into movement which, in turn, produces minute pressure changes in the surrounding air. We call these pressure changes a sound wave.

The movements of the vocal organs generate a speech sound wave that travels through the air between speaker and listener. Pressure changes at the ear activate the listener's hearing mechanism and produce nerve impulses that travel along the acoustic nerve to the listener's brain. In the listener's brain, a considerable amount of nerve activity is already taking place, and this activity is modified by the nerve impulses arriving from the ear. This modification of brain activity, in ways we do not fully understand, brings about recognition of the speaker's message. We see, therefore, that speech communications consists of a chain of events linking the speaker's brain with the listener's brain. We shall call this chain of events *the speech chain*. (See figure, p. 7.)

It might be worthwhile to mention at this point that the speech chain has an important side link. In the simple speaker-listener situation just described, there are really two listeners, not one, because the speaker not only speaks, he also listens to his own voice. In listening, he continuously compares the quality of the sounds he produces with the sound qualities he intended to produce and makes the adjustments necessary to match the results with his intentions.

There are many ways to show that a speaker is his own listener. Perhaps the most amusing is to delay the sound "fed-back" to the speaker. This can be done simply by recording the speaker's voice on a tape re-

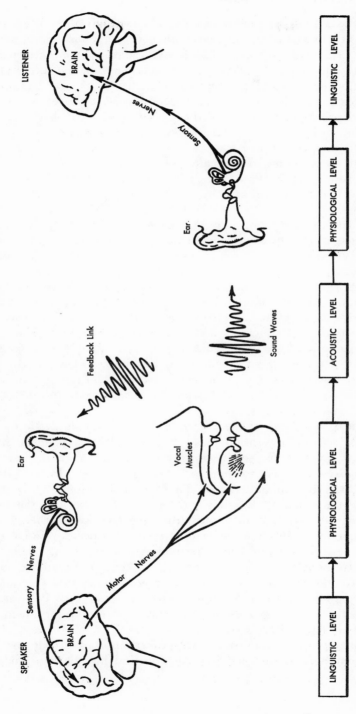

THE SPEECH CHAIN

THE SPEECH CHAIN: the different forms in which a spoken message exists in its progress from the mind of the speaker to the mind of the listener.

corder and playing it back a fraction of a second later. The speaker listens to the delayed version over earphones. Under such circumstances, the unexpected delay in the fed-back sound makes the speaker stammer and slur. This is the so-called delayed speech feed-back effect. Another example of the importance of "feed-back" is the general deterioration of the speech of people who have suffered prolonged deafness. Deafness, of course, deprives these people of the speech chain's feed-back link. To some limited extent, we can tell the kind of deafness from the type of speech deterioration it produces.

Let us go back now to the main speech chain, the links that connect speaker with listener. We have seen that the transmission of a message begins with the selection of suitable words and sentences. This can be called the *linguistic level* of the speech chain.

The speech event continues on the *physiological level,* with neural and muscular activity, and ends, on the speaker's side, with the generation and transmission of a sound wave, the *physical level* of the speech chain.

At the listener's end of the chain, the process is reversed. Events start on the physical level, when the incoming sound wave activates the hearing mechanism. They continue on the physiological level with neural activity in the hearing and perceptual mechanisms. The speech chain is completed on the linguistic level when the listener recognizes the words and sentences transmitted by the speaker. The speech chain, therefore, involves activity on at least three different levels, the linguistic, physiological, and physical, first on the speaker's side and then at the listener's end.

We may also think of the speech chain as a communication system in which ideas to be transmitted are represented by a code that undergoes transformations as speech events proceed from one level to another. We can draw an analogy here between speech and Morse Code. In Morse Code, certain patterns of dots and dashes stand for different letters of the alphabet; the dots and dashes are a code for the letters. This code can also be transformed from one form to another. For example, a series of dots and dashes on a piece of paper can be converted into an acoustic sequence, like "beep-bip-bip-beep." In the same way, the words of our language are a code for concepts and material objects. The word "dog" is the code for a four-legged animal that wags its tail, just as "dash-dash-dash" is Morse Code for the letter "O." We learn the code words of a language—and the rules for combining them into sentences—when we learn to speak.

During speech transmission, the speaker's linguistic code of words and sentences is transformed into physiological and physical codes—in other words, into corresponding sets of muscle movements and air vibrations—before being reconverted into a linguistic code at the listener's end. This is analogous to translating the written "dash-dash-dash" of Morse Code into the sounds, "beep-beep-beep."

Although we can regard speech transmission as a chain of events in which a code for certain ideas is transformed from one level or medium to another, it would be a great mistake to think that corresponding events at the different levels are the same. There is some relationship, to be sure, but the events are far from being identical. For example, there is no guarantee that people will produce sound waves with identical characteristics when they pronounce the same word. In fact, they are more likely to produce sound waves of different characteristics when they pronounce the same word. By the same token, they may very well generate similar sound waves when pronouncing different words.

This state of affairs was clearly demonstrated in an experiment carried out a few years ago. A group of people listened to the same sound wave, representing a word, on three occasions when the word was used in three different-sounding sentences. The listeners agreed that the test word was either "bit" or "bet" or "bat," depending on which of the three sentences was used.

The experiment clearly shows that the general circumstances (context) under which we listen to speech profoundly affect the kind of words we associate with particular sound waves. In other words, the relationship between a word and a particular sound wave, or between a word and a particular muscle movement or pattern of nerve impulses, is not unique. There is no label on a speech sound wave that invariably associates it with a particular word. Depending on context, we recognize a particular sound wave as one word or another. A good example of this is reported by people who speak several languages fluently. They sometimes recognize indistinctly heard phrases as being spoken in one of their languages, but realize later that the conversation was in another of their languages.

Knowledge of the right context can even make the difference between understanding and not understanding a particular sound wave sequence. You probably know that at some airports you can pay a dime and listen in on the conversations between pilots and the control tower. The chances are that many of the sentences would be incomprehensible to you because of noise and distortion. Yet this same speech wave would be clearly intelligible to the pilots simply because they have more knowledge of context than you. In this case, the context is provided by their experience in listening under conditions of distortion, and by their greater knowledge of the kind of messages to expect.

The strong influence of circumstance on what you recognize is not confined to speech. When you watch television or movies, you probably consider the scenes you see as quite life-like. But pictures on television are much smaller than life-size and much larger on a movie screen. Context will make the small television picture, the life-sized original and the huge movie scene appear to be the same size. Black-and-white television and movies also appear quite life-like, despite their lack of true color. Once again, context makes the multicolored original and the black and white screen seem similar. In speech, as in these examples, we are quite unaware of our heavy reliance on context.

We can say, therefore, that speakers will not generally produce identical sound waves when they pronounce the same words on different occasions. The listener, in recognizing speech, does not rely solely on information derived from the speech wave he receives. He also relies on his knowledge of an intricate communication system subject to the rules of language and speech, and on cues provided by the subject matter and the identity of the speaker.

In speech communication, then, we do not actually rely on a precise knowledge of specific cues. Instead, we relate a great variety of ambiguous cues against the background of the complex system we call our common language. When you think about it, there is really no other way speech could function efficiently. It does seem unlikely that millions of speakers, with all their different voice qualities, speaking habits, and accents, would ever produce anything like identical sound waves when they say the same words. People engaged in speech research know this only too well, much to their regret. Even though our instruments for measuring the characteristics of sound waves are considerably more accurate and flexible than the human ear, we are still unable to build a machine that will recognize speech. We can measure characteristics of speech waves with great accuracy, but we do not know the nature and rules of the contextual system against which the results of our measurements must be related, as they are so successfully related in the brains of listeners.

For Discussion

1. Denes and Pinson argue that speech is a more important communication medium than is writing. Do you agree with their position? What arguments could you advance for or against their position?

2. How do the systems of speech and writing differ from each other? More specifically, what means of communication does our speech system have that

our writing system does not and vice-versa? For what communication purposes and in what communication situations is speech more appropriate than writing? When is writing more appropriate than speech?

3. Denes and Pinson provide a simplified diagram of the communication process which omits many significant elements and processes. What other elements and processes should be included? What is their function in communication?

4. At what points in this model of the speech chain may breakdowns in communication occur? Identify some of the possible communication breakdowns—their causes and remedies.

How
Communication
Works

WILBUR SCHRAMM

Wilbur Schramm here provides an overview of the elements and processes which are common to all forms of communication—communication with ourselves, communication with one person or a group of persons, or communication with a mass audience of thousands or even millions. The concepts which Schramm introduces, such as encoder, decoder, redundancy, feedback, and the like provide us with a useful beginning vocabulary for conceptualizing and talking about communication and communication processes.

Communication comes from the Latin *communis,* common. When we communicate we are trying to establish a "commonness" with someone. That is, we are trying to share information, an idea, or an attitude. At this moment I am trying to communicate to you the idea that the essence of communication is getting the receiver and the sender "tuned" together for a particular message. At this same moment, someone somewhere is excitedly phoning the fire department that the house is on fire. Somewhere else a young man in a parked automobile is trying to convey the understanding that he is moon-eyed because he loves the young lady. Somewhere else a newspaper is trying to persuade its readers to believe as it does about the Republican Party. All these are forms of communication, and the process in each case is essentially the same.

Communication always requires at least three elements—the source, the message, and the destination. A *source* may be an individual (speaking, writing, drawing, gesturing) or a communication organization (like a newspaper, publishing house, television station, or motion picture studio). The *message* may be in the form of ink on paper, sound waves in the air, impulses in an electric current, a wave of the hand, a flag in the air, or any other signal capable of being interpreted meaningfully. The *destination* may be an *individual* listening, watching, or reading; or a member of a *group,* such as a discussion group, a lecture audience, a football crowd, or a mob; or an individual member of the particular group we call the *mass audience,* such as the reader of a newspaper or a viewer of television.

Now what happens when the source tries to build up this "commonness" with his intended receiver? First, the source encodes his message. That is, he takes the information or feeling he wants to share and puts

"How Communication Works." From Wilbur Schramm, "How Communication Works," in The Process and Effects of Mass Communication, *ed., Wilbur Schramm (Urbana, Illinois: University of Illinois Press, 1954), pp. 3–10. Reprinted by permission of University of Illinois Press.*

it into a form that can be transmitted. The "pictures in our heads" can't be transmitted until they are coded. When they are coded into spoken words, they can be transmitted easily and effectively, but they can't travel very far unless radio carries them. If they are coded into written words, they go more slowly than spoken words, but they go farther and last longer. Indeed, some messages long outlive their senders—the *Iliad*, for instance; the Gettysburg address; Chartres cathedral. Once coded and sent, a message is quite free of its sender, and what it does is beyond the power of the sender to change. Every writer feels a sense of helplessness when he finally commits his story or his poem to print; you doubtless feel the same way when you mail an important letter. Will it reach the right person? Will he understand it as you intend him to? Will he respond as you want him to? For in order to complete the act of communication the message must be decoded. And there is good reason, as we shall see, for the sender to wonder whether his receiver will really be in tune with him, whether the message will be interpreted without distortion, whether the "picture in the head" of the receiver will bear any resemblance to that in the head of the sender.

We are talking about something very like a radio or telephone circuit. In fact, it is perfectly possible to draw a picture of the human communication system that way:

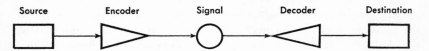

Substitute "microphone" for encoder, and "earphone" for decoder and you are talking about electronic communication. Consider that the "source" and "encoder" are one person, "decoder" and "destination" are another, and the signal is language, and you are talking about human communication.

Now it is perfectly possible by looking at those diagrams to predict how such a system will work. For one thing, such a system can be no stronger than its weakest link. In engineering terms, there may be filtering or distortion at any stage. In human terms, if the source does not have adequate or clear information; if the message is not encoded fully, accurately, effectively in transmittable signs; if these are not transmitted fast enough and accurately enough, despite interference and competition, to the desired receiver; if the message is not decoded in a pattern that corresponds to the encoding; and finally, if the destination is unable to handle the decoded message so as to produce the desired response— then, obviously, the system is working at less than top efficiency. When we realize that *all* these steps must be accomplished with relatively high efficiency if any communication is to be successful, the everyday act of explaining something to a stranger, or writing a letter, seems a minor miracle.

A system like this will have a maximum capacity for handling information and this will depend on the separate capacities of each unit on the chain—for example, the capacity of the channel (how fast can one talk?) or the capacity of the encoder (can your student understand something explained quickly?). If the coding is good (for example, no unnecessary words) the capacity of the channel can be approached, but it can never be exceeded. You can readily see that one of the great skills of communication will lie in knowing how near capacity to operate a channel.

This is partly determined for us by the nature of the language. English, like every other language, has its sequences of words and sounds governed by certain probabilities. If it were organized so that no set of probabilities governed the likelihood that certain words would follow certain other words (for example, that a noun would follow an adjective, or that "States" or "Nations" would follow "United") then we would have nonsense. As a matter of fact, we can calculate the relative amount of freedom open to us in writing any language. For English, the freedom is about 50 per cent. (Incidentally, this is about the required amount of freedom to enable us to construct interesting crossword puzzles. Shannon has estimated that if we had about 70 per cent freedom, we could construct three-dimensional crossword puzzles. If we had only 20 per cent, crossword puzzle making would not be worth while).

So much for language *redundancy,* as communication theorists call it, meaning the percentage of the message which is not open to free choice. But there is also the communicator's redundancy, and this is an important aspect of constructing a message. For if we think our audience may have a hard time understanding the message, we can deliberately introduce more redundancy; we can repeat (just as the radio operator on a ship may send "SOS" over and over again to make sure it is heard and decoded), or we can give examples and analogies. In other words, we always have to choose between transmitting more information in a given time, or transmitting less and repeating more in the hope of being better understood. And as you know, it is often a delicate choice, because too slow a rate will bore an audience, whereas too fast a rate may confuse them.

Perhaps the most important thing about such a system is one we have been talking about all too glibly—the fact that receiver and sender must be in tune. This is clear enough in the case of a radio transmitter and receiver, but somewhat more complicated when it means that a human receiver must be able to understand a human sender.

Let us redraw our diagram in very simple form, like this:

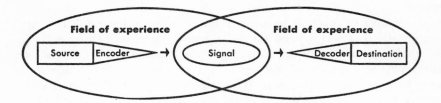

Think of those circles as the accumulated experience of the two individuals trying to communicate. The source can encode, and the destination can decode, only in terms of the experience each has had. If we have never learned any Russian, we can neither code nor decode in that language. If an African tribesman has never seen or heard of an airplane, he can only decode the sight of a plane in terms of whatever experience he has had. The plane may seem to him to be a bird, and the aviator a god borne on wings. If the circles have a large area in common, then communication is easy. If the circles do not meet—if there has been no common experience—then communication is impossible. If the circles have only a small area in common—that is, if the experiences of source and destination have been strikingly unlike—then it is going to be very difficult to get an intended meaning across from one to the other. This is the difficulty we face when a non-science-trained person tries to read Einstein, or when we try to communicate with another culture much different from ours.

The source, then, tries to encode in such a way as to make it easy for the destination to tune in the message—to relate it to parts of his experience which are much like those of the source. What does he have to work with?

Messages are made up of signs. A sign is a signal that stands for something in experience. The word "dog" is a sign that stands for our generalized experience with dogs. The word would be meaningless to a person who came from a dog-less island and had never read of or heard of a dog. But most of us have learned that word by association, just as we learn most signs. Someone called our attention to an animal, and said "dog." When we learned the word, it produced in us much the same response as the object it stood for. That is, when we heard "dog" we could recall the appearance of dogs, their sound, their feel, perhaps their smell. But there is an important difference between the sign and the object: the sign always represents the object at a reduced level of cues. By this we mean simply that the sign will not call forth all the responses that the object itself will call forth. The sign "dog," for example, will probably not call forth in us the same wariness or attention a strange dog might attract if it wandered into our presence. This is the price we pay for portability in language. We have a sign system that we can use in place of the less portable originals (for example, Margaret Mitchell could re-create the burning of Atlanta in a novel, and a photograph could transport world-wide the appearance of a bursting atomic bomb), but our sign system is merely a kind of shorthand. The coder has to be able to write the shorthand, the decoder to read it. And no two persons have learned exactly the same system. For example, a person who has known only Arctic huskies will not have learned exactly the same meaning for the shorthand sign "dog" as will a person who comes from a city where he has known only pekes and poms.

We have come now to a point where we need to tinker a little more with our diagram of the communication process. It is obvious that each person in the communication process is both an encoder and a decoder. He receives and transmits. He must be able to write a readable shorthand, and to read other people's shorthand. Therefore, it is possible to describe either sender or receiver in a human communication system thus:

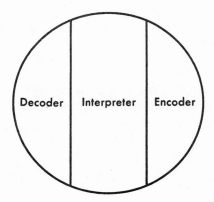

What happens when a signal comes to you? Remember that it comes in the form of a sign. If you have learned the sign, you have learned certain responses with it. We can call these mediatory responses, because they mediate what happens to the message in your nervous system. These responses are the *meaning* the sign has for you. They are learned from experience, as we said, but they are affected by the state of your organism at the moment. For example, if you are hungry, a picture of a steak may not arouse exactly the same response in you as when you are overfed.

But subject to these effects, the mediatory responses will then determine what you do about the sign. For you have learned other sets of reactions connected to the mediatory responses. A sign that means a certain thing to you will start certain other processes in your nerves and muscles. A sign that means "fire," for example, will certainly trigger off some activity in you. A sign that means you are in danger may start the process in your nerves and muscles that makes you say "help!" In other words, the meaning that results from your decoding of a sign will start you *en*coding. Exactly *what* you encode will depend on your choice of the responses available in the situation and connected with the meaning.

Whether this encoding actually results in some overt communication or action depends partly on the barriers in the way. You may think it better to keep silent. And if an action does occur, the nature of the action will also depend on the avenues for action available to you and the barriers in your way. The code of your group may not sanction the action you want to take. The meaning of a sign may make you want to hit the person who has said it, but he may be too big, or you may be in the wrong social situation. You may merely ignore him, or "look murder at him," or say something nasty about him to someone else.

But whatever the exact result, this is the process in which you are constantly engaged. You are constantly decoding signs from your environment, interpreting these signs, and encoding something as a result. In fact, it is misleading to think of the communication process as starting somewhere and ending somewhere. It is really endless. We are little switchboard centers handling and rerouting the great endless current of communication. We can accurately think of communication as passing through us—changed, to be sure, by our interpretations, our habits, our abilities and capabilities, but the input still being reflected in the output.

We need now to add another element to our description of the communication process. Consider what happens in a conversation between two people. One is constantly communicating back to the other, thus:

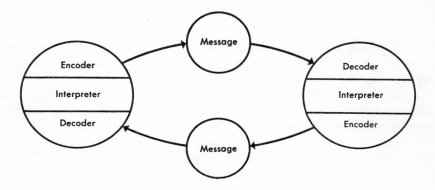

The return process is called *feedback,* and plays a very important part in communication because it tells us how our messages are being interpreted. Does the hearer say, "Yes, yes, that's right," as we try to persuade him? Does he nod his head in agreement? Does a puzzled frown appear on his forehead? Does he look away as though he were losing interest? All these are feedback. So is a letter to the editor of a newspaper, protesting an editorial. So is an answer to a letter. So is the applause of a lecture audience. An experienced communicator is attentive to feedback, and constantly modifies his messages in light of what he observes in or hears from his audience.

At least one other example of feedback, also, is familiar to all of us. We get feedback from our own messages. That is, we hear our own voices and can correct mispronunciations. We see the words we have written on paper, and can correct misspellings or change the style. When we do that, here is what is happening:

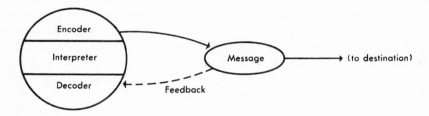

It is clear that in any kind of communication we rarely send out messages in a single channel, and this is the final element we must add to our account of the communication process. When you speak to me, the sound waves from your voice are the primary message. But there are others: the expression on your face, your gestures, the relation of a given message to past messages. Even the primary message conveys information on several levels. It gives me words to decode. It emphasizes certain words above others. It presents the words in a pattern of intonation and timing which contribute to the total meaning. The quality of your voice (deep, high, shrill, rasping, rich, thin, loud, soft) itself carries information about you and what you are saying.

This multiple channel situation exists even in printed mass communication, where the channels are perhaps most restricted. Meaning is conveyed, not only by the words in a news item, but also by the size of the headline, the position on the page and the page in the paper, the association with pictures, the use of boldface and other typographical devices. All these tell us something about the item. Thus we can visualize the typical channel of communication, not as a simple telegraph circuit, in which current does or does not flow, but rather as a sort of coaxial cable in which many signals flow in parallel from source toward the destination.

These parallel relationships are complex, but you can see their general pattern. A communicator can emphasize a point by adding as many parallel messages as he feels are deserved. If he is communicating by speaking, he can stress a word, pause just before it, say it with a rising inflection, gesture while he says it, look earnestly at his audience. Or he can keep all the signals parallel—except *one*. He can speak solemnly, but wink, as Lowell Thomas sometimes does. He can stress a word in a way that makes it mean something else—for example, "That's a *fine* job you did!" And by so doing he conveys secondary meanings of sarcasm or humor or doubt.

The same thing can be done with printed prose, with broadcast, with television or films. The secondary channels of the sight-sound media are especially rich. I am reminded of a skillful but deadly job done entirely with secondary channels on a certain political candidate. A sidewalk interview program was filmed to run in local theaters. Ostensibly it was a completely impartial program. An equal number of followers of each candidate were interviewed—first, one who favored Candidate A, then one who favored Candidate B, and so on. They were asked exactly the same questions, and said about the same things, although on opposite sides of the political fence, of course. But there was one interesting difference. Whereas the supporters of Candidate A were ordinary folks, not outstandingly attractive or impressive, the followers of Candidate B who were chosen to be interviewed invariably had something slightly wrong with them. They looked wildeyed, or they stuttered, or they wore unpressed suits. The extra meaning was communicated. Need I say which candidate won?

But this is the process by which communication works, whether it is mass communication, or communication in a group, or communication between individuals.

For Discussion

1. Schramm cites Chartres cathedral as an example of a communication message. What properties does this cathedral possess which would qualify it as a message? In what ways does it differ from speeches, letters, books, and what we would traditionally classify as messages? Do you agree with Schramm that it would be considered a "message"?

2. "We always have to choose," says Schramm, "between transmitting more information in a given time, or transmitting less and repeating more in the

hope of being better understood. . . . it is often a delicate choice, because too slow a rate will bore an audience, whereas too fast a rate may confuse them." Analyze the communication patterns and habits of the instructors you have this term. Do some try to communicate too much while others communicate too little? Are these instructors aware of the capacity of their students for taking in information? From observing their communications, what assumptions do you think these different instructors have made about their students' abilities?

3. In discussing the importance of the fields of experience between source and receiver Schramm notes that communication is possible only to the degree that these fields overlap. Relate this concept to the problems of children communicating with their parents. How might parent-child communication be improved? Are these same problems present in teacher-student communication? How might such communication be improved?

4. During a class lecture observe the role of feedback. What kinds of feedback do the students give the instructor? What kinds does the instructor give the students? Is the instructor aware of the feedback from students? Does he modify his messages on the basis of this feedback? In what ways? Might the ability to perceive and act on the basis of feedback be used as one standard with which to measure effectiveness in communicating and teaching? Why?

5. What elements would you include in a model of communication which Schramm has not included? Diagram the process of communication as you understand it at present. Of what value is your model?

The Fateful Process
of Mr. A
Talking to Mr. B

WENDELL JOHNSON

In the past twenty years the field of communication has been literally flooded with models and diagrams of the communication process. The model presented here by Wendell Johnson is clearly among the best of these. The model describes not only the elements and processes which enter into the communication act but also defines those areas where communication breakdowns are most likely to occur and suggests both reasons and remedies for these failures to communicate. While the illustrations are drawn primarily from the field of business and industry, the communication process, problems, and preventives discussed are basically the same for all forms of interpersonal and group interaction.

It is a source of never-ending astonishment to me that there are so few men who possess in high degree the peculiar pattern of abilities required for administrative success. There are hundreds who can "meet people well" for every one who can gain the confidence, goodwill, and deep esteem of his fellows. There are thousands who can speak fluently and pleasantly for every one who can make statements of clear significance. There are tens of thousands who are cunning and clever for every one who is wise and creative.

Why is this so? The two stock answers which I have heard so often in so many different contexts are: (1) administrators are born, and (2) administrators are made.

The trouble with the first explanation—entirely apart from the fact that it contradicts the second—is that those who insist that only God can make a chairman of the board usually think themselves into unimaginative acceptance of men as they find them. Hence any attempt at improving men for leadership is automatically ruled out.

Meanwhile, those who contend that administrators can be tailor-made are far from omniscient in their varied approaches to the practical job of transforming bright young men into the inspired leaders without which our national economy could not long survive. Nevertheless, it is in the self-acknowledged but earnest fumblings of those who would seek out and train our future executives and administrators that we may find our finest hopes and possibilities.

This article does not propose to wrap up the problem of what will make men better administrators. Such an attempt would be presumptuous and foolhardy on anyone's part; there are too many side issues, too many far-reaching ramifications. Rather, this is simply an exploration into one of the relatively uncharted areas of the subject, made with the

"The Fateful Process of Mr. A Talking to Mr. B." From Wendell Johnson, "The Fateful Process of Mr. A Talking to Mr. B," Harvard Business Review, XXXI (1953), 49–56. © 1952 by the President and Fellows of Harvard College; all rights reserved. Reprinted by permission of Harvard Business Review.

thought that the observations presented may help others to find their way a little better. At the same time, the objective of our exploration can perhaps be described as an oasis of insight in what otherwise is a rather frightening expanse of doubt and confusion.

The ability to respond to and with symbols would seem to be the single most important attribute of great administrators. Adroitness in reading and listening, in speaking and writing, in figuring, in drawing designs and diagrams, in smoothing the skin to conceal and wrinkling it to express inner feelings, and in making the pictures inside the head by means of which thinking, imagining, pondering, and evaluating are carried on—these are the fundamental skills without which no man may adequately exercise administrative responsibilities.

Many of the more significant aspects of these administrative prerequisites may be brought into focus by means of a consideration of what is probably the most fateful of all human functions, and certainly the one function indispensable to our economic life: communication. So let us go on, now, to look at the process of communication and to try to understand the difficulties and disorders that beset us in our efforts to communicate with one another.

THE PROCESS DIAGRAMED

Several years ago I spent five weeks as a member of a group of university professors who had the job of setting up a project concerned with the study of speech. In the course of this academic exploring party we spent a major part of our time talking—or at least making noises—about "communication." By the second or third day it had become plain, and each day thereafter it became plainer, that we had no common and clear notion of just what the word "communication" meant.

After several days of deepening bewilderment, I recalled an old saying: "If you can't diagram it, you don't understand it." The next day I made a modest attempt to bring order out of the chaos—for myself, at least—by drawing on the blackboard a simple diagram representing what seemed to me to be the main steps in the curious process of Mr. A talking to Mr. B. Then I tried to discuss communication by describing what goes on at each step—and what might go wrong. Since sketching that first diagram on the blackboard eight or nine years ago, I have refined and elaborated it, and I have tried from time to time, as I shall again here, to discuss the process of communication in terms of it (see figure, p. 25).[1]

[1] The diagram, with a discussion of it, was first published in my book *People in Quandaries* (New York, Harper & Brothers, 1946), Chapter 18, "The

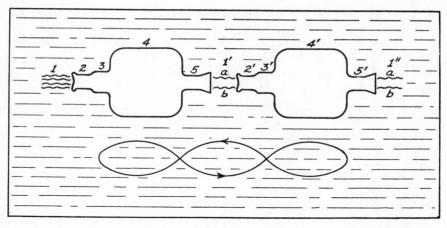

KEY: Stage 1, event, or source of stimulation, external to the sensory end organs of the speaker; Stage 2, sensory stimulation; Stage 3, pre-verbal neurophysiological state; Stage 4, transformation of pre-verbal into symbolic forms; Stage 5, verbal formulations in "final draft" for overt expression; Stage 1', transformation of verbal formulations into (a) air waves and (b) light waves, which serve as sources of stimulation for the listener (who may be either the speaker himself or another person); Stages 2' through 1" correspond, in the listener, to Stages 2 through 1'. The arrowed loops represent the functional interrelationships of the stages in the process as a whole.

INSIDE MR. A

What appears to take place when Mr. A talks to Mr. B is that first of all, at Stage 1, some event occurs which is external to Mr. A's eyes, ears, taste buds, or other sensory organs. This event arouses the sensory stimulation that occurs at Stage 2. The dotted lines are intended to represent the fact that the process of communication takes place in a "field of reality," a context of energy manifestations external to the communica-

---

Urgency of Paradise." I developed it further in *The Communication of Ideas,* edited by Lyman Bryson (New York, Harper & Brothers, 1948), Chapter 5, "Speech and Personality." It was also reproduced in *Mass Communications,* edited by Wilbur Schramm (Urbana, University of Illinois Press, 1949), pp. 261–274. The most recent statement is to be found in my article, "The Spoken Word and the Great Unsaid," *Quarterly Journal of Speech,* December 1951, pp. 419–429. The form of the diagram reproduced here, together with a substantial portion of the text, are used by permission of the *Quarterly Journal of Speech.*

tion process and in major part external to both the speaker and the listener.

The importance of this fact is evident in relation to Stage 2 (or Stage 2'). The small size of the "opening" to Stage 2 in relation to the magnitude of the "channel" of Stage 1 represents the fact that our sensory receptors are capable of responding only to relatively small segments of the total ranges of energy radiations.

Sensory Limitations

The wave lengths to which the eye responds are but a small part of the total spectrum of such wave lengths. We register as sound only a narrow band of the full range of air vibrations. Noiseless dog whistles, "electronic eyes," and radar mechanisms—to say nothing of homing pigeons—underscore the primitive character of man's sensory equipment. Indeed, we seem little more than barely capable of tasting and smelling, and the narrowness of the temperature range we can tolerate is downright sobering to anyone dispassionately concerned with the efficiency of survival mechanisms.

The situation with regard to the normal individual may appear to be sufficiently dismal; let us not forget, however, how few of us are wholly normal in sensory acuity. We are familiar with the blind and partially sighted, the deaf and hard of hearing; we notice less the equally if not more numerous individuals who cannot taste the difference between peaches and strawberries, who cannot smell a distraught civet cat, or feel a fly bite.

All in all, the degree to which we can know directly, through sensory avenues, the world outside (and this includes the world outside the sensory receptors but inside the body) is impressively restricted.

Any speaker is correspondingly limited in his physical ability to know what he is talking about. Relatively sophisticated listeners are likely to judge a speaker's dependability as a communicating agent by the degree to which he discloses his awareness of this limitation. The executive who demonstrates a realistic awareness of his own ignorance will in the long run acquire among his peers and subordinates a far better reputation for good judgment than the one who reveals his limitations by refusing to acknowledge them.

Pre-Verbal State

Once a sensory receptor has been stimulated, nerve currents travel quickly into the spinal cord and normally up through the base of the brain to the higher reaches of the cortex, out again along return tracts to the muscles and glands. The contractions and secretions they cause bring about new sensory stimulations which are "fed back" into the cord and brain and effect still further changes. The resulting reverberations of stimulation and response define what we may call a pre-verbal state of affairs within the organism. This state is represented at Stage 3 of the diagram.

Two statements about this pre-verbal state are fundamental: (1) we need to realize that our direct knowledge of this state is slight; (2) at the same time we are justified in assuming that it does occur.

No one has ever trudged through the spinal cord and brain with gun and camera, at least not while the owner of those organs was alive. Nevertheless, we are reasonably sure of certain facts about the nervous system. Observations have been reported by neurosurgeons, electro-encephalographers, nerve physiologists, and anatomists. Thousands of laboratory animals have been sacrified on the altars of scientific inquiry. We know that there are nerve currents, that they travel at known rates of speed, exhibit certain electrical properties, and are functionally re-lated to specific kinds and loci of stimulation and to specified kinds and loci of response.

Thus, though our factual information is meager as yet, certainly it is sufficient to demonstrate that the nervous system is not merely a hypo-thetical construct. We can say with practical assurance that stimulation of our sensory end organs is normally followed by the transmission of nerve currents into the central nervous system, with a consequent re-verberation effect, as described above, and the resulting state of affairs within the organism.

Two specific observations about this state of affairs are crucial: (1) it is truly pre-verbal, or silent; (2) it is this noiseless bodily state that gets transformed into words (or other symbols). Therefore—and these next few words should be read at a snail's pace and pondered long and fret-fully—besides talking always to ourselves (although others may be listen-ing more or less too), and whatever else we may also be striving to sym-bolize, *we inevitably talk about ourselves.*

The Individual's Filter

What the speaker—whether he be a junior executive or the general manager—directly symbolizes, *what he turns into words,* are physiological or electrochemical goings-on inside his own body. His organism, in this sense, operates constantly as a kind of filter through which facts (in the sense of things that arouse sensory impulses) must pass before they can become known to him and before they can be *communicated* by him to others in some symbolic form, such as standard English speech.

It follows, to present a single, seemingly trivial, but quite representative example, that when the junior executive says to the general manager, "It's certainly a fine day," he is exhibiting an elaborate variety of confusion; indeed, he appears literally not to know what he is talking about. In the meantime, he is talking about himself—or at least about the weather only as "filtered" by himself. He is symbolizing an inner state, first of all. In this he is the brother of all of us who speak.

I do not mean to imply that we talk solely about our inner states. We often talk about the world outside; but when we do, we filter it through our inner states. To the degree that our individual filters are standardized and alike, we will agree in the statements we make about the world outside—allowing, of course, for differences in time, place, observational set, equipment, sensory acuity, perceptive skill, and manner of making verbal reports.

The existence of the filter at Stage 3 of the process of communication is the basic fact. We may differ in our manner of appreciating and interpreting the significance of the filter, and in so doing make ourselves interesting to each other. But when the administrator—when anyone at all —simply never learns that the filter is there, or forgets or disregards it, he becomes, as a speaker, a threat to his own sanity and a potential or actual menace in a public sense.

Self-Projection

Because the filter is there in each of us, self-projection is a basic bodily process that operates not only in all our speaking but in other kinds of communicative behavior. To claim to speak literally, then, a person must always say "as I see it," or "as I interpret the facts," or "as I filter the world" if you please, or simply "to me."

An administrator whose language becomes too "is"-y tends to persuade himself that what he says the facts are is the same thing as the facts, and under the numbing spell of this illusion he may become quite incapable of evaluating his own judgments. If he is aware of projection, he must make clear, first of all to himself, that he is not speaking about reality in some utterly impersonal or disembodied and "revealed" sense, but only about reality as the prism of his own nervous system projects it upon the gray screen of his own language—and he must realize that this projection, however trustworthy or untrustworthy, must still be received, filtered, and reprojected by each of his listeners.

Sufficient contemplation of this curious engineering scheme renders one sensitive to the hazards involved in its use. As with any other possibility of miracle, one is well advised not to expect too much of it.

Patterns and Symbols

Stage 4, the first stage of symbolization, is represented in our diagram as a great enlargement in the tunnel through which "the world" passes from Stage 1 to Stage 1'. The words ultimately selected for utterance (at Stage 5) are a very small part of the lush abundance of possible verbalizations from which they are abstracted. Moreover, the bulge is intended to suggest that the state of affairs at Stage 3 becomes in a peculiarly human way much more significant by virtue of its symbolization at Stage 4.

At Stage 4 the individual's symbolic system and the pattern of evaluation reflected in its use come into play. The evaluative processes represented at this stage have been the object of much and varied study and speculation:

> *Freud*—Here, it would appear, was the location of Freud's chief preoccupations, as he attempted to explain them in terms of the so-called unconscious depths of the person, the struggle between the Id and the Super-Ego from which the Ego evolves, the ceaseless brewing of dreamstuff, wish and counterwish, the fabulous symbolism of the drama that we call the human personality.[2] Indeed, at this stage there is more than meets the eye—incredibly more so far as we may dimly but compellingly surmise.
>
> *Korzybski*—Here, too, were the major preoccupations of the founder of general semantics, Alfred Korzybski: the symbol; the creation of symbols and of systems of symbols; the appalling distortions of experience wrought by the culturally imposed semantic crippling of the young through the witless and artful indoctrination of each new generation by the fateful words of the elders—the words which are the carriers of prejudice, unreasoning aspiration, delusional absolutes, and the resulting attitudes of self-abandonment. But also here we find the unencompassable promise of all that *human* can suggest, and this Korzybski called upon all men to see, to cherish, and to cultivate with fierce tenderness.[3]

[2] Sigmund Freud, *A General Introduction to Psychoanalysis*, translated by Joan Riviere (New York, Liveright Publishing Corporation, 1935).

[3] Alfred Korzybski, *Science and Sanity: An Introduction to Non-Aristotelian Systems and General Semantics* (Lancaster, Pennsylvania, Science Press, 3rd ed. 1948).

Pavlov—The father of the modern science of behavior, Pavlov, also busied himself with ingenious explanations of occurrences at what we have called Stage 4.[4] In human beings, at least, the learning processes, as well as the drives and goals that power and direct them, appear to function at this stage of incipient symbolization.

It seems useful to conjecture that perhaps the general *patterns* of symbolic conditioning are formed at Stage 4, in contrast to the conditioning of specific symbolic responses (i.e., particular statements) produced at Stage 5. We may put it this way: at Stage 4 the syllogism, for example, as a *pattern* or *form* of possible symbolic response, is laid down, while at Stage 5 there occur the specific verbal responses patterned in this syllogistic mold.

Again, at Stage 4 we find the general form, "X affects Y"; at Stage 5 we see its specific progeny in such statements as "John Loves Mary," "germs cause disease," "clothes make the man," and so on. In this relationship between general forms or patterns at Stage 4 and the corresponding specific utterances at Stage 5 we find the substantial sense of the proposition that our language does our thinking for us.

In fact, one of the grave disorders that we may usefully locate at Stage 4 consists in a lack of awareness of the influence on one's overt speech of the general symbolic forms operating at Stage 4. The more the individual knows about these forms, the more different forms he knows— or originates—and the more adroit he is in the selective and systematic use of them in patterning specific statements at Stage 5, the more control he exercises over "the language that does his thinking for him." The degree of such control exercised over the verbal responses at Stage 5 represents one of the important dimensions along which speakers range themselves, all the way from the naïveté of the irresponsible robot—or compulsive schizophrenic patient—to the culture-shaping symbolic sophistication of the creative genius.

(Generally speaking, most of the disorders of abstracting described and emphasized by the general semanticists are to be most usefully thought of as operating chiefly at Stage 4. These disorders include those involving identification or lack of effective discrimination for purposes of sound evaluation.[5])

[4] I. P. Pavlov, *Conditioned Reflexes: An Investigation of the Physiological Activity of the Cerebral Cortex*, translated and edited by G. V. Anrep (London, Oxford University Press, 1927).

[5] See Alfred Korzybski, *op. cit.*, and Wendell Johnson, *People in Quandaries*, particularly Chapters 5 through 10.

The Final Draft

The fact has been mentioned, and should be emphasized, that the "final draft" formulated at Stage 5, the words that come to be spoken, represents as a rule a highly condensed abstract of all that might have been spoken. What enters into this final draft is determined, in a positive sense, by the speaker's available knowledge of fact and relationship, his vocabulary, and his flexibility in using it, his purposes, and (to use the term in a broad sense) his habits. What enters into it is determined negatively by the repressions, inhibitions, taboos, semantic blockages, and ignorances, as well as the limiting symbolic forms, operating at Stage 4.

MR. A TO MR. B

As the communication process moves from Stage 5 to Stage 1', it undergoes another of the incredible transformations which give it a unique and altogether remarkable character: the words, phrases, and sentences at Stage 5 are changed into air waves (and light waves) at Stage 1'. At close quarters, Mr. A may at times pat the listener's shoulder, tug at his coat lapels, or in some other way try to inject his meaning into Mr. B by hand, as it were, but this transmission of meaning through mechanical pressure may be disregarded for present purposes.

Inefficiency of Air Waves

In general, it seems a valid observation that we place an unwarranted trust in spoken words, partly because we disregard, or do not appreciate, the inefficiency of air waves as carriers of information and evaluation. The reasons for this inefficiency lie both in the speaker and in the listener, of course, as well as in the air waves themselves. What the listener ends up with is necessarily a highly abstracted version of what the speaker intends to convey.

The speaker who sufficiently understands this—the wise administrator —expects to be misunderstood and, as a matter of fact, predicts quite well the particular misunderstandings with which he will need to contend. Consequently, he is able not only to forestall confusion to some extent but also to give himself a chance to meet misunderstanding with the poise essential to an intelligent handling of the relationships arising out of it. A minimal requirement for the handling of such relationships is that either the speaker or the listener (or, better, both) recognize that the fault lies not so much in either one of them as in the process of communication itself—including particularly the fragile and tenuous air waves, whose cargo of meaning, whether too light to be retained or too heavy to be borne, is so often lost in transit.

Such an executive takes sufficiently into account the fact that words, whether spoken or written, are not foolproof. He will do all he can, within reason, to find out how his statements, his letters and press releases, his instructions to subordinates, and so on are received and interpreted. He will not take for granted that anyone else thinks he means what he himself thinks he means. And when he discovers the misunderstandings and confusions he has learned to expect, he reacts with disarming and constructive forbearance to the resentments and disturbed human relationships that he recognizes as being due, not to men, but to the far from perfect communications by means of which men try to work and live together.

INSIDE MR. B

The air waves (and light waves) that arrive at Stage 2′—that is, at the ears and eyes of the listener—serve to trigger the complex abstracting process which we have just examined, except that now it moves from 2′ through 5′ instead of 2 through 5. That is, the various stages sketched in the speaker are now repeated in the listener. To understand speech, or the communication process in general, is to be aware of the various functions and the disorders operating at each stage in the process—and to be conscious of the complex pattern of relationships among the various stages, as represented schematically by the double-arrowed loops in the diagram.

Effect of Feedback

Always important, these relationships become particularly significant when the speaker and listener are one and the same individual. And this, of course, is always the case, even when there are other listeners. The speaker is always affected by "feedback": he hears himself. What is significant is precisely the degree to which he is affected by feedback. It may, in fact, be ventured as a basic principle that the speaker's responsiveness to feedback—or, particularly important, the *administrator's* responsiveness to feedback—is crucial in determining the soundness of his spoken evaluations. It is crucial, also, in determining his effectiveness in maintaining good working relationships with his associates.

APPLICATION TO PROBLEMS

This view of the process of Mr. A speaking to Mr. B may be applied to any one of a great many specific problems and purposes. The diagram can be used especially well as a means of directing attention to the disorders of communication, such as those encountered daily in the world of trade and industry.

Preventing Troubles

In this connection, let me call attention to the fact that Professor Irving Lee of the School of Speech at Northwestern University has written a book on *How to Talk with People*,[6] which is of particular interest to anyone concerned with such disorders. Its subtitle describes it as "a program for preventing troubles that come when people talk together." The sorts of troubles with which Professor Lee is concerned in this book are among those of greatest interest and importance to personnel managers and business administrators and executives generally, and there would seem to be no better way to make my diagram take on a very practical kind of meaning than to sketch briefly what Professor Lee did and what he found in his studies of men in the world of business trying to communicate with one another.

Over a period of nearly ten years Professor Lee listened to the deliberations of more than 200 boards of directors, committees, organization staffs, and other similar groups. He made notes of the troubles he observed, and in some cases he was able to get the groups to try out his suggestions for reducing such troubles as they were having; and as they tried out his suggestions, he observed what happened and took more notes.

Among the many problems he describes in *How to Talk with People* there are three of special interest, which can be summarized thus:

1. First of all, misunderstanding results when one man assumes that another uses words just as he does. Professor Quine of Harvard once referred to this as "the uncritical assumption of mutual understanding." It is, beyond question, one of our most serious obstacles to effective thinking and communication. Professor Lee suggests a remedy, decep-

[6] New York, Harper & Brothers, 1952.

tively simple but profoundly revolutionary: better habits of listening. We must learn, he says, not only how to define our own terms but also how to ask others what they are talking about. He is advising us to pay as much attention to the righthand side of our diagram as to the lefthand side of it.

2. Another problem is represented by the person who takes it for granted that anyone who does not feel the way he does about something is a fool. "What is important here," says Lee, "is not that men disagree, but that they become disagreeable about it." The fact is, of course, that the very disagreeable disagreer is more or less sick, from a psychological and semantic point of view. Such a person is indulging in "unconscious projection." As we observed in considering the amazing transformation of the physiological goings-on at Stage 3 into words or other symbols at Stage 4, the only way we can talk about the world outside is to filter it through our private inner states. The disagreeable disagreer is one who has never learned that he possesses such a filter, or has forgotten it, or is so desperate, demoralized, drunk, or distracted as not to care about it.

A trained consciousness of the projection process would seem to be essential in any very effective approach to this problem. The kind of training called for may be indicated by the suggestion to any administrator who is inclined to try it out that he qualify any important statements he makes, with which others may disagree, by such phrases as "to my way of thinking," "to one with my particular background," "as I see it," and the like.

3. One more source of trouble is found in the executive who thinks a meeting should be "as workmanlike as a belt line." He has such a business-only attitude that he simply leaves out of account the fact that "people like to get things off their chests almost as much as they like to solve problems." Professor Lee's sensible recommendation is this: "If people in a group want to interrupt serious discussion with some diversion or personal expression—let them. Then bring them back to the agenda. Committees work best when the talk swings between the personal and the purposeful."

Constructive Factors

Professor Lee saw something, however, in addition to the "troubles that come when people talk together." He has this heartening and important observation to report:

"In sixteen groups we saw illustrations of men and women talking together, spontaneously, cooperatively, constructively. There was team-play and team-work. We tried to isolate some of the factors we found there: (1) The leader did not try to tell the others what to do or how to think; he was thinking along with them. (2) No one presumed to know it all; one might be eager and vigorous in his manner of talking, but he was amenable and attentive when others spoke. (3) The people thought of the accomplishments of the group rather than of their individual exploits."

This can happen—and where it does not happen, something is amiss. The diagram presented on page 25, along with the description of the process of communication fashioned in terms of it, is designed to help us figure out what might be at fault when such harmony is not to be found. And it is intended to provide essential leads to better and more fruitful communication in business and industry, and under all other circumstances as well.

CONCLUSION

Mr. A talking to Mr. B is a deceptively simple affair, and we take it for granted to a fantastic and tragic degree. It would surely be true that our lives would be longer and richer if only we were to spend a greater share of them in the tranquil hush of thoughtful listening. We are a noisy lot; and of what gets said among us, far more goes unheard and unheeded than seems possible. We have yet to learn on a grand scale how to use the wonders of speaking and listening in our own best interests and for the good of all our fellows. It is the finest art still to be mastered by men.

For Discussion

1. Johnson notes that "besides talking always to ourselves (although others may be listening more or less too), and whatever else we may also be striving to symbolize, *we inevitably talk about ourselves.*" How and in what ways might your own communications reveal information about yourself?

2. In his discussion of self-projection Johnson argues that we do not speak about reality in an impersonal and objective sense but rather about reality as it is filtered through our own unique nervous systems. Consequently, no two persons can ever perceive "reality" in exactly the same way. With this notion in mind consider some recent disagreements in which you engaged, for example, over the value of a particular motion picture or tele-

vision program or about a particular course or instructor or about another individual. In such disagreements did the communicators *act as if* they were talking about reality in a purely objective sense or did they *act as if* they were talking about reality as filtered and as influenced by their own nervous systems, their own experiences, personalities, needs, interests, and so on? Do such different points of view make a difference in communication? How?

3. Johnson discusses three communication problems described by Irving Lee: the assumption of mutual understanding, the tendency to disagree disagreeably, and the business-only attitude. Examine your own communication behavior in groups. Do you contribute to these problems? Have you observed others who are particularly prone to these weaknesses? What are the effects of such behaviors on the subsequent actions of the group? How might such problems be eliminated?

4. The diagram of the communication process presented in this article, says Johnson, "is intended to provide essential leads to better and more fruitful communication in business and industry, and under all other circumstances as well." Apply this model to the classroom situation. What might both teacher and student learn about effective and meaningful communication from this model? What communication problems seem to be particularly pervasive in the classroom? Can these problems be located on the model? Does the model suggest solutions for these communication problems?

Information
Theory

DONALD K. DARNELL

The concepts and postulates of information theory have influenced and, in fact, revolutionized the entire field of communication as well as such allied sciences as psychology, sociology, and linguistics. Here Donald Darnell explains some of the fundamentals of this theory and suggests a few of its numerous possible applications.

It is always dangerous to attempt to popularize a technical masterpiece like *The Mathematical Theory of Communication*. Such an attempt will necessarily be less precise, less elegant, and less adequate than the original. But, if it were not for the availability of cheap copies, which suffer from all these defects, great art would only be available to the very rich who would, for lack of personal suffering, be unable to appreciate it.

This attempt to increase the availability of the concepts of information theory is a mistake if it (1) fails to produce a new interest and new insight into communication, or (2) it is mistakenly accepted as a satisfactory substitute for extensive reading on the subject.

"Information theory" is the popular, generic name for a body of concepts, assumptions, and propositions about communication to which several thinkers have made contributions. J. R. Pierce, in Chapter Two of *Symbols, Signals and Noise*, presents a readable historical perspective, which readers with a sense of irony may find amusing. But, the purpose of this paper is neither to amuse nor to teach history. C. E. Shannon is commonly credited with being the originator of information theory, probably because his paper, which first appeared in the *Bell System Technical Journal* in 1948, had a clear purpose and it constituted a general, though elegant, attack on a number of technical communication problems. This paper will attempt to explain, without the mathematical proofs, some of the basic concepts and theorums of Shannon's work and give some notion of their current relevance.

One of Shannon's contributions was a description of the essential functions of a general communication system. The basic idea is that an information source has a message that it is trying to get through some channel to some destination. It employs two transducers, a transmitter, and a complementary receiver, to convert the message into a transmittable signal and recover it from the channel. It must contend with certain disruptive forces represented by a noise source.

"Information Theory." Prepared especially for this volume by Donald K. Darnell and printed with the author's permission.

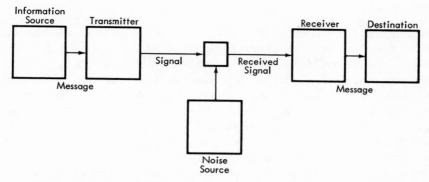

Schematic diagram of a general communication system. Claude Shannon and Warren Weaver, *The Mathematical Theory of Communication* (Urbana, Illinois: University of Illinois Press, 1949), p. 5.

Perhaps the clearest example of such a system is a simple two-person exchange. Suppose that a gentleman notes that a lady has a smudge on her nose, and he would like for her to become aware of that fact. He can activate his vocal transmitter which, by means of a complex set of muscle contractions, converts that message into a series of vibrations, "You have a smudge on your nose." These vibrations (the signal) mingled with other vibrations present in the situation (noise) are carried to the lady's pressure sensitive ear. Her cochlea performs an inverse translation converting the vibrations in the air to a patterned electrical stimulation which, if everything goes well, creates in her brain (destination) the desired awareness. If there is much noise in the system, she may "hear" "You have mud in your nose." If he anticipates such a problem he may, instead of talking at all, hand her his handkerchief, point to his own nose, and smile. If he is very cautious, he may do all these things to minimize the risk of being misunderstood.

The question is, "How does an information source get his message through to the destination with an acceptable minimum of distortion or error in spite of the characteristics of the channel, the transducers, and the noise source?" The general answer is, "By encoding the message with sufficient redundancy so that the receiver can reconstruct the message from the composit of transmitted signal and noise that is received." The rest of information theory is an elaboration of this answer.

Probably because he was not entangled in preconceptions about real language and because he was concerned only with the technical transmission problems of communication systems, Shannon arrived at a concept of "information" that was unusual. This unusual concept of information is fundamental to the ensuing explanation. He reasoned that the crucial fact about an *information source* is that it *makes choices.* And, the crucial thing that a destination *needs to know* is what it does *not* already know, namely, what those choices were. In an ideal system, in which the source and destination start from the same set of presumptions (more or less true of mechanical systems and probably less true about human communication systems), the destination's *uncertainty* about the transmitted message is precisely equal to the source's *freedom-of-choice* in constructing the message. The mathematical concept of *information,* then, encompasses the concepts of uncertainty and freedom-of-choice. In this context, information is specifically *about* the source's freedom-of-choice and is designed to remove a destination's uncertainty. Another word that is sometimes used for this concept, because of certain mathematical similarities to a concept in thermodynamics, is *entropy.* The common mathematical symbol for it is H.

To illustrate these abstract concepts, let us assume that the lady in our previous example asks, "Do I have a smudge on my nose?" Assuming that this message was accurately transmitted and decoded, the respondent (now the information source) has, within normal linguistic restraints, two possible answers, "yes" or "no." Considering only the linguistic restraints (disregarding his observation of her nose), his freedom-of-choice is precisely equal to her uncertainty or the entropy of the situation. If she trusts his powers of observation and the communication system, the information carried by his signal (response) will exactly remove her uncertainty. Whether she, in fact, has a smudge on her nose is beside the point.

The information value of a specific transmission (or symbol) is the logarithm of the reciprocal of its probability of occurrence. Which is to say, the less likely something is to happen the more informative it is when it does. The *average* information, entropy, uncertainty, freedom-of-choice, or H of a system (call it what you will) is a function of the number of alternatives from which choices are made *and* the probabilities of all the possible choices. In general, the more alternatives there are the more information is involved in a choice among them, and the maximum freedom-of-choice for any specific number of alternatives is reached when the options are equally probable. The mathematical equation that precisely satisfies these conditions (and several others) is the weighted average of the logarithms of the probabilities of all the alternatives:

$$H = - \Sigma \, p_i \log p_i$$

By introducing the base two logarithm ($\log_2$) into this statement, Shannon *defined* the unit of measurement of information (the *bit*) as the amount of information involved in a choice between two equally probable alternatives. That is, the value of the equation is unity (one) when exactly two alternatives are considered, each has the probability of .5, and the $\log_2$ is used. It is convenient that the simplest possible choice involves exactly one bit of information or uncertainty.

To continue the previous example, we can now say that the "yes" or "no" answer transmitted approximately one bit of information. If the lady had some a priori reason to suspect the existence or nonexistence of a smudge, then, the "expected" answer would carry somewhat less than one bit of information, the "unexpected" answer somewhat more. If we consider averaging over a number of similar situations, the average information-uncertainty in such two choice situations would be equal to or less than one bit per message. No matter how many words are used to differentiate the affirmative and negative responses, the information transmitted is the same. It is determined by the number of available choices and their probabilities. The number of symbols used to specify this choice is, as you will soon see, a matter of coding efficiency.

The mathematical concept of information made it possible to define the *capacity of a channel* (C) as the maximum number of bits of information it can handle per symbol or per unit of time. An advantage of this concept of capacity over one, say, stated in symbols per second is that it introduces efficiency of encoding as a variable. The problem of coding efficiency becomes the problem of utilizing the channel capacity. This leads to the very general statement that by efficient encoding it is possible to transmit in a noiseless channel at a rate which approaches but cannot exceed C bits per second. The proportion of the channel capacity that is actually utilized is a measure of coding efficiency.

In a noise free channel, then, the most efficient way to operate is to make successive choices independent of each other and to use all the different options with equal frequency. That way each signal transmitted and received bears the maximum amount of information.

It is immediately apparent, however, that *noise* (which creates a discrepancy between the signal transmitted and the signal received) has the greatest disruptive effect in the otherwise maximally efficient system. When each signal bears a maximum amount of information, any distortion of the signal causes a maximum probable error in the reconstructed message. Inefficiency (commonly called *redundancy*), then, takes on a positive value in the presence of noise. It is, Shannon assures us, possible to encode with sufficient redundancy that an arbitrarily small frequency of errors may be obtained even under the noisiest of conditions.

Normal English (and probably most other natural languages) seems to have evolved a happy compromise between efficiency and redundancy —about fifty-fifty. About half of what we say is necessary for the reconstruction of the message, and the other half is *noise insurance*. (Redundancy doesn't prevent noise, but it reduces the risk for a price. Health insurance doesn't prevent illness, but it makes available the best possible treatment and facilitates recovery by reducing worry and responsibility. Some people never appreciate insurance or redundancy until they need it and don't have it.) When we talk long distance or to a computer, when we are charged by the symbol (in time units or storage area), we tend to reduce the redundancy of our transmissions to an absolute minimum. Consider the following two versions of a message. In a cablegram we might say, "Meet TWA 234 JFK 2-2." In a letter we might say, "Please meet me at Kennedy International Airport on Monday, February 2, at 2:10 p.m. I will arrive from London on Trans World Airlines flight number 234." Anyone with an airline schedule book or a friendly travel agent could construct the second from the first. So, they carry the same information but differ in efficiency-redundancy.

In air traffic control operations, for example, where even a "small" error is intolerable, we tend to disregard the value of efficiency. Crucial messages may be spelled out in a system which employs a word for each alphabetic character (for example, alpha, bravo, charley, delta, easy, fox, golf) and numbers are pronounced in exaggerated stylized fashion (for example, thu-ree, fi-ive, nin-er). Whole messages may be repeated, and confirmation is routinely required before a specified maneuver is executed. Information theory provides a neat justification for these intuitively right decisions.

Although Shannon specifically claimed that the "semantic aspects of communication are irrelevant to the engineering problem," it is quite clear that the converse is not the case. An *ambiguous* message, for instance, may be viewed as one in which there is a choice available among alternative interpretations. The statement, "My dog has a brown coat," may be taken to refer to his natural coat or a manufactured garment. By changing "brown" to "green" or by adding "with matching ear muffs," the probability of the garment interpretation can be greatly increased and the ambiguity reduced. Insertion of the adjective "slick" almost resolves the ambiguity of the original statement in the other way, but in combination with "green" raises a third alternative of the "natural" coat in an unnatural color. Many English sentences allow both a literal and a metaphorical interpretation. Idiomatic expressions such as "How are you?" are, almost by definition, ambiguous. When the ambiguity disappears the metaphor is dead and the idiom becomes just another irregularity of the language. If a set of alternatives can be specified and their probabilities (relative strength) estimated, then Shannon's measure of information can be applied as a measure of ambiguity. It is a short step from there to measuring the value of a pun.

In dealing with problems of effect of messages, one may find it useful to consider the freedom-of-choice of response available to the destination for a given reconstruction of a message and a given interpretation of that reconstruction. The information measure may be applied (or misapplied if you're a purist) to this too. We may find, ultimately, that in human communication at least three independent sources of "uncertainty" must be controlled or accounted for before the process is satisfactorily explained.

D. E. Berlyne in *Conflict, Arousal, and Curiosity* (p. 34) has found "information" to be an apt description of what he calls "cognitive conflict." If, for example, an individual learns a number of incompatible responses (to distinctive stimuli), then they are called for simultaneously (multiple stimuli), he will experience "cognitive conflict" which is a function of the number of competing responses and their relative response strengths. A person who speaks more than one language would, then, be subject to cognitive conflict and the conflict would be maximum for any given number of languages when the speaker enjoys *equal facility* in all of them. Would this account for the common difficulty in second language acquisition?

Given Berlyne's application of "information," the impulse is irresistible to apply the same measure to social conflict, ambivalence, decision difficulty, etc., in fact, to any situation whatsoever involving a choice among a set of alternatives.

The vagueness of McLuhan's "hot" and "cool" media ("Hot media are, therefore, low in participation, and cool media are high in participation or completion by the audience." p. 23) may be reduced by substituting "redundant" and "entropic" and, I think, without serious distortion.

A slight manipulation of information statistics (to obtain a difference between the information value of a specific outcome and the average uncertainty of a system) produces a measure of "abnormality" or "compatibility" which Darnell has successfully applied to the assessment of "language proficiency."

Finally, in the mathematical concept of information, I find a precise criterion for evaluating arguments, scientific theories, or pieces of evidence which is an alternative to the archaic notion of "formal adequacy." In fact, the criterion of formal adequacy may be stated in information terms. An *adequate* argument (in the formal sense) establishes a claim or proposition conclusively, admitting no alternative. That is, an adequate argument is one which reduces uncertainty about a claim to zero. Arguments which do not meet this criterion are called invalid, inconclusive, inductive, or even rhetorical. It is the case, however, that arguments which do not meet this criterion are often quite persuasive—are good enough to permit a more or less confident judgment among a set of competing alternatives.

At least in those instances, then, in which an argument, theory, or piece of evidence is put forward to modify the relative tenability of a set of alternative claims or positions (for example, guilty or not guilty), the value (strength) of the argument, theory, or evidence may be determined by its effect on the uncertainty in the situation—the amount of information it transmits—whether or not the end result is a zero uncertainty state (that is, perfect confidence). Such a relative criterion of value readily lends itself to the assessment of progress in an extended communication campaign or a continuing program of scientific research.

References

D. E. Berlyne, *Conflict, Arousal, and Curiosity*. New York: McGraw-Hill, 1960.

A. R. Broadhurst and D. K. Darnell, "Introduction to Cybernetics and Information Theory," *Quarterly Journal of Speech*, LI (December, 1965), 441–53.

D. K. Darnell, "CLOZENTROPY: A Procedure for Testing English Language Proficiency of Foreign Students," *Speech Monographs*, XXXVII (March, 1970), 36–46.

Marshall McLuhan, *Understanding Media: The Extensions of Man*. New York: McGraw-Hill, 1964.

J. R. Pierce, *Symbols, Signals, and Noise*. New York: Harper Torchbooks, 1961.

C. E. Shannon and Warren Weaver, *The Mathematical Theory of Communication*. Urbana: University of Illinois Press, 1949.

For Discussion

1. Select an example of two-person communication and trace it through the model presented in this paper. Does this procedure help at all in your understanding of the *process* character of communication? How?

2. "Noise" can be present in both oral and written communications. Identify as many types of noise as possible which can enter into (1) oral and (2) written communication. What effects does each type of noise have? What remedies or "noise insurance" measures might be used to combat the effects of noise?

3. What type of noise does an instructor have to deal with during a class lecture? Describe the methods one of your instructors uses to deal with noise. Is he successful?

4. In *Communication: The Social Matrix of Psychiatry* by Jurgen Ruesch and Gregory Bateson (New York: W. W. Norton, 1951), Bateson, in referring to the notion that "information" and "negative entropy" are synonymous, says: "this statement, in the opinion of the writers, marks the greatest single shift in human thinking since the days of Plato and Aristotle" (p. 177). Why is the very simple formula—information = negative entropy—so important?

5. Darnell says: "Given Berlyne's application of 'information,' the impulse is irresistible to apply the same measure to social conflict, ambivalence, decision difficulty, etc., in fact, to any situation whatsoever involving a choice among a set of alternatives." How might this be done?

6. What one concept of information theory do you feel is most important for an understanding of effective and meaningful communication? Why?

COMMUNICATION
MESSAGES
AND
CHANNELS

How to Say Nothing in Five Hundred Words

PAUL ROBERTS

Writing compositions is undoubtedly one of the most hated tasks students face in their entire college careers. It is probably the most frequently postponed assignment and the one which seems to bring the least rewards. Here Paul Roberts, writing with a keen understanding of these difficulties and problems, offers an entertaining and perceptive account of some of the most frequently encountered problems in writing compositions. What he says here, however, is not limited to the written composition; rather, it pertains with equal validity to preparing speeches and, in fact, to communication in all its forms.

It's Friday afternoon, and you have almost survived another week of classes. You are just looking forward dreamily to the week end when the English instructor says: "For Monday you will turn in a five-hundred word composition on college football."

Well, that puts a good big hole in the week end. You don't have any strong views on college football one way or the other. You get rather excited during the season and go to all the home games and find it rather more fun than not. On the other hand, the class has been reading Robert Hutchins in the anthology and perhaps Shaw's "Eighty-Yard Run," and from the class discussion you have got the idea that the instructor thinks college football is for the birds. You are no fool, you. You can figure out what side to take.

After dinner you get out the portable typewriter that you got for high school graduation. You might as well get it over with and enjoy Saturday and Sunday. Five hundred words is about two double-spaced pages with normal margins. You put in a sheet of paper, think up a title, and you're off:

WHY COLLEGE FOOTBALL SHOULD BE ABOLISHED

College football should be abolished because it's bad for the school and also bad for the players. The players are so busy practicing that they don't have any time for their studies.

This, you feel, is a mighty good start. The only trouble is that it's only thirty-two words. You still have four hundred and sixty-eight to go, and you've pretty well exhausted the subject. It comes to you that you do your best thinking in the morning, so you put away the typewriter and go to the movies. But the next morning you have to do your washing and some math problems, and in the afternoon you go to the game. The

"How to Say Nothing in Five Hundred Words." From Paul Roberts, Understanding English *(New York: Harper & Row, Publishers, 1958), pp. 404–20. Copyright © 1958 by Paul Roberts. Reprinted by permission of Harper & Row, Publishers.*

English instructor turns up too, and you wonder if you've taken the right side after all. Saturday night you have a date, and Sunday morning you have to go to church. (You shouldn't let English assignments interfere with your religion.) What with one thing and another, it's ten o'clock Sunday night before you get out the typewriter again. You make a pot of coffee and start to fill out your views on college football. Put a little meat on the bones.

Why College Football Should Be Abolished

In my opinion, it seems to me that college football should be abolished. The reason why I think this to be true is because I feel that football is bad for the colleges in nearly every respect. As Robert Hutchins says in his article in our anthology in which he discusses college football, it would be better if the colleges had race horses and had races with one another, because then the horses would not have to attend classes. I firmly agree with Mr. Hutchins on this point, and I am sure that many other students would agree too.

One reason why it seems to me that college football is bad is that it has become too commercial. In the olden times when people played football just for the fun of it, maybe college football was all right, but they do not play football just for the fun of it now as they used to in the old days. Nowadays college football is what you might call a big business. Maybe this is not true at all schools, and I don't think it is especially true here at State, but certainly this is the case at most colleges and universities in America nowadays, as Mr. Hutchins points out in his very interesting article. Actually the coaches and alumni go around to the high schools and offer the high school stars large salaries to come to their colleges and play football for them. There was one case where a high school star was offered a convertible if he would play football for a certain college.

Another reason for abolishing college football is that it is bad for the players. They do not have time to get a college education, because they are so busy playing football. A football player has to practice every afternoon from three to six, and then he is so tired that he can't concentrate on his studies. He just feels like dropping off to sleep after dinner, and then the next day he goes to his classes without having studied and maybe he fails the test.

(Good ripe stuff so far, but you're still a hundred and fifty-one words from home. One more push.)

Also I think college football is bad for the colleges and the universities because not very many students get to participate in it. Out of a college of ten thousand students only seventy-five or a hundred play football, if that many. Football is what you might call a spectator sport. That means that most people go to watch it but do not play it themselves.

(Four hundred and fifteen. Well, you still have the conclusion, and when you retype it, you can make the margins a little wider.)

These are the reasons why I agree with Mr. Hutchins that college football should be abolished in American colleges and universities.

On Monday you turn it in, moderately hopeful, and on Friday it comes back marked "weak in content" and sporting a big "D."

This essay is exaggerated a little, not much. The English instructor will recognize it as reasonably typical of what an assignment on college football will bring in. He knows that nearly half of the class will contrive in five hundred words to say that college football is too commercial and bad for the players. Most of the other half will inform him that college football builds character and prepares one for life and brings prestige to the school. As he reads paper after paper all saying the same thing in almost the same words, all bloodless, five hundred words dripping out of nothing, he wonders how he allowed himself to get trapped into teaching English when he might have had a happy and interesting life as an electrician or a confidence man.

Well, you may ask, what can you do about it? The subject is one on which you have few convictions and little information. Can you be expected to make a dull subject interesting? As a matter of fact, this is precisely what you are expected to do. This is the writer's essential task. All subjects, except sex, are dull until somebody makes them interesting. The writer's job is to find the argument, the approach, the angle, the wording that will take the reader with him. This is seldom easy, and it is particularly hard in subjects that have been much discussed: College Football, Fraternities, Popular Music, Is Chivalry Dead?, and the like. You will feel that there is nothing you can do with such subjects except repeat the old bromides. But there are some things you can do which will make your papers, if not throbbingly alive, at least less insufferably tedious than they might otherwise be.

AVOID THE OBVIOUS CONTENT

Say the assignment is college football. Say that you've decided to be against it. Begin by putting down the arguments that come to your mind: it is too commercial, it takes the students' minds off their studies, it is hard on the players, it makes the university a kind of circus instead of an intellectual center, for most schools it is financially ruinous. Can you think of any more arguments just off hand? All right. Now when you write your paper, *make sure that you don't use any of the material on this list.* If these are the points that leap to your mind, they will leap to everyone else's too, and whether you get a "C" or a "D" may depend on whether the instructor reads your paper early when he is fresh and tolerant or late, when the sentence "In my opinion, college football has become too commercial," inexorably repeated, has brought him to the brink of lunacy.

Be against college football for some reason or reasons of your own. If they are keen and perceptive ones, that's splendid. But even if they are trivial or foolish or indefensible, you are still ahead so long as they are not everybody else's reasons too. Be against it because the colleges don't spend enough money on it to make it worth while, because it is bad for the characters of the spectators, because the players are forced to attend classes, because the football stars hog all the beautiful women, because it competes with baseball and is therefore unAmerican and possibly Communist inspired. There are lots of more or less unused reasons for being against college football.

Sometimes it is a good idea to sum up and dispose of the trite and conventional points before going on to your own. This has the advantage of indicating to the reader that you are going to be neither trite nor conventional. Something like this:

> We are often told that college football should be abolished because it has become too commercial or because it is bad for the players. These arguments are no doubt very cogent, but they don't really go to the heart of the matter.

Then you go to the heart of the matter.

TAKE THE LESS USUAL SIDE

One rather simple way of getting interest into your paper is to take the side of the argument that most of the citizens will want to avoid. If the assignment is an essay on dogs, you can, if you choose, explain that dogs are faithful and lovable companions, intelligent, useful as guardians of the house and protectors of children, indispensable in police work—in short, when all is said and done, man's best friends. Or you can suggest that those big brown eyes conceal, more often than not, a vacuity of mind and an inconstancy of purpose; that the dogs you have known most intimately have been mangy, ill-tempered brutes, incapable of instruction;

and that only your nobility of mind and fear of arrest prevent you from kicking the flea-ridden animals when you pass them on the street.

Naturally, personal convictions will sometimes dictate your approach. If the assigned subject is "Is Methodism Rewarding to the Individual?" and you are a pious Methodist, you have really no choice. But few assigned subjects, if any, will fall in this category. Most of them will lie in broad areas of discussion with much to be said on both sides. They are intellectual exercises, and it is legitimate to argue now one way and now another, as debaters do in similar circumstances. Always take the side that looks to you hardest, least defensible. It will almost always turn out to be easier to write interestingly on that side.

This general advice applies where you have a choice of subjects. If you are to choose among "The Value of Fraternities" and "My Favorite High School Teacher" and "What I Think About Beetles," by all means plump for the beetles. By the time the instructor gets to your paper, he will be up to his ears in tedious tales about the French teacher at Bloombury High and assertions about how fraternities build character and prepare one for life. Your views on beetles, whatever they are, are bound to be a refreshing change.

Don't worry too much about figuring out what the instructor thinks about the subject so that you can cuddle up with him. Chances are his views are no stronger than yours. If he does have convictions and you oppose them, his problem is to keep from grading you higher than you deserve in order to show he is not biased. This doesn't mean that you should always cantankerously dissent from what the instructor says; that gets tiresome too. And if the subject assigned is "My Pet Peeve," do not begin, "My pet peeve is the English instructor who assigns papers on 'my pet peeve.' " This was still funny during the War of 1812, but it has sort of lost its edge since then. It is in general good manners to avoid personalities.

SLIP OUT OF ABSTRACTION

If you will study the essay on college football on page 51, you will perceive that one reason for its appalling dullness is that it never gets down to particulars. It is just a series of not very glittering generalities: "football is bad for the colleges," "it has become too commercial," "football is a big business," "it is bad for the players," and so on. Such round phrases thudding against the reader's brain are unlikely to convince him, though they may well render him unconscious.

If you want the reader to believe that college football is bad for the players, you have to do more than say so. You have to display the evil.

Take your roommate, Alfred Simkins, the second-string center. Picture poor old Alfy coming home from football practice every evening, bruised and aching, agonizingly tired, scarcely able to shovel the mashed potatoes into his mouth. Let us see him staggering up to the room, getting out his econ textbook, peering desperately at it with his good eye, falling asleep and failing the test in the morning. Let us share his unbearable tension as Saturday draws near. Will he fail, be demoted, lose his monthly allowance, be forced to return to the coal mines? And if he succeeds, what will be his reward? Perhaps a slight ripple of applause when the third-string center replaces him, a moment of elation in the locker room if the team wins, of despair if it loses. What will he look back on when he graduates from college? Toil and torn ligaments. And what will be his future? He is not good enough for pro football, and he is too obscure and weak in econ to succeed in stocks and bonds. College football is tearing the heart from Alfy Simkins and, when it finishes with him, will callously toss aside the shattered hulk.

This is no doubt a weak enough argument for the abolition of college football, but it is a sight better than saying, in three or four variations, that college football (in your opinion) is bad for the players.

Look at the work of any professional writer and notice how constantly he is moving from the generality, the abstract statement, to the concrete example, the facts and figures, the illustration. If he is writing on juvenile delinquency, he does not just tell you that juveniles are (it seems to him) delinquent and that (in his opinion) something should be done about it. He shows you juveniles being delinquent, tearing up movie theatres in Buffalo, stabbing high school principals in Dallas, smoking marijuana in Palo Alto. And more than likely he is moving toward some specific remedy, not just a general wringing of the hands.

It is no doubt possible to be *too* concrete, too illustrative or anecdotal, but few inexperienced writers err this way. For most the soundest advice is to be seeking always for the picture, to be always turning general remarks into seeable examples. Don't say, "Sororities teach girls the social graces." Say, "Sorority life teaches a girl how to carry on a conversation while pouring tea, without sloshing the tea into the saucer." Don't say, "I like certain kinds of popular music very much." Say, "Whenever I hear Gerber Spinklittle play 'Mississippi Man' on the trombone, my socks creep up my ankles."

GET RID OF OBVIOUS PADDING

The student toiling away at his weekly English theme is too often tormented by a figure: five hundred words. How, he asks himself, is he to achieve this staggering total? Obviously by never using one word when he can somehow work in ten.

He is therefore seldom content with a plain statement like "Fast driving is dangerous." This has only four words in it. He takes thought, and the sentence becomes:

> In my opinion, fast driving is dangerous.

Better, but he can do better still:

> In my opinion, fast driving would seem to be rather dangerous.

If he is really adept, it may come out:

> In my humble opinion, though I do not claim to be an expert on this complicated subject, fast driving, in most circumstances, would seem to be rather dangerous in many respects, or at least so it would seem to me.

Thus four words have been turned into forty, and not an iota of content has been added.

Now this is a way to go about reaching five hundred words, and if you are content with a "D" grade, it is as good a way as any. But if you aim higher, you must work differently. Instead of stuffing your sentences with straw, you must try steadily to get rid of the padding, to make your sentences lean and tough. If you are really working at it, your first draft will greatly exceed the required total, and then you will work it down, thus:

> It is thought in some quarters that fraternities do not contribute as much as might be expected to campus life.
> Some people think that fraternities contribute little to campus life.

> The average doctor who practices in small towns or in the country must toil night and day to heal the sick.
> Most country doctors work long hours.

> When I was a little girl, I suffered from shyness and embarrassment in the presence of others.
> I was a shy little girl.

> It is absolutely necessary for the person employed as a marine fireman to give the matter of steam pressure his undivided attention at all times.
> The fireman has to keep his eye on the steam gauge.

You may ask how you can arrive at five hundred words at this rate. Simply. You dig up more real content. Instead of taking a couple of obvious points off the surface of the topic and then circling warily around them for six paragraphs, you work in and explore, figure out the details. You illustrate. You say that fast driving is dangerous, and then you prove it. How long does it take to stop a car at forty and at eighty? How far can you see at night? What happens when a tire blows? What happens in a head-on collision at fifty miles an hour? Pretty soon your paper will be full of broken glass and blood and headless torsos, and reaching five hundred words will not really be a problem.

CALL A FOOL A FOOL

Some of the padding in freshman themes is to be blamed not on anxiety about the word minimum but on excessive timidity. The student writes, "In my opinion, the principal of my high school acted in ways that I believe every unbiased person would have to call foolish." This isn't exactly what he means. What he means is, "My high school principal was a fool." If he was a fool, call him a fool. Hedging the thing about with "in-my-opinion's" and "it-seems-to-me's" and "as-I-see-it's" and "at-least-from-my-point-of-view's" gains you nothing. Delete these phrases whenever they creep into your paper.

The student's tendency to hedge stems from a modesty that in other circumstances would be commendable. He is, he realizes, young and inexperienced, and he half suspects that he is dopey and fuzzy-minded beyond the average. Probably only too true. But it doesn't help to announce your incompetence six times in every paragraph. Decide what you want to say and say it as vigorously as possible, without apology and in plain words.

Linguistic diffidence can take various forms. One is what we call *euphemism*. This is the tendency to call a spade "a certain garden implement" or women's underwear "unmentionables." It is stronger in some eras than others and in some people than others but it always operates more or less in subjects that are touchy or taboo: death, sex, madness, and so on. Thus we shrink from saying "He died last night" but say instead "passed away," "left us," "joined his Maker," "went to his reward." Or we try to take off the tension with a lighter cliché: "kicked the bucket," "cashed in his chips," "handed in his dinner pail." We have found all sorts of ways to avoid saying *mad:* "mentally ill," "touched," "not quite right upstairs," "feeble-minded," "innocent," "simple," "off his trolley," "not in his right mind." Even such a now plain word as *insane* began as a euphemism with the meaning "not healthy."

Modern science, particularly psychology, contributes many poly-syllables in which we can wrap our thoughts and blunt their force. To many writers there is no such thing as a bad schoolboy. Schoolboys are maladjusted or unoriented or misunderstood or in need of guidance or lacking in continued success toward satisfactory integration of the personality as a social unit, but they are never bad. Psychology no doubt makes us better men or women, more sympathetic and tolerant, but it doesn't make writing any easier. Had Shakespeare been confronted with psychology, "To be or not to be" might have come out, "To continue as a social unit or not to do so. That is the personality problem. Whether 'tis a better sign of integration at the conscious level to display a psychic tolerance toward the maladjustments and repressions induced by one's lack of orientation in one's environment or—" But Hamlet would never have finished the soliloquy.

Writing in the modern world, you cannot altogether avoid modern jargon. Nor, in an effort to get away from euphemism, should you salt your paper with four-letter words. But you can do much if you will mount guard against those roundabout phrases, those echoing polysylla-bles that tend to slip into your writing to rob it of its crispness and force.

BEWARE OF THE PAT EXPRESSION

Other things being equal, avoid phrases like "other things being equal." Those sentences that come to you whole, or in two or three doughy lumps, are sure to be bad sentences. They are no creation of yours but pieces of common thought floating in the community soup.

Pat expressions are hard, often impossible, to avoid, because they come too easily to be noticed and seem too necessary to be dispensed with. No writer avoids them altogether, but good writers avoid them more often than poor writers.

By "pat expressions" we mean such tags as "to all practical intents and purposes," "the pure and simple truth," "from where I sit," "the time of his life," "to the ends of the earth," "in the twinkling of an eye," "as sure as you're born," "over my dead body," "under cover of darkness," "took the easy way out," "when all is said and done," "told him time and time again," "parted the best of friends," "stand up and be counted," "gave him the best years of her life," "worked her fingers to the bone." Like other clichés, these expressions were once forceful. Now we should use them only when we can't possibly think of anything else.

Some pat expressions stand like a wall between the writer and thought. Such a one is "the American way of life." Many student writers feel that when they have said that something accords with the American way of life or does not they have exhausted the subject. Actually, they have stopped at the highest level of abstraction. The American way of life is the complicated set of bonds between a hundred and eighty million ways. All of us know this when we think about it, but the tag phrase too often keeps us from thinking about it.

So with many another phrase dear to the politician: "this great land of ours," "the man in the street," "our national heritage." These may prove our patriotism or give a clue to our political beliefs, but otherwise they add nothing to the paper except words.

COLORFUL WORDS

The writer builds with words, and no builder uses a raw material more slippery and elusive and treacherous. A writer's work is a constant struggle to get the right word in the right place, to find that particular word that will convey his meaning exactly, that will persuade the reader or soothe him or startle or amuse him. He never succeeds altogether—sometimes he feels that he scarcely succeeds at all—but such successes as he has are what make the thing worth doing.

There is no book of rules for this game. One progresses through everlasting experiment on the basis of ever-widening experience. There are few useful generalizations that one can make about words as words, but there are perhaps a few.

Some words are what we call "colorful." By this we mean that they are calculated to produce a picture or induce an emotion. They are dressy instead of plain, specific instead of general, loud instead of soft. Thus, in place of "Her heart beat," we may write "Her heart *pounded, throbbed, fluttered, danced.*" Instead of "He sat in his chair," we may say, "He *lounged, sprawled, coiled.*" Instead of "It was hot," we may say, "It was *blistering, sultry, muggy, suffocating, steamy, wilting.*"

However, it should not be supposed that the fancy word is always better. Often it is as well to write "Her heart beat" or "It was hot" if that is all it did or all it was. Ages differ in how they like their prose. The nineteenth century liked it rich and smoky. The twentieth has usually preferred it lean and cool. The twentieth century writer, like all writers, is forever seeking the exact word, but he is wary of sounding feverish. He tends to pitch it low, to understate it, to throw it away. He knows that if he gets too colorful, the audience is likely to giggle.

See how this strikes you: "As the rich, golden flow of the sunset died away along the eternal western hills, Angela's limpid blue eyes looked softly and trustingly into Montague's flashing brown ones, and her heart

pounded like a drum in time with the joyous song surging in her soul."
Some people like that sort of thing, but most modern readers would say,
"Good grief," and turn on the television.

COLORED WORDS

Some words we would call not so much colorful as colored—that is,
loaded with associations, good or bad. All words—except perhaps
structure words—have associations of some eventualities, like a grade of
"D." Notice also what "etc." means. It means "I'd like to make this list
longer, but I can't think of any more examples."

For Discussion

1. Roberts implies that students will take the position they feel the instructor
holds—if he's against college football students will write their themes arguing against football. From your own experience do you find this to be true?
Would you write for the position your instructor holds simply because it is
his position and he is the one who will grade you? Can you identify those
instructors who will give better grades to those compositions which agree
with their position? From what evidence do you draw this conclusion? How
sure are you of this conclusion? Ask your instructor if he favors (with
higher grades) those papers which agree with his position.

2. Assignments, says Roberts, are "intellectual exercises, and it is legitimate to
argue now one way and now another, as debaters do in similar circumstances." Do you agree with this? Is it ethical to argue in favor of something you do not believe is right? Is it ethical to debate both sides of the
question? (You may be interested in the following articles in which this
question is considered: Richard Murphy, "The Ethics of Debating Both
Sides," *Speech Teacher*, VI (January 1957), 1–9; Nicholas M. Cripe, "Debating Both Sides in Tournaments is Ethical," *Speech Teacher*, VI (September
1957), 209–12; George W. Dell, "In Defense of Debating Both Sides,"
Speech Teacher, VII (January 1958), 31–34; Douglas Ehninger, "The Debate About Debating," *Quarterly Journal of Speech*, XLIV (April 1958),
128–36; Richard Murphy, "The Ethics of Debating Both Sides II," *Speech
Teacher*, XII (September 1963), 242–47.)

3. Examine one of your own compositions or speech manuscripts or outlines
for the faults Roberts discusses. Can you identify specific examples of these
faults in your own writing? Rewrite the composition or speech so as to
eliminate as many of these problems as possible.

4. What criteria do you feel should be employed in evaluating a written composition? What criteria should be employed in evaluating a speech? Should the criteria be the same or different? Why?

5. When you write a composition, for whom are you writing? That is, who is your audience? In what ways would changes in your audience lead to changes in your style of writing? Why? Why do you suppose speech texts give more attention to audience than do written composition texts?

Gobbledygook

STUART CHASE

In this article Stuart Chase discusses a perennial problem,
that of gobbledygook—using too many and too big words
where fewer and shorter words would do a better job.

Said Franklin Roosevelt, in one of his early presidential speeches: "I see one-third of a nation ill-housed, ill-clad, ill-nourished." Translated into standard bureaucratic prose his statement would read:

> It is evident that a substantial number of persons within the Continental boundaries of the United States have inadequate financial resources with which to purchase the products of agricultural communities and industrial establishments. It would appear that for a considerable segment of the population, possibly as much as 33.3333* of the total, there are inadequate housing facilities, and an equally significant proportion is deprived of the proper types of clothing and nutriment.
>
> * Not carried beyond four places.

This rousing satire on gobbledygook—or talk among the bureaucrats —is adapted from a report[1] prepared by the Federal Security Agency in an attempt to break out of the verbal squirrel cage. "Gobbledygook" was coined by an exasperated Congressman, Maury Maverick of Texas, and means using two, or three, or ten words in the place of one, or using a five-syllable word where a single syllable would suffice. Maverick was censuring the forbidding prose of executive departments in Washington, but the term has now spread to windy and pretentious language in general.

"Gobbledygook" itself is a good example of the way a language grows. There was no word for the event before Maverick's invention; one had to say: "You know, that terrible, involved, polysyllabic lan-

[1] This and succeeding quotations from F.S.A. report by special permission of the author, Milton Hall.

"Gobbledygook." From Stuart Chase, The Power of Words (*New York: Harcourt Brace Jovanovich, Inc., 1954*), *pp. 249– 59. Copyright 1953, 1954 by Stuart Chase. Reprinted by permission of Harcourt Brace Jovanovich, Inc.*

guage those government people use down in Washington." Now one word takes the place of a dozen.

A British member of Parliament, A. P. Herbert, also exasperated with bureaucratic jargon, translated Nelson's immortal phrase, "England expects every man to do his duty":

> England anticipates that, as regards the current emergency, personnel will face up to the issues, and exercise appropriately the functions allocated to their respective occupational groups.

A New Zealand official made the following report after surveying a plot of ground for an athletic field:[2]

> It is obvious from the difference in elevation with relation to the short depth of the property that the contour is such as to preclude any reasonable developmental potential for active recreation.

Seems the plot was too steep.

An office manager sent this memo to his chief:

> Verbal contract with Mr. Blank regarding the attached notification of promotion has elicited the attached representation intimating that he prefers to decline the assignment.

Seems Mr. Blank didn't want the job.

> A doctor testified at an English trial that one of the parties was suffering from "circumorbital haematoma."

Seems the party had a black eye.

> In August 1952 the U.S. Department of Agriculture put out a pamphlet entitled: "Cultural and Pathogenic Variability in Single-Condial and Hyphaltip Isolates of Hemlin-Thosporium Turcicum Pass."

Seems it was about corn leaf disease.

On reaching the top of the Finsteraarhorn in 1845, M. Dollfus-Ausset, when he got his breath, exclaimed:

---

[2] This item and the next two are from the piece on gobbledygook by W. E. Farbstein, New York *Times,* March 29, 1953.

> The soul communes in the infinite with those icy peaks which seem to have their roots in the bowels of eternity.

Seems he enjoyed the view.

A government department announced:

> Voucherable expenditures necessary to provide adequate dental treatment required as adjunct to medical treatment being rendered a pay patient in in-patient status may be incurred as required at the expense of the Public Health Service.

Seems you can charge your dentist bill to the Public Health Service. Or can you?

Legal Talk

Gobbledygook not only flourishes in government bureaus but grows wild and lush in the law, the universities, and sometimes among the literati. Mr. Micawber was a master of gobbledygook, which he hoped would improve his fortunes. It is almost always found in offices too big for face-to-face talk. Gobbledygook can be defined as squandering words, packing a message with excess baggage and so introducing semantic "noise." Or it can be scrambling words in a message so that meaning does not come through. The directions on cans, bottles, and packages for putting the contents to use are often a good illustration. Gobbledygook must not be confused with double talk, however, for the intentions of the sender are usually honest.

I offer you a round fruit and say, "Have an orange." Not so an expert in legal phraseology, as parodied by editors of *Labor:*

> I hereby give and convey to you, all and singular, my estate and interests, right, title, claim and advantages of and in said orange, together with all rind, juice, pulp and pits, and all rights and advantages therein . . . anything hereinbefore or hereinafter or in any other deed or deeds, instrument or instruments of whatever nature or kind whatsoever, to the contrary, in any wise, notwithstanding.

The state of Ohio, after five years of work, has redrafted its legal code in modern English, eliminating 4,500 sections and doubtless a blizzard of "whereases" and "hereinafters." Legal terms of necessity must be closely tied to their referents, but the early solons tried to do this the hard way, by adding synonyms. They hoped to trap the physical event in a net of words, but instead they created a mumbo-jumbo beyond the power of the layman, and even many a lawyer, to translate. Legal talk is studded with tautologies, such as "cease and desist," "give and convey," "irrelevant, incompetent, and immaterial." Furthermore, legal jargon is a dead language; it is not spoken and it is not growing. An official of one of the big insurance companies calls their branch of it "bafflegab." Here is a sample from his collection:[3]

> One-half to his mother, if living, if not to his father, and one-half to his mother-in-law, if living, if not to his mother, if living, if not to his father. Thereafter payment is to be made in a single sum to his brothers. On the one-half payable to his mother, if living, if not to his father, he does not bring in his mother-in-law as the next payee to receive, although on the one-half to his mother-in-law, he does bring in the mother or father.

You apply for an insurance policy, pass the tests, and instead of a straightforward "here is your policy," you receive something like this:

> This policy is issued in consideration of the application therefor, copy of which application is attached hereto and made part hereof, and of the payment for said insurance on the life of the above-named insured.

Academic Talk

The pedagogues may be less repetitious than the lawyers, but many use even longer words. It is a symbol of their calling to prefer Greek and Latin derivatives to Anglo-Saxon. Thus instead of saying: "I like short clear words," many a professor would think it more seemingly to say: "I prefer an abbreviated phraseology, distinguished for its lucidity." Your professor is sometimes right, the longer word may carry the meaning better—but not because it is long. Allen Upward in his book *The New Word* warmly advocates Anglo-Saxon English as against what he calls "Mediterranean" English, with its polysyllables built up like a skyscraper.

Professional pedagogy, still alternating between the Middle Ages and modern science, can produce what Henshaw Ward once called the

---

[3] Interview with Clifford B. Reeves by Sylvia F. Porter, New York *Evening Post*, March 14, 1952.

most repellent prose known to man. It takes an iron will to read as much as a page of it. Here is a sample of what is known in some quarters as "pedageese":

> Realization has grown that the curriculum or the experiences of learners change and improve only as those who are most directly involved examine their goals, improve their understandings and increase their skill in performing the tasks necessary to reach newly defined goals. This places the focus upon teacher, lay citizen and learner as partners in curricular improvement and as the individuals who must change, if there is to be curriculum change.

I think there is an idea concealed here somewhere. I think it means: "If we are going to change the curriculum, teacher, parent, and student must all help." The reader is invited to get out his semantic decoder and check on my translation. Observe there is no technical language in this gem of pedageese, beyond possibly the word "curriculum." It is just a simple idea heavily ververbalized.

In another kind of academic talk the author may display his learning to conceal a lack of ideas. A bright instructor, for instance, in need of prestige may select a common sense proposition for the subject of a learned monograph—say, "Modern cities are hard to live in" and adorn it with imposing polysyllables: "Urban existence in the perpendicular declivities of megalopolis . . ." et cetera. He coins some new terms to transfix the reader—"mega-decibel" or "strato-cosmopolis"—and works them vigorously. He is careful to add a page or two of differential equations to show the "scatter." And then he publishes, with 147 footnotes and a bibliography to knock your eye out. If the authorities are dozing, it can be worth an associate professorship.

While we are on the campus, however, we must not forget that the technical language of the natural sciences and some terms in the social sciences, forbidding as they may sound to the layman, are quite necessary. Without them, specialists could not communicate what they find. Trouble arises when experts expect the uninitiated to understand the words; when they tell the jury, for instance, that the defendant is suffering from "circumorbital haematoma."

Here are two authentic quotations. Which was written by a distinguished modern author, and which by a patient in a mental hospital? You will find the answer at the end of the chapter.

> 1. Have just been to supper. Did not knowing what the woodchuck sent me here. How when the blue blue blue on the said anyone can do it that tries. Such is the presidential candidate.

2. No history of a family to close with those and close. Never shall he be
   alone to be alone to be alone to be alone to be alone to lend a hand
   and leave it left and wasted.

REDUCING THE GOBBLE

As government and business offices grow larger, the need for doing
something about gobbledygook increases. Fortunately the biggest office
in the world is working hard to reduce it. The Federal Security Agency
in Washington,[4] with nearly 100 million clients on its books, began
analyzing its communication lines some years ago, with gratifying results.
Surveys find trouble in three main areas: correspondence with clients
about their social security problems, office memos, official reports.

Clarity and brevity, as well as common humanity, are urgently
needed in this vast establishment which deals with disability, old age,
and unemployment. The surveys found instead many cases of long-
windedness, foggy meanings, clichés, and singsong phrases, and gross
neglect of the reader's point of view. Rather than talking to a real person, the writer was talking to himself. "We often write like a man walking on stilts."

Here is a typical case of long-windedness:

> *Gobbledygook as found:* "We are wondering if sufficient time has
> passed so that you are in a position to indicate whether favorable
> action may now be taken on our recommendation for the reclassifi-
> cation of Mrs. Blank, junior clerk-stenographer, CAF 2, to assistant
> clerk-stenographer, CAF 3?"
>
> *Suggested improvement:* "Have you yet been able to act on our
> recommendation to reclassify Mrs. Blank?"

Another case:

> Although the Central Efficiency Rating Committee recognizes
> that there are many desirable changes that could be made in the
> present efficiency rating system in order to make it more realistic and
> more workable than it now is, this committee is of the opinion that
> no further change should be made in the present system during the
> current year. Because of conditions prevailing throughout the coun-
> try and the resultant turnover in personnel, and difficulty in admin-
> istering the Federal programs, further mechanical improvement in
> the present rating system would require staff retraining and other

---

[4] Now the Department of Health, Education, and Welfare.

administrative expense which would seem best withheld until the official termination of hostilities, and until restoration of regular operations.

The F.S.A. invites us to squeeze the gobbledygook out of this statement. Here is my attempt:

> The Central Efficiency Rating Committee recognizes that desirable changes could be made in the present system. We believe, however, that no change should be attempted until the war is over.

This cuts the statement from 111 to 30 words, about one-quarter of the original, but perhaps the reader can do still better. What of importance have I left out?

Sometimes in a book which I am reading for information—not for literary pleasure—I run a pencil through the surplus words. Often I can cut a section to half its length with an improvement in clarity. Magazines like *The Reader's Digest* have reduced this process to an art. Are long-windedness and obscurity a cultural lag from the days when writing was reserved for priests and cloistered scholars? The more words and the deeper the mystery, the greater their prestige and the firmer the hold on their jobs. And the better the candidate's chance today to have his doctoral thesis accepted.

The F.S.A. surveys found that a great deal of writing was obscure although not necessarily prolix. Here is a letter sent to more than 100,000 inquirers, a classic example of murky prose. To clarify it, one needs to *add* words, not cut them:

> In order to be fully insured, an individual must have earned $50 or more in covered employment for as many quarters of coverage as half the calendar quarters elapsing between 1936 and the quarter in which he reaches age 65 or dies, whichever first occurs.

Probably no one without the technical jargon of the office could translate this: nevertheless, it was sent out to drive clients mad for seven years. One poor fellow wrote back: "I am no longer in covered employment. I have an outside job now."

Many words and phrases in officialese seem to come out automatically, as if from lower centers of the brain. In this standardized prose people never *get jobs*, they "secure employment"; *before* and *after* become "prior to" and "subsequent to"; one does not *do*, one "performs"; nobody *knows* a thing, he is "fully cognizant"; one never *says*, he "indicates." A great favorite at present is "implement."

Some charming boners occur in this talking-in-one's-sleep. For instance:

> The problem of extending coverage to all employees, regardless of size, is not as simple as surface appearances indicate.
> Though the proportions of all males and females in ages 16–45 are essentially the same . . .
> Dairy cattle, usually and commonly embraced in dairying . . .

In its manual to employees, the F.S.A. suggests the following:

Instead of	Use
give consideration to	consider
make inquiry regarding	inquire
is of the opinion	believes
comes into conflict with	conflicts
information which is of a confidential nature	confidential information

Professional or office gobbledygook often arises from using the passive rather than the active voice. Instead of looking you in the eye, as it were, and writing "This act requires . . ." the office worker looks out of the window and writes: "It is required by this statute that . . ." When the bureau chief says, "We expect Congress to cut your budget," the message is only too clear; but usually he says, "It is expected that the departmental budget estimates will be reduced by Congress."

> *Gobbled:* "All letters prepared for the signature of the Administrator will be single spaced."
> *Ungobbled:* "Single space all letters for the Administrator."
> (Thus cutting 13 words to 7.)

Only People Can Read

The F.S.A. surveys pick up the point, stressed in Chapter 15, that human communication involves a listener as well as a speaker. Only people can read, though a lot of writing seems to be addressed to beings in outer space. To whom are you talking? The sender of the officialese message often forgets the chap on the other end of the line.

A woman with two small children wrote the F.S.A. asking what she should do about payments, as her husband had lost his memory. "If he never gets able to work," she said, "and stays in an institution would I be able to draw any benefits? . . . I don't know how I am going to live and raise my children since he is disable to work. Please give me some information. . . ."

To this human appeal, she received a shattering blast of gobbledygook, beginning, "State unemployment compensation laws do not provide any benefits for sick or disabled individuals . . . in order to qualify an individual must have a certain number of quarters of coverage . . ." et cetera, et cetera. Certainly if the writer had been thinking about the poor woman he would not have dragged in unessential material about old-age insurance. If he had pictured a mother without means to care for her children, he would have told her where she might get help—from the local office which handles aid to dependent children, for instance.

Gobbledygook of this kind would largely evaporate if we thought of our messages as two way—in the above case, if we pictured ourselves talking on the doorstep of a shabby house to a woman with two children tugging at her skirts, who in her distress does not know which way to turn.

Results of the Survey

The F.S.A. survey showed that office documents could be cut 20 to 50 per cent, with an improvement in clarity and a great saving to taxpayers in paper and payrolls.

A handbook was prepared and distributed to key officials.[5] They read it, thought about it, and presently began calling section meetings to discuss gobbledygook. More booklets were ordered, and the local output of documents began to improve. A Correspondence Review Section was established as a kind of laboratory to test murky messages. A supervisor could send up samples for analysis and suggestions. The handbook is now used for training new members; and many employees keep it on their desks along with the dictionary. Outside the Bureau some 25,000 copies have been sold (at 20 cents each) to individuals, governments, business firms, all over the world. It is now used officially in the Veterans Administration and in the Department of Agriculture.

The handbook makes clear the enormous amount of gobbledygook which automatically spreads in any large office, together with ways and means to keep it under control. I would guess that at least half of all the words circulating around the bureaus of the world are "irrelevant, incompetent, and immaterial"—to use a favorite legalism; or are just plain "unnecessary"—to ungobble it.

[5] By Milton Hall.

My favorite story of removing the gobble from gobbledygook concerns the Bureau of Standards at Washington. I have told it before but perhaps the reader will forgive the repetition. A New York plumber wrote the Bureau that he had found hydrochloric acid fine for cleaning drains, and was it harmless? Washington replied: "The efficacy of hydrochloric acid is indisputable, but the chlorine residue is incompatible with metallic permanence."

The plumber wrote back that he was mighty glad the Bureau agreed with him. The Bureau replied with a note of alarm: "We cannot assume responsibility for the production of toxic and noxious residues with hydrochloric acid, and suggest that you use an alternate procedure." The plumber was happy to learn that the Bureau still agreed with him.

Whereupon Washington exploded: "Don't use hydrochloric acid; it eats hell out of the pipes!"

Note: The second quotation on page 68 comes from Gertrude Stein's *Lucy Church Amiably.*

For Discussion

1. College catalogues are notorious for gobbledygook. Read through a few pages, identifying the instances of gobbledygook and rewrite them in plain, simple English.

2. Chase is undoubtedly correct in advocating short, simple words for communicating information. Would the same principle apply to persuasive messages? Most textbooks on persuasion, for example, claim that the language must be clearly understood before the audience will be persuaded. Do you agree with this? Can you identify instances where persuasion was achieved even when the message was not understood?

3. One procedure for reducing gobbledygook, Chase suggests, is to pencil through the excess words. Do this for one page in one of your textbooks. How many words were you able to eliminate? Would the textbook be clearer if the author had done this for every page?

4. Gobbledygook, says Chase, often results from using the passive rather than the active voice. What are the advantages of using the active voice? What are the disadvantages? What are the advantages and disadvantages of using the passive voice?

5. Chase suggests that by viewing communication as a two-way process we are less likely to fall into the gobbledygook trap and earlier in the article he

noted that college professors were particularly prone to gobbledygook. Examine one of your textbooks (this one if you prefer) with Chase's observations in mind. Does the author conform to Chase's characterization of the gobbledygook professor? What specific indications can you find in the book to support your position?

The Medium
Is the Message

MARSHALL MC LUHAN

The following excerpt comes from one of the most
provocative and controversial books of our time,
Understanding Media: The Extensions of Man. In it
Marshall McLuhan argues that the most important
element in communication is not the content—as most
theorists hold—but rather the medium; the medium is so
important that it is, in fact, the message. The entire book
and especially the first chapter which is reprinted here is
intellectually exhausting to read. Although it takes
considerable energy to get through his prose, it is well
worth the effort. McLuhan is not only provocative;
very probably he's right.

In a culture like ours, long accustomed to splitting and dividing all things as a means of control, it is sometimes a bit of a shock to be reminded that, in operational and practical fact, the medium is the message. This is merely to say that the personal and social consequences of any medium—that is, of any extension of ourselves—result from the new scale that is introduced into our affairs by each extension of ourselves, or by any new technology. Thus, with automation, for example, the new patterns of human association tend to eliminate jobs, it is true. That is the negative result. Positively, automation creates roles for people, which is to say depth of involvement in their work and human association that our preceding mechanical technology had destroyed. Many people would be disposed to say that it was not the machine, but what one did with the machine, that was its meaning or message. In terms of the ways in which the machine altered our relations to one another and to ourselves, it mattered not in the least whether it turned out cornflakes or Cadillacs. The restructuring of human work and association was shaped by the technique of fragmentation that is the essence of machine technology. The essence of automation technology is the opposite. It is integral and decentralist in depth, just as the machine was fragmentary, centralist, and superficial in its patterning of human relationships.

The instance of the electric light may prove illuminating in this connection. The electric light is pure information. It is a medium without a message, as it were, unless it is used to spell out some verbal ad or name. This fact, characteristic of all media, means that the "content" of any medium is always another medium. The content of writing is speech, just as the written word is the content of print, and print is the content of the telegraph. If it is asked, "What is the content of speech?," it is necessary to say, "It is an actual process of thought, which is in

"The Medium Is the Message." From Marshall McLuhan, Understanding Media: The Extensions of Man (*New York: McGraw-Hill, 1964*), *pp. 7–21. Reprinted by permission of McGraw-Hill Book Company.*

itself nonverbal." An abstract painting represents direct manifestation of creative thought processes as they might appear in computer designs. What we are considering here, however, are the psychic and social consequences of the designs or patterns as they amplify or accelerate existing processes. For the "message" of any medium or technology is the change of scale or pace or pattern that it introduces into human affairs. The railway did not introduce movement or transportation or wheel or road into human society, but it accelerated and enlarged the scale of previous human functions, creating totally new kinds of cities and new kinds of work and leisure. This happened whether the railway functioned in a tropical or a northern environment, and is quite independent of the freight or content of the railway medium. The airplane, on the other hand, by accelerating the rate of transportation, tends to dissolve the railway form of city, politics, and association, quite independently of what the airplane is used for.

Let us return to the electric light. Whether the light is being used for brain surgery or night baseball is a matter of indifference. It could be argued that these activities are in some way the "content" of the electric light, since they could not exist without the electric light. This fact merely underlines the point that "the medium is the message" because it is the medium that shapes and controls the scale and form of human association and action. The content or uses of such media are as diverse as they are ineffectual in shaping the form of human association. Indeed, it is only too typical that the "content" of any medium blinds us to the character of the medium. It is only today that industries have become aware of the various kinds of business in which they are engaged. When IBM discovered that it was not in the business of making office equipment or business machines, but that it was in the business of processing information, then it began to navigate with clear vision. The General Electric Company makes a considerable portion of its profits from electric light bulbs and lighting systems. It has not yet discovered that, quite as much as A.T.&T., it is in the business of moving information.

The electric light escapes attention as a communication medium just because it has no "content." And this makes it an invaluable instance of how people fail to study media at all. For it is not till the electric light is used to spell out some brand name that it is noticed as a medium. Then it is not the light but the "content" (or what is really another medium) that is noticed. The message of the electric light is like the message of electric power in industry, totally radical, pervasive, and decentralized. For electric light and power are separate from their uses, yet they eliminate time and space factors in human association exactly as do radio, telegraph, telephone, and TV, creating involvement in depth.

A fairly complete handbook for studying the extensions of man could be made up from selections from Shakespeare. Some might quibble about whether or not he was referring to TV in these familiar lines from *Romeo and Juliet:*

> But soft! What light through yonder window breaks?
> It speaks, and yet says nothing.

In *Othello,* which, as much as *King Lear,* is concerned with the torment of people transformed by illusions, there are these lines that bespeak Shakespeare's intuition of the transforming powers of new media:

> Is there not charms
> By which the property of youth and maidhood
> May be abus'd? Have you not read Roderigo,
> Of some such thing?

In Shakespeare's *Troilus and Cressida,* which is almost completely devoted to both a psychic and social study of communication, Shakespeare states his awareness that true social and political navigation depend upon anticipating the consequences of innovation:

> The providence that's in a watchful state
> Knows almost every grain of Plutus' gold,
> Finds bottom in the uncomprehensive deeps,
> Keeps place with thought, and almost like the gods
> Does thoughts unveil in their dumb cradles.

The increasing awareness of the action of media, quite independently of their "content" or programming, was indicated in the annoyed and anonymous stanza:

> In modern thought, (if not in fact)
> Nothing is that doesn't act,
> So that is reckoned wisdom which
> Describes the scratch but not the itch.

The same kind of total, configurational awareness that reveals why the medium is socially the message has occurred in the most recent and radical medical theories. In his *Stress of Life,* Hans Selye tells of the dismay of a research colleague on hearing of Selye's theory:

> When he saw me thus launched on yet another enraptured description of what I had observed in animals treated with this or that impure, toxic material, he looked at me with desperately sad eyes

and said in obvious despair: "But Selye, try to realize what you are doing before it is too late! You have now decided to spend your entire life studying the pharmacology of dirt!"

(Hans Selye, *The Stress of Life*)

As Selye deals with the total environmental situation in his "stress" theory of disease, so the latest approach to media study considers not only the "content" but the medium and the cultural matrix within which the particular medium operates. The older unawareness of the psychic and social effects of media can be illustrated from almost any of the conventional pronouncements.

In accepting an honorary degree from the University of Notre Dame a few years ago, General David Sarnoff made this statement: "We are too prone to make technological instruments the scapegoats for the sins of those who wield them. The products of modern science are not in themselves good or bad; it is the way they are used that determines their value." That is the voice of the current somnambulism. Suppose we were to say, "Apple pie is in itself neither good nor bad; it is the way it is used that determines its value." Or, "The smallpox virus is in itself neither good nor bad; it is the way it is used that determines its value." Again, "Firearms are in themselves neither good nor bad; it is the way they are used that determines their value." That is, if the slugs reach the right people firearms are good. If the TV tube fires the right ammunition at the right people it is good. I am not being perverse. There is simply nothing in the Sarnoff statement that will bear scrutiny, for it ignores the nature of the medium, of any and all media, in the true Narcissus style of one hypnotized by the amputation and extension of his own being in a new technical form. General Sarnoff went on to explain his attitude to the technology of print, saying that it was true that print caused much trash to circulate, but it had also disseminated the Bible and the thoughts of seers and philosophers. It has never occurred to General Sarnoff that any technology could do anything but *add* itself on to what we already are.

Such economists as Robert Theobald, W. W. Rostow, and John Kenneth Galbraith have been explaining for years how it is that "classical economics" cannot explain change or growth. And the paradox of mechanization is that although it is itself the cause of maximal growth and change, the principle of mechanization excludes the very possibility of growth or the understanding of change. For mechanization is achieved by fragmentation of any process and by putting the fragmented parts in a series. Yet, as David Hume showed in the eighteenth century, there is no principle of causality in a mere sequence. That one thing follows another accounts for nothing. Nothing follows from following, except change. So the greatest of all reversals occurred with electricity, that ended sequence by making things instant. With instant speed the causes of things began to emerge to awareness again, as they had not done with things in sequence and in concatenation accordingly. Instead of asking which came first, the chicken or the egg, it suddenly seemed that a chicken was an egg's idea for getting more eggs.

Just before an airplane breaks the sound barrier, sound waves become visible on the wings of the plane. The sudden visibility of sound just as sound ends is an apt instance of that great pattern of being that reveals new and opposite forms just as the earlier forms reach their peak performance. Mechanization was never so vividly fragmented or sequential as in the birth of the movies, the moment that translated us beyond mechanism into the world of growth and organic interrelation. The movie, by sheer speeding up the mechanical, carried us from the world of sequence and connections into the world of creative configuration and structure. The message of the movie medium is that of transition from lineal connections to configurations. It is the transition that produced the now quite correct observation: "If it works, it's obsolete." When electric speed further takes over from mechanical movie sequences, then the lines of force in structures and in media become loud and clear. We return to the inclusive form of the icon.

To a highly literate and mechanized culture the movie appeared as a world of triumphant illusions and dreams that money could buy. It was at this moment of the movie that cubism occurred, and it has been described by E. H. Gombrich (*Art and Illusion*) as "the most radical attempt to stamp out ambiguity and to enforce one reading of the picture—that of a man-made construction, a colored canvas." For cubism substitutes all facets of an object simultaneously for the "point of view" or facet of perspective illusion. Instead of the specialized illusion of the third dimension on canvas, cubism sets up an interplay of planes and contradiction or dramatic conflict of patterns, lights, textures that "drives home the message" by involvement. This is held by many to be an exercise in painting, not in illusion.

In other words, cubism, by giving the inside and outside, the top, bottom, back, and front and the rest, in two dimensions, drops the illusion of perspective in favor of instant sensory awareness of the whole. Cubism, by seizing on instant total awareness, suddenly announced that *the medium is the message*. Is it not evident that the moment that sequence yields to the simultaneous, one is in the world of the structure and of configuration? Is that not what has happened in physics as in painting, poetry, and in communication? Specialized segments of attention have shifted to total field, and we can now say, "The medium is the message" quite naturally. Before the electric speed and total field, it was not obvious that the medium is the message. The message, it seemed, was the "content," as people used to ask what a painting was *about*. Yet they never thought to ask what a melody was about, nor what a house or a dress was about. In such matters, people retained some sense of the whole pattern, of form and function as a unity. But in the electric age this integral idea of structure and configuration has become so prevalent that educational theory has taken up the matter. Instead of working with specialized "problems" in arithmetic, the structural approach now follows the linea of force in the field of number and has small children meditating about number theory and "sets."

Cardinal Newman said of Napoleon, "He understood the grammar of gunpowder." Napoleon had paid some attention to other media as well, especially the semaphore telegraph that gave him a great advantage over his enemies. He is on record for saying that "Three hostile newspapers are more to be feared than a thousand bayonets."

Alexis de Tocqueville was the first to master the grammar of print and typography. He was thus able to read off the message of coming change in France and America as if he were reading aloud from a text that had been handed to him. In fact, the nineteenth century in France and in America was just such an open book to de Tocqueville because he had learned the grammar of print. So he, also, knew when that grammar did not apply. He was asked why he did not write a book on England, since he knew and admired England. He replied:

> One would have to have an unusual degree of philosophical folly to believe oneself able to judge England in six months. A year always seemed to me too short a time in which to appreciate the United States properly, and it is much easier to acquire clear and precise notions about the American Union than about Great Britain. In America all laws derive in a sense from the same line of thought. The whole of society, so to speak, is founded upon a single fact; everything springs from a simple principle. One could compare America to a forest pierced by a multitude of straight roads all converging on the same point. One has only to find the center and everything is revealed at a glance. But in England the paths run criss-cross, and it is only by travelling down each one of them that one can build up a picture of the whole.

De Tocqueville, in an earlier work on the French Revolution, had explained how it was the printed word that, achieving cultural saturation in the eighteenth century, had homogenized the French nation. Frenchmen were the same kind of people from north to south. The typographic principles of uniformity, continuity, and lineality had overlaid the complexities of ancient feudal and oral society. The Revolution was carried out by the new literati and lawyers.

In England, however, such was the power of the ancient oral traditions of common law, backed by the medieval institution of Parliament, that no uniformity or continuity of the new visual print culture could take complete hold. The result was that the most important event in English history has never taken place; namely, the English Revolution on the lines of the French Revolution. The American Revolution had no medieval legal institutions to discard or to root out, apart from monarchy. And many have held that the American Presidency has become very much more personal and monarchical than any European monarch ever could be.

De Tocqueville's contrast between England and America is clearly based on the fact of typography and of print culture creating uniformity and continuity. England, he says, has rejected this principle and clung to the dynamic or oral common-law tradition. Hence the discontinuity and unpredictable quality of English culture. The grammar of print cannot help to construe the message of oral and nonwritten culture and institutions. The English aristocracy was properly classified as barbarian by Matthew Arnold because its power and status had nothing to do with literacy or with the cultural forms of typography. Said the Duke of Gloucester to Edward Gibbon upon the publication of his *Decline and Fall:* "Another damned fat book, eh, Mr. Gibbon? Scribble, scribble, scribble, eh, Mr. Gibbon?" De Tocqueville was a highly literate aristocrat who was quite able to be detached from the values and assumptions of typography. That is why he alone understood the grammar of typography. And it is only on those terms, standing aside from any structure or medium, that its principles and lines of force can be discerned. For any medium has the power of imposing its own assumption on the unwary. Prediction and control consist in avoiding this subliminal state of Narcissus trance. But the greatest aid to this end is simply in knowing that the spell can occur immediately upon contact, as in the first bars of a melody.

A Passage to India by E. M. Forster is a dramatic study of the inability of oral and intuitive oriental culture to meet with the rational, visual European patterns of experience. "Rational," of course, has for the West long meant "uniform and continuous and sequential." In other words, we have confused reason with literacy, and rationalism with a single technology. Thus in the electric age man seems to the conventional West to become irrational. In Forster's novel the moment of truth and dislocation from the typographic trance of the West comes in the Marabar Caves. Adela Quested's reasoning powers cannot cope with the total inclusive field of resonance that is India. After the Caves: "Life went on as usual, but had no consequences, that is to say, sounds did not echo nor thought develop. Everything seemed cut off at its root and therefore infected with illusion."

A Passage to India (the phrase is from Whitman, who saw America headed Eastward) is a parable of Western man in the electric age, and is only incidentally related to Europe or the Orient. The ultimate conflict between sight and sound, between written and oral kinds of perception and organization of existence is upon us. Since understanding stops action, as Nietzsche observed, we can moderate the fierceness of this conflict by understanding the media that extend us and raise these wars within and without us.

Detribalization by literacy and its traumatic effects on tribal man is the theme of a book by the psychiatrist J. C. Carothers, *The African Mind in Health and Disease* (World Health Organization, Geneva, 1953). Much of his material appeared in an article in *Psychiatry* magazine, November, 1959: "The Culture, Psychiatry, and the Written Word." Again, it is electric speed that has revealed the lines of force operating from Western technology in the remotest areas of bush, savannah, and desert. One example is the Bedouin with his battery radio on board the camel. Submerging natives with floods of concepts for which nothing has prepared them is the normal action of all of our technology. But with electric media Western man himself experiences exactly the same inundation as the remote native. We are no more prepared to encounter radio and TV in our literate milieu than the native of Ghana is able to cope with the literacy that takes him out of his collective tribal world and beaches him in individual isolation. We are as numb in our new electric world as the native involved in our literate and mechanical culture.

Electric speed mingles the cultures of prehistory with the dregs of industrial marketeers, the nonliterate with the semiliterate and the postliterate. Mental breakdown of varying degrees is the very common result of uprooting and inundation with new information and endless new patterns of information. Wyndham Lewis made this a theme of his group of novels called *The Human Age*. The first of these, *The Childermass,* is concerned precisely with accelerated media change as a kind of massacre of the innocents. In our own world as we become more aware of the effects of technology on psychic formation and manifestation, we are losing all confidence in our right to assign guilt. Ancient prehistoric societies regard violent crime as pathetic. The killer is regarded as we do a cancer victim. "How terrible it must be to feel like that," they say. J. M. Synge took up this idea very effectively in his *Playboy of the Western World.*

If the criminal appears as a nonconformist who is unable to meet the demand of technology that we behave in uniform and continuous patterns, literate man is quite inclined to see others who cannot conform as somewhat pathetic. Especially the child, the cripple, the woman, and the colored person appear in a world of visual and typographic technology as victims of injustice. On the other hand, in a culture that assigns roles instead of jobs to people—the dwarf, the skew, the child create their own spaces. They are not expected to fit into some uniform and repeatable niche that is not their size anyway. Consider the phrase "It's a man's world." As a quantitative observation endlessly repeated from within a homogenized culture, this phrase refers to the men in such a culture who have to be homogenized Dagwoods in order to belong at all. It is in our I.Q. testing that we have produced the greatest flood of misbegotten standards. Unaware of our typographic cultural bias, our testers assume that uniform and continuous habits are a sign of intelligence, thus eliminating the ear man and the tactile man.

C. P. Snow, reviewing a book of A. L. Rowse (*The New York Times Book Review,* December 24, 1961) on *Appeasement* and the road to Munich, describes the top level of British brains and experience in the 1930s. "Their I.Q.'s were much higher than usual among political bosses. Why were they such a disaster?" The view of Rowse, Snow approves: "They would not listen to warnings because they did not wish to hear." Being anti-Red made it impossible for them to read the message of Hitler. But their failure was as nothing compared to our present one. The American stake in literacy as a technology or uniformity applied to every level of education, government, industry, and social life is totally threatened by the electric technology. The threat of Stalin or Hitler was external. The electric technology is within the gates, and we are numb, deaf, blind, and mute about its encounter with the Gutenberg technology, on and through which the American way of life was formed. It is, however, no time to suggest strategies when the threat has not even been acknowledged to exist. I am in the position of Louis Pasteur telling doctors that their greatest enemy was quite invisible, and quite unrecognized by them. Our conventional response to all media, namely that it is how they are used that counts, is the numb stance of the technological idiot. For the "content" of a medium is like the juicy piece of meat carried by the burglar to distract the watchdog of the mind. The effect of the medium is made strong and intense just because it is given another medium as "content." The content of a movie is a novel or a play or an opera. The effect of the movie form is not related to its program content. The "content" of writing or print is speech, but the reader is almost entirely unaware either of print or of speech.

Arnold Toynbee is innocent of any understanding of media as they have shaped history, but he is full of examples that the student of media can use. At one moment he can seriously suggest that adult education, such as the Workers Educational Association in Britain, is a useful counterforce to the popular press. Toynbee considers that although all of the oriental societies have in our time accepted the industrial technology and its political consequences: "On the cultural plane, however, there is no uniform corresponding tendency" (Somervell, I. 267). This is like the voice of the literate man, floundering in a milieu of ads, who boasts, "Personally, I pay no attention to ads." The spiritual and cultural reservations that the oriental peoples may have toward our technology will avail them not at all. The effects of technology do not occur at the level of opinions or concepts, but alter sense ratios or patterns of perception steadily and without any resistance. The serious artist is the only person able to encounter technology with impunity, just because he is an expert aware of the changes in sense perception.

The operation of the money medium in seventeenth-century Japan had effects not unlike the operation of typography in the West. The penetration of the money economy, wrote G. B. Sansom (in *Japan*, Cresset Press, London, 1931) "caused a slow but irresistible revolution, culminating in the breakdown of feudal government and the resumption of intercourse with foreign countries after more than two hundred years of seclusion." Money has reorganized the sense life of peoples just because it is an *extension* of our sense lives. This change does not depend upon approval or disapproval of those living in the society.

Arnold Toynbee made one approach to the transforming power of media in his concept of "etherialization," which he holds to be the principle of progressive simplification and efficiency in any organization or technology. Typically, he is ignoring the *effect* of the challenge of these forms upon the response of our senses. He imagines that it is the response of our opinions that is relevant to the effect of media and technology in society, a "point of view" that is plainly the result of the typographic spell. For the man in a literate and homogenized society ceases to be sensitive to the diverse and discontinuous life of forms. He acquires the illusion of the third dimension and the "private point of view" as part of his Narcissus fixation, and is quite shut off from Blake's awareness or that of the Psalmist, that we become what we behold.

Today when we want to get our bearings in our own culture, and have need to stand aside from the bias and pressure exerted by any technical form of human expression, we have only to visit a society where that particular form has not been felt, or a historical period in which it was unknown. Professor Wilbur Schramm made such a tactical move in studying *Television in the Lives of Our Children*. He found areas where TV had not penetrated at all and ran some tests. Since he had made no study of the peculiar nature of the TV image, his tests were of "content" preferences, viewing time, and vocabulary counts. In a word, his approach to the problem was a literary one, albeit unconsciously so.

Consequently, he had nothing to report. Had his methods been employed in 1500 A.D. to discover the effects of the printed book in the lives of children or adults, he could have found out nothing of the changes in human and social psychology resulting from typography. Print created individualism and nationalism in the sixteenth century. Program and "content" analysis offer no clues to the magic of these media or to their subliminal charge.

Leonard Doob, in his report *Communication in Africa*, tells of one African who took great pains to listen each evening to the BBC news, even though he could understand nothing of it. Just to be in the presence of those sounds at 7 P.M. each day was important for him. His attitude to speech was like ours to melody—the resonant intonation was meaning enough. In the seventeenth century our ancestors still shared this native's attitude to the forms of media, as is plain in the following sentiment of the Frenchman Bernard Lam expressed in *The Art of Speaking* (London, 1696):

> 'Tis an effect of the Wisdom of God, who created Man to be happy, that whatever is useful to his conversation (way of life) is agreeable to him . . . because all victual that conduces to nourishment is relishable, whereas other things that cannot be assimilated and be turned into our substance are insipid. A Discourse cannot be pleasant to the Hearer that is not easie to the Speaker; nor can it be easily pronounced unless it be heard with delight.

Here is an equilibrium theory of human diet and expression such as even now we are only striving to work out again for media after centuries of fragmentation and specialism.

Pope Pius XII was deeply concerned that there be serious study of the media today. On February 17, 1950, he said:

> It is not an exaggeration to say that the future of modern society and the stability of its inner life depend in large part on the maintenance of an equilibrium between the strength of the techniques of communication and the capacity of the individual's own reaction.

Failure in this respect has for centuries been typical and total for mankind. Subliminal and docile acceptance of media impact has made them prisons without walls for their human users. As A. J. Liebling remarked in his book *The Press*, a man is not free if he cannot see where he is going, even if he has a gun to help him get there. For each of the media is also a powerful weapon with which to clobber other media and other groups. The result is that the present age has been one of multiple civil wars that are not limited to the world of art and entertainment. In *War and Human Progress,* Professor J. U. Nef declared: "The total wars of our time have been the result of a series of intellectual mistakes . . ."

If the formative power in the media are the media themselves, that raises a host of large matters that can only be mentioned here, although they deserve volumes. Namely, that technological media are staples or natural resources, exactly as are coal and cotton and oil. Anybody will concede that society whose economy is dependent upon one or two major staples like cotton, or grain, or lumber, or fish, or cattle is going to have some obvious social patterns of organization as a result. Stress on a few major staples creates extreme instability in the economy but great endurance in the population. The pathos and humor of the American South are embedded in such an economy of limited staples. For a society configured by reliance on a few commodities accepts them as a social bond quite as much as the metropolis does the press. Cotton and oil, like radio and TV, become "fixed charges" on the entire psychic life of the community. And this pervasive fact creates the unique cultural flavor of any society. It pays through the nose and all its other senses for each staple that shapes its life.

That our human senses, of which all media are extensions, are also fixed charges on our personal energies, and that they also configure the awareness and experience of each one of us, may be perceived in another connection mentioned by the psychologist C. G. Jung:

> Every Roman was surrounded by slaves. The slave and his psychology flooded ancient Italy, and every Roman became inwardly, and of course unwittingly, a slave. Because living constantly in the atmosphere of slaves, he became infected through the unconscious with their psychology. No one can shield himself from such an influence (*Contributions to Analytical Psychology,* London, 1928).

For Discussion

1. Although this will be a particularly difficult task, try to state in one paragraph what McLuhan means by "the medium is the message."

2. What does McLuhan mean when he says: "For any medium has the power of imposing its own assumption on the unwary. Prediction and control consist in avoiding this subliminal state of Narcissus trance. But the greatest

aid to this end is simply in knowing that the spell can occur immediately upon contact, as in the first bars of a melody."

3. In his various other writings McLuhan has commented extensively on the present educational system. What do you suppose McLuhan's opinions are regarding our educational system? What changes would he make? Do you think these changes are worthwhile? Why?

4. Do you agree with McLuhan's observation that "program and 'content' analysis offer no clues to the magic of these media or to their subliminal charge"? Why?

5. What implications does McLuhan's "the medium is the message" concept have for your present communication course? What changes would McLuhan make in this course? Why? Would these changes be for the better? for the worse? Why?

Other Ways of Packaging Information

In this article Randall P. Harrison discusses and, most importantly, illustrates other ways in which information may be communicated and reviews some of the attempts of communication theorists to provide models of the ways in which information may be transmitted from one person to another. This article also provides an excellent concrete example of how messages may be made more meaningful by combining the visual with the verbal.

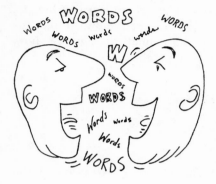

· We *are* a verbal lot. Not only we communicators, in conclave, but we human beings—the communicating animals. The words flow trippingly off the tongue; they cascade endlessly upon the ear.

We are somewhat surprised when someone like Ray Birdwhistell [1] estimates that in a normal, two-person conversation the verbal band carries less than 35% of the social meaning of the situation; more than 65% is transmitted via nonverbal bands. This doesn't square very well with our common sense notions about the communication process.

"Other Ways of Packaging Information." From Randall P. Harrison, "Other Ways of Packaging Information," in Communication-Spectrum *'7, ed., Lee Thayer (Lawrence, Kansas: International Communication Association, 1968), pp. 121–36. Reprinted by permission of the author and the International Communication Association.*

We, after all, spend a good deal of time packaging—and unpackaging—verbal messages. It takes a lot of conscious thought. It's real work. We spend years in school learning how to read, how to spell, how to put together a grammatical sentence, how to make a speech.

We tend to be less aware of the other packages of information we produce—and use. We tend to learn these packaging procedures in what Ed Hall [2] calls an "informal" manner. They are often "out-of-awareness." They are learned by imitation or accident. They are not taught explicitly.

This lack of awareness has been one stumbling block for the communication theorist who would like to examine the communication process. He's often tripped up by a nonverbal element. But he doesn't have the tools for analysis. He doesn't even have a conceptual perspective—so he knows what to look for.

Recently, several trends have forced nonverbal communication upon our attention. In the mass media, we've seen the advent of powerful new institutions with strong nonverbal components—first, film, and then its younger, big brother—television. Even the old print media have taken on a new look. Books, magazines, newspapers—all have been treated to a pictorial facelift. And now they're cosmetically color co-ordinated.

From an audience viewpoint—(emphasis on the *view*)—we find the average American spending 30 to 40 hours a week with television—and two to four hours a week with the print media.

But even in esoteric communication areas such as the man-computer interface, we're finding a nonverbal trend. Once the computer's output was totally digital—in the form of a "print-out." But now, we may soon see the day when 50% of the computer's output will be in the form of "visual display"—charts, drawings, graphs—presented on a cathode-ray tube or even on animated film. [3] (Parenthetically, the computer was originally called a "computer" because it could compute. Perhaps it would be more appropriate to call the present generation "informers.")

Advances in computer technology are important to the communication scholar, but there's another spot where nonverbal communication is apparently hitting the researcher where he lives . . .

This is work—such as Rosenthal's at Harvard [4]—which shows the extent to which the experimenter may be influencing the outcome of his experiments—often nonverbally. From some of Rosenthal's research we might conclude that sometimes the only naïve subject in the lab is the experimenter. What we've said so far bears on the first problem. I see before us, namely . . .

HOW IMPORTANT ?

How important is nonverbal communication? How important are these other ways of packaging information? It seems the answer to this question should be reflected to some extent in the amount of time, energy, and resources we invest in studying nonverbal communication. By several criteria it would appear that nonverbal communication is quite important.

QUANTITY

We've touched, for instance, on quantity. Apparently, a great deal of nonverbal communication goes on about us. In fact, the domain of communication seems to be spreading into areas that once we didn't define as communication. And in these areas much of the communication is nonverbal. Too, we've seen trends—particularly in the mass media—which lead us to believe that the quantity of nonverbal communication may be increasing.

PRIMACY

We might next mention primacy. And here we mean both that nonverbal communication is first in development, setting the pattern for later communication developments in the individual—and primacy in the sense that "seeing is believing." Often, the nonverbal messages take precedence because of sheer stimulus strength. In a somewhat related vein, it's often assumed by a receiver that the nonverbal message is harder to "fake" —whether it's a photo or a facial expression.

SUBTLETY

Finally, nonverbal communication acts with subtlety. We may be unaware that we are sending nonverbal messages. In complex nonverbal messmessages. We may be unaware that we are receiving nonverbal messages. In complex nonverbal messages, we may not know to what we respond. This subtlety makes communication breakdowns hard to analyze. It makes the process of nonverbal communication hard to teach.

This then leads to our second major problem area: How to study nonverbal communication? This comprises the twin problems of how to research and how to teach. Although we often assume these are identical problems, the goals of research and teaching may be quite different. Research moves toward fruitful and comprehensive theories which in turn lead to more research. Meanwhile, teaching is concerned with effective operation in some context. The role of research *in* teaching may be quite a separate issue. . . .

HOW STUDY ?

RESEARCH

TEACH

But we might assume that to study nonverbal communication we will need to go through some steps—which we might label: sensitize, analyze, organize, utilize. Within the research frame, *sensitize* means problem awareness, an articulation of relevant variables. *Analyze* means the operationalization of variables—the sorting, the labeling, the sifting of relevant from irrelevant. *Organize* introduces theorizing, the integration and structuring of conceptual systems. Finally, *utilize* refers to testing, to hypotheses and experiment. For the teacher, perhaps a parallel process occurs, ending with application.

In attacking the problem, the process is perhaps not so neatly linear. To the extent, for instance, that we have a well-articulated nomenclature, we will find it easier to sensitize ourselves. And to the degree we're sensitive we're better able to analyze. And so on. But let us start with "sensitize."

For both the researcher and the would-be practitioner, we have a growing battery of tools that help focus attention on nonverbal cues, that help us dissect the on-going nonverbal process. Included are videotapes—with instant re-play—motion pictures, still photos, recordings, and so on. We can produce these ourselves, and a growing list of already produced materials is becoming available. (As one sensitizing technique, we have taken a standard film—such as the Nixon-Kennedy debates—and played it without the sound. In a few moments, the viewer feels he's seen "everything." But as he watches, he becomes aware of more and more.)

For the researcher, sensitizing—as well as analyzing and organizing—frequently begins with a review of the literature. Fortunately, there's a growing—although far-flung—body of research, representing several frames of reference. . . .

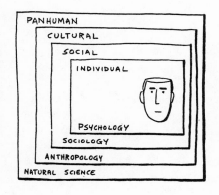

Certain panhuman characteristics emerge from the study of natural science—mapping the boundaries of what can be perceived, what can be performed, what biological needs undergird communication. Similarly, we find determinants—constraints—at the cultural, at the social, and at the individual level. To sample briefly from each level, we might start with . . .

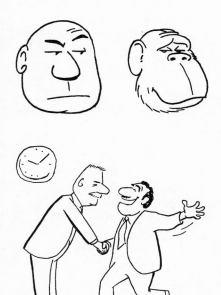

. . . Charles Darwin, [5] who made an early attempt to link expression in man to expression in other animals. He tried to isolate human universals and make the link to earlier noncommunicative functions. This work continues today in animal studies of emotion, learning, cooperation, territoriality, and so on.

Anthropologist Edward Hall [6] points out cultural differences in the use of time and space and what he calls the "primary message systems." He most recently has articulated the area of "proxemics"—the language of space.

Ray Birdwhistell, [7] working in the anthropological and linguistic traditions, has focused on "kinesics" —the study of gestural communication. In his cross-cultural research, he notes that the eye and hand are important "situation definers" in our culture, but not in all.

At a sociological level, scholars like Erving Goffman [8] point to the "management of personal front" that goes on in any social "gathering"— the socialization of potential communication performance depending on status, age, role, and group norms. The work of Hall, Birdwhistell, and Goffman has filtered into the psychological area, particularly in . . .

Psychiatric communication—in the interview situation between counselor and client—and also in communication between emotionally disturbed individuals. Men in the clinical tradition—like Jurgen Ruesch [9] and Joel Davitz [10]—have increasingly explored the nonverbal domain. Davitz, for instance, was frustrated at the non-specific advice given fledgling psychiatrists: "be sensitive" or "grow a third ear. . . ." He tried experimentally to isolate some of the nonverbal cues being used by experienced clinicians.

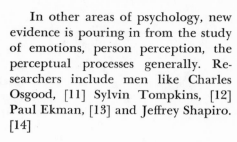

In other areas of psychology, new evidence is pouring in from the study of emotions, person perception, the perceptual processes generally. Researchers include men like Charles Osgood, [11] Sylvin Tompkins, [12] Paul Ekman, [13] and Jeffrey Shapiro. [14]

Recently, an additional frame of analysis has emerged, namely . . .

. . . Communication theory and research itself. This frame partakes deeply in the levels of analysis already mentioned, and adds new perspectives—drawing from the spectrum of communication arts and tapping relevant disciplines ranging from the philosophy of language to electrical engineering.

This audience hardly needs a review of communication models, but let me touch briefly on what I see as the unique calculus underlying communication theory.

Perhaps the simplest communication model possible is what we might call the A-B model—where two systems join—sharing an interface—so that changes in the states of one system influence the states of the other system. This diagram, of course, could apply equally to a mechanical system, a hydraulic system, etc. The communication theorist, however, is primarily interested in those systems where the flow across the interface is information, not merely energy or matter.

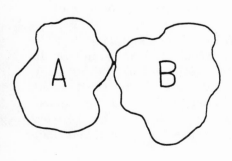

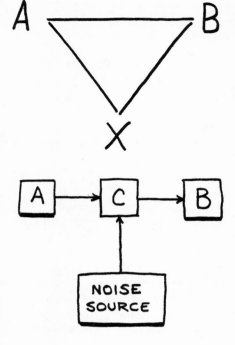

Newcomb's A-B-X model [15] is an early elaboration which adds an X component—some referent of orientation in the environment. This model, of course, was elaborated further in the Westley-MacLean model [16] to apply to more complex mass media phenomena.

The Shannon-Weaver model [17] might be termed an A-B-C model—the C standing for "channel." Shannon, of course, was particularly interested in channel capacity and the problems of communicating in the face of various noise levels.

Berlo's S-M-C-R model [18] might be called an A-B-C-M model—with the M standing for "message." With the emergence of the M component we seem to be squarely in a communication framework—no longer in electrical engineering, in physical systems, or even in traditional social psychology. For our present topic—other ways of packaging information—it is this message component which we will wish to explore in some detail.

Berlo originally suggested that a message could be analyzed in terms of its code, its content, and its treatment. What we have been calling "packaging" is first a coding problem —but with implications for the selection of content, treatment, and channel.

MESSAGE

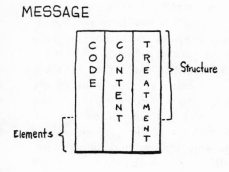

Berlo also noted that code, content, and treatment can all be analyzed in terms of, first, elements. And elements combine to form structure. The concept of "levels" becomes important here since elements at one level combine to form structures, which—at the next level of analysis—become elements which, in turn, combine into structures. Any given message can be analyzed at several levels and it can be considered a miniature system—with interrelated code, content, and treatment.

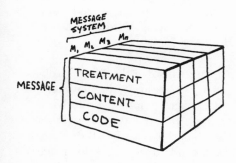

In many of the situations which interest us most, however, the receiver is being bombarded with simultaneous messages which to some extent are interrelated. These multiple messages—bounded by time, place, receiving communicator, or producing communicator—can be analyzed as one level of message system.

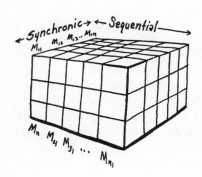

But in addition to this synchronic message system we are frequently interested in message chains—i.e., sequential message systems. We can go on to map more encompassing message systems—on up to national and international levels—as indeed George Gerbner [19] has done. But in terms of our present topic, we can begin by focusing on three small cells. . .

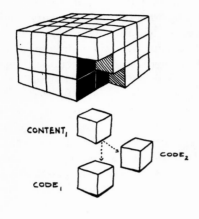

CONTENT₁

CODE₂

CODE₁

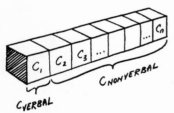

C_{VERBAL}

$C_{NONVERBAL}$

$$C_2 \simeq C_3 \simeq C_n \ ?$$

$$C_v \simeq C_{nv} \ ?$$

LINGUISTICS
KINESICS
PROXEMICS
PICTICS
VIDISTICS
GLYPTICS
PLASTICS
TECTONICS
MELODICS
HAPTICS
AROMATICS
EDETICS

Phrased as "other ways of packaging information" we have the underlying assumption that there is some block of content which could be encoded in either Code One or Code Two. Now to the extent that we are dealing with a system, we might not expect to shift from one code to another without eliminating—or adding —some information, and indeed without changing the treatment. We have much anecdotal speculation on this point—including Marshall McLuhan's dictum that "the medium is the message." [20] But at the moment we seem to lack adequate data on the problem—partly because of inadequate information measures—and partly because alternative code systems have not been thoroughly articulated.

In trying to solve the latter problem, two issues arise immediately. First, are there enough underlying similarities among the nonverbal codes so that they can be studied together? Second, does our knowledge of the verbal code system provide a useful model for the analysis of nonverbal code systems? If the answer to those two questions is "yes" we've made some giant strides forward; if not, we've a lot of basic conceptualizing to do.

So far, the linguistic analog has been best pursued by Birdwhistell in his kinesics. Hall has moved in a similar direction with his proxemics. We've done some work on "pictics" —an analysis of the pictorial code [21]. Sol Worth [22] is pursuing a parallel analysis of cinema, which he calls "vidistics." And Martin Krampen [23] has suggested a nomenclature for several other areas, such as glyptics, plastics, tectonics, haptics, aromatics, and edetics.

Looking down the road, it seems very likely that verbal and nonverbal codes will diverge in important ways. Similarly, key differences are likely to divide the various nonverbal codes. I'm hoping that we can profitably pursue a common path—although some theorists feel that already differences far outweigh similarities—that we are following deadened trails —and we need to remap our research strategy.

In particular, we hear the arguments that verbal codes are "discrete" while nonverbal codes tend to be "continuous." In the semantic dimension, verbal codes are "arbitrary" while nonverbal codes are "natural." It's suggested that for the nonverbal codes, greater variability persists in both encoding and decoding. And similarly, the nonverbal codes tend to be strongly connotative whereas verbal codes are more abstractly denotative. Each proposition raises interesting research questions. Many of these questions, however, rest on appropriate information measures.

Looking at the receiver at any given moment in the communication process, we might assume that he has certain uncertainties—needs for various types of information. At one level is technical uncertainty: what was sent? Next, semantic uncertainty: what was meant? Finally, pragmatic uncertainty: what is the appropriate response?

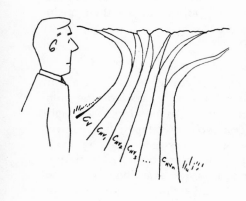

VERBAL

DISCRETE	CONTINUOUS
ARBITRARY	NATURAL
INVARIABLE	VARIABLE
DENOTATIVE	CONNOTATIVE

SENT?
MEANT?
RESPONSE?

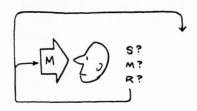

This, in turn, leads to higher level, or longer-range uncertainties. If communicator B makes response X, what will communicator A send next? And how will this relate to previous messages? Does it modify their meanings, etc.?

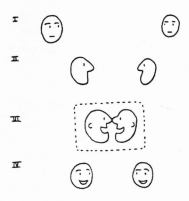

This, in turn, feeds into a still higher level of analysis of the communication system. Here, we might suggest successive stages: I. Pre-initiation, when messages relate to availability for interaction; II. Initiation, when messages examine reward potentials and establish communication traffic patterns; III. Interaction, the main body of communication, where messages relate to goal achievement and interaction maintenance; IV. Termination, where the communication system suspends its current interaction. Each stage may have certain uncertainty-reducing priorities. At each stage, different code systems may be brought into play. And similar cues may shift their meaning from stage to stage.

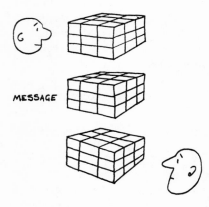

MESSAGE

For each communication system, then, we have a message space which reflects the information or uncertainty space of the communicators. This complex matrix changes from stage to stage. And it changes as we introduce more communicators or change the means of interposing our communicators.

Returning to our original topic—other ways of packaging information —it seems that many superficial tips might be given. But perhaps our central problem is that, on one hand, we are still struggling to conceptualize that key communication variable: information. And on the other hand, we have all too little knowledge of alternative ways of packaging—i.e., the code systems available to man. Meanwhile, the state of our art—like Venus de Milo—may be beautiful to look at, but it lacks the hands that are needed for an effective science.

References

1. Birdwhistell, Ray L., "Paralanguage: 25 Years After Sapir." Unpublished (1959).

2. Hall, Edward T., *The Silent Language*. Garden City, N.Y.: Doubleday, 1959.

3. Sutherland, Ivan E., "Computer Inputs and Outputs," in Scientific American Editors, *Information*. San Francisco: W. H. Freeman, 1966, pp. 40–55.

4. Rosenthal, Robert, *Experimenter Effects in Behavioral Research*. New York: Appleton-Century-Crofts, 1966.

5. Darwin, Charles, *Expression of Emotions in Man and Animals*. New York: Philosophical Library, 1955.

6. Hall, *op. cit.,* and Edward T. Hall, *The Hidden Dimension*. Garden City, N.Y.: Doubleday, 1966.

7. Birdwhistell, Ray L., "Background to Kinesics," *ETC.*, 13 (1955), pp. 10–18.

8. Goffman, Erving, *The Presentation of Self in Everyday Life*. Garden City, N.Y.: Doubleday, 1959; and *Behavior in Public Places*. London: Collier-Macmillan, 1963.

9. Ruesch, Jurgen, and Weldon Kees, *Nonverbal Communication*. Berkeley: University of California Press, 1956.

10. Davitz, Joel R., *The Communication of Emotional Meaning*. New York: McGraw-Hill, 1964.

11. Osgood, Charles E., "Dimensionality of the Semantic Space for Communica-

tion via Facial Expressions," *Scandinavian Journal of Psychology,* 7 (1966), pp. 1–30.

12. Tompkins, S. S., and Robert McCarter, "What and Where Are the Primary Affects? Some Evidence for a Theory," *Perceptual and Motor Skills,* 18 (1964), pp. 119–58.

13. Ekman, Paul, "Body Position, Facial Expression and Verbal Behavior During Interviews," *Journal of Abnormal and Social Psychology,* 68 (1964), pp. 295–301.

14. Shapiro, Jeffrey, "Responsivity to Facial and Linguistic Cues." Unpublished, privately distributed (1966).

15. Newcomb, T. M., "An Approach to the Study of Communicative Acts," *Psychological Review,* 60 (1953), pp. 393–404.

16. Westley, Bruce H., and Malcolm S. MacLean, "A Conceptual Model for Communication Research," *Journalism Quarterly,* 34 (1957), pp. 31–38.

17. Shannon, Claude E., and Warren Weaver, *The Mathematical Theory of Communication.* Urbana: Univ. of Illinois Press, 1963.

18. Berlo, David K., *The Process of Communication.* New York: Holt, Rinehart and Winston, 1960.

19. Gerbner, George, *Mass Communications and Popular Conceptions of Education: A Cross-Cultural Study,* Cooperative Research Project No. 876, Office of Education, U.S. Department of Health, Education and Welfare, 1964.

20. McLuhan, Marshall, *Understanding Media.* New York: McGraw-Hill, 1964.

21. Harrison, Randall, "Pictic Analysis: Toward a Vocabulary and Syntax for the Pictorial Code; with Research on Facial Communication." Unpublished Ph.D. dissertation, Michigan State University (1964).

22. Worth, Sol, "Cognitive Aspects of Sequence in Visual Communication." Unpublished, privately distributed (1965).

23. Harrison, Randall, and Clyde D. J. Morris, "Communication Theory and Typographic Research," *Journal of Typographic Research,* 1 (1967), pp. 115–24.

24. Harrison, *op. cit.*

For Discussion

1. What are some of the implications of learning how to "package information" in an informal manner or "out-of-awareness" for communicating with persons from other cultures?

2. Harrison mentions the work of Charles Darwin as "an early attempt to link expression in man to expression in other animals." Today a great deal of work is being done analyzing the communication systems of bees, dolphins, monkeys, and other animals and also in trying to teach various animals human language. From your own observations what types of communication do you think animals are capable of? That is, what kinds of information can they communicate? What kinds of communication do you think animals are incapable of? Put differently, what (if anything) distinguishes human from animal communication?

3. Erving Goffman has pointed out that communication depends in great part on such factors as status and age. How do you think these factors influence the form and content of both verbal and nonverbal communication? Analyze your own behavior when communicating with persons younger and older and of higher and lower status than you. How does your communicative behavior vary as a function of the status and age of your listener?

4. Roger P. Wilcox in his *Oral Reporting in Business and Industry* (Englewood Cliffs, New Jersey: Prentice-Hall, 1967) lists five basic requirements of visual aids. They should: (1) serve a need, (2) play a subordinate role, (3) be adapted to the listening-viewing audience, (4) have a professional appearance, and (5) be practical. Do the visuals in this article meet these requirements? Explain.

5. What implications does Harrison's article have for education? What might teachers and textbook writers learn from this article? If you wrote a paper for a course in sociology or history or some other subject in the same format as this article what do you suppose would be your instructor's reaction? How might you attempt to justify this way of communicating? What advantages are there in this kind of format which are not present in the traditional text-only term paper? Consider this from the point of view of both writer and reader.

Communication Without Words

ALBERT MEHRABIAN

Too often communication is equated with speaking and writing; words are often viewed as the primary if not the only means by which information may be conveyed from one person to another. In this brief article Albert Mehrabian discusses communication *without* words—communication by facial expression, by tone of voice, by touch, and the like. The author argues that words actually convey very little information when compared with that communicated by facial and vocal means. And although we may disagree with the relative importance he places on these different means of communication, his article provides a healthy antidote to our tendency to think of communication and words as synonymous.

Suppose you are sitting in my office listening to me describe some research I have done on communication. I tell you that feelings are communicated less by the words a person uses than by certain nonverbal means—that, for example, the verbal part of a spoken message has considerably less effect on whether a listener feels liked or disliked than a speaker's facial expression or tone of voice.

So far so good. But suppose I add, "In fact, we've worked out a formula that shows exactly how much each of these components contributes to the effect of the message as a whole. It goes like this: Total Impact = .07 verbal + .38 vocal + .55 facial."

What would you say to *that?* Perhaps you would smile good-naturedly and say, with some feeling, "Baloney!" Or perhaps you would frown and remark acidly, "Isn't science grand." My own response to the first answer would probably be to smile back: the facial part of your message, at least, was positive (55 per cent of the total). The second answer might make me uncomfortable: only the verbal part was positive (seven per cent).

The point here is not only that my reactions would lend credence to the formula but that most listeners would have mixed feelings about my statement. People like to see science march on, but they tend to resent its intrusion into an "art" like the communication of feelings, just as they find analytical and quantitative approaches to the study of personality cold, mechanistic, and unacceptable.

The psychologist himself is sometimes plagued by the feeling that he is trying to put a rainbow into a bottle. Fascinated by a complicated and emotionally rich human situation, he begins to study it, only to find in the course of his research that he has destroyed part of the

"Communication Without Words." From Albert Mehrabian, "Communication Without Words." Reprinted from Psychology Today *Magazine, II (September 1968), 53–55. Copyright ©* Communications/Research/Machines/Inc. *Reprinted by permission of Communications/Research/Machines/Inc.*

mystique that originally intrigued and involved him. But despite a certain nostalgia for earlier, more intuitive approaches, one must acknowledge that concrete experimental data have added a great deal to our understanding of how feelings are communicated. In fact, as I hope to show, analytical and intuitive findings do not so much conflict as complement each other.

It is indeed difficult to know what another person really feels. He says one thing and does another; he seems to mean something but we have an uneasy feeling it isn't true. The early psychoanalysts, facing this problem of inconsistencies and ambiguities in a person's communications, attempted to resolve it through the concepts of the conscious and the unconscious. They assumed that contradictory messages meant a conflict between superficial, deceitful, or erroneous feelings on the one hand and true attitudes and feelings on the other. Their role, then, was to help the client separate the wheat from the chaff.

The question was, how could this be done? Some analysts insisted that inferring the client's unconscious wishes was a completely intuitive process. Others thought that some nonverbal behavior, such as posture, position, and movement, could be used in a more objective way to discover the client's feelings. A favorite technique of Frieda Fromm-Reichmann, for example, was to imitate a client's posture herself in order to obtain some feeling for what he was experiencing.

Thus began the gradual shift away from the idea that communication is primarily verbal, and that the verbal message includes distortions or ambiguities due to unobservable motives that only experts can discover.

Language, though, can be used to communicate almost anything. By comparison, nonverbal behavior is very limited in range. Usually, it is used to communicate feelings, likings, and preferences, and it customarily reinforces or contradicts the feelings that are communicated verbally. Less often, it adds a new dimension of sorts to a verbal message, as when a salesman describes his product to a client and simultaneously conveys, nonverbally, the impression that he likes the client.

A great many forms of nonverbal behavior can communicate feelings: touching, facial expression, tone of voice, spatial distance from the addressee, relaxation of posture, rate of speech, number of errors in speech. Some of these are generally recognized as informative. Untrained adults and children easily infer that they are liked or disliked from certain facial expressions, from whether (and how) someone touches them, and from a speaker's tone of voice. Other behavior, such as posture, has a more subtle effect. A listener may sense how someone feels about him from the way the person sits while talking to him, but he may have trouble identifying precisely what his impression comes from.

Correct intuitive judgments of the feelings or attitudes of others are especially difficult when different degrees of feeling, or contradictory kinds of feeling, are expressed simultaneously through different forms of behavior. As I have pointed out, there is a distinction between verbal and vocal information (vocal information being what is lost when speech is written down—intonation, tone, stress, length and frequency of pauses, and so on), and the two kinds of information do not always communicate the same feeling. This distinction, which has been recognized for some time, has shed new light on certain types of communication. Sarcasm, for example, can be defined as a message in which the information transmitted vocally contradicts the information transmitted verbally. Usually the verbal information is positive and the vocal is negative, as in "Isn't science grand."

Through the use of an electronic filter, it is possible to measure the degree of liking communicated vocally. What the filter does is eliminate the higher frequencies of recorded speech, so that words are unintelligible but most vocal qualities remain. (For women's speech, we eliminate frequencies higher than about 200 cycles per second; for men, frequencies over about 100 cycles per second.) When people are asked to judge the degree of liking conveyed by the filtered speech, they perform the task rather easily and with a significant amount of agreement.

This method allows us to find out, in a given message, just how inconsistent the information communicated in words and the information communicated vocally really are. We ask one group to judge the amount of liking conveyed by a transcription of what was said, the verbal part of the message. A second group judges the vocal component, and a third group judges the impact of the complete recorded message. In one study of this sort we found that, when the verbal and vocal components of a message agree (both positive or both negative), the message as a whole is judged a little more positive or a little more negative than either component by itself. But when vocal information contradicts verbal, vocal wins out. If someone calls you "honey" in a nasty tone of voice, you are likely to feel disliked; it is also possible to say "I hate you" in a way that conveys exactly the opposite feeling.

Besides the verbal and vocal characteristics of speech, there are other, more subtle, signals of meaning in a spoken message. For example, everyone makes mistakes when he talks—unnecessary repetitions, stutterings, the omission of parts of words, incomplete sentences, "ums" and "ahs." In a number of studies of speech errors, George Mahl of Yale University has found that errors become more frequent as the speaker's discomfort or anxiety increases. It might be interesting to apply this index in an attempt to detect deceit (though on some occasions it might be risky: confidence men are notoriously smooth talkers).

Timing is also highly informative. How long does a speaker allow silent periods to last, and how long does he wait before he answers his partner? How long do his utterances tend to be? How often does he interrupt his partner, or wait an inappropriately long time before speaking? Joseph Matarazzo and his colleagues at the University of Oregon have found that each of these speech habits is stable from person to person, and each tells something about the speaker's personality and about his feelings toward and status in relation to his partner.

Utterance duration, for example, is a very stable quality in a person's speech; about 30 seconds long on the average. But when someone talks to a partner whose status is higher than his own, the more the high-status person nods his head the longer the speaker's utterances become. If the high-status person changes his own customary speech pattern toward longer or shorter utterances, the lower-status person will change his own speech in the same direction. If the high-status person often interrupts the speaker, or creates long silences, the speaker is likely to become quite uncomfortable. These are things that can be observed outside the laboratory as well as under experimental conditions. If you have an employee who makes you uneasy and seems not to respect you, watch him the next time you talk to him—perhaps he is failing to follow the customary low-status pattern.

Immediacy or directness is another good source of information about feelings. We use more distant forms of communication when the act of communicating is undesirable or uncomfortable. For example, some people would rather transmit discontent with an employee's work through a third party than do it themselves, and some find it easier to communicate negative feelings in writing than by telephone or face to face.

Distance can show a negative attitude toward the message itself, as well as toward the act of delivering it. Certain forms of speech are more distant than others, and they show fewer positive feelings for the subject referred to. A speaker might say "Those people need help," which is more distant than "These people need help," which is in turn even more distant than "These people need our help." Or he might say "Sam and I have been having dinner," which has less immediacy than "Sam and I are having dinner."

Facial expression, touching, gestures, self-manipulation (such as scratching), changes in body position, and head movements—all these express a person's positive and negative attitudes, both at the moment and in general, and many reflect status relationships as well. Movements of the limbs and head, for example, not only indicate one's attitude toward a specific set of circumstances but relate to how dominant, and how anxious, one generally tends to be in social situations. Gross changes in body position, such as shifting in the chair, may show negative feelings toward the person one is talking to. They may also be cues: "It's your turn to talk," or "I'm about to get out of here, so finish what you're saying."

Posture is used to indicate both liking and status. The more a person leans toward his addressee, the more positively he feels about him. Relaxation of posture is a good indicator of both attitude and status, and one that we have been able to measure quite precisely. Three categories have been established for relaxation in a seated position: least relaxation is indicated by muscular tension in the hands and rigidity of posture; moderate relaxation is indicated by a forward lean of about 20 degrees and a sideways lean of less than 10 degrees, a curved back, and, for women, an open arm position; and extreme relaxation is indicated by a reclining angle greater than 20 degrees and a sideways lean greater than 10 degrees.

Our findings suggest that a speaker relaxes either very little or a great deal when he dislikes the person he is talking to, and to a moderate degree when he likes his companion. It seems that extreme tension occurs with threatening addressees, and extreme relaxation with non-threatening, disliked addressees. In particular, men tend to become tense when talking to other men whom they dislike; on the other hand, women talking to men *or* women and men talking to women show dislike through extreme relaxation. As for status, people relax most with a low-status addressee, second-most with a peer, and least with someone of higher status than their own. Body orientation also shows status: in both sexes, it is least direct toward women with low status and most direct toward disliked men of high status. In part, body orientation seems to be determined by whether one regards one's partner as threatening.

The more you like a person, the more time you are likely to spend looking into his eyes as you talk to him. Standing close to your partner and facing him directly (which makes eye contact easier) also indicate positive feelings. And you are likely to stand or sit closer to your peers than you do to addressees whose status is either lower or higher than yours.

What I have said so far has been based on research studies performed, for the most part, with college students from the middle and upper-middle classes. One interesting question about communication, however, concerns young children from lower socioeconomic levels. Are these children, as some have suggested, more responsive to implicit channels of communication than middle- and upper-class children are?

Morton Wiener and his colleagues at Clark University had a group of middle- and lower-class children play learning games in which the reward for learning was praise. The child's responsiveness to the verbal and vocal parts of the praise-reward was measured by how much he learned. Praise came in two forms: the objective words "right" and "correct," and the more affective or evaluative words, "good" and "fine." All four words were spoken sometimes in a positive tone of voice and sometimes neutrally.

Positive intonation proved to have a dramatic effect on the learning rate of the lower-class group. They learned much faster when the vocal part of the message was positive than when it was neutral. Positive intonation affected the middle-class group as well, but not nearly as much.

If children of lower socioeconomic groups are more responsive to facial expression, posture, and touch as well as to vocal communication, that fact could have interesting applications to elementary education. For example, teachers could be explicitly trained to be aware of, and to use, the forms of praise (nonverbal or verbal) that would be likely to have the greatest effect on their particular students.

Another application of experimental data on communication is to the interpretation and treatment of schizophrenia. The literature on schizophrenia has for some time emphasized that parents of schizophrenic children give off contradictory signals simultaneously. Perhaps the parent tells the child in words that he loves him, but his posture conveys a negative attitude. According to the "double-bind" theory of schizophrenia, the child who perceives simultaneous contradictory feelings in his parent does not know how to react: should he respond to the positive part of the message, or to the negative? If he is frequently placed in this paralyzing situation, he may learn to respond with contradictory communications of his own. The boy who sends a birthday card to his mother and signs it "Napoleon" says that he likes his mother and yet denies that he is the one who likes her.

In an attempt to determine whether parents of disturbed children really do emit more inconsistent messages about their feelings than other parents do, my colleagues and I have compared what these parents communicate verbally and vocally with what they show through posture. We interviewed parents of moderately and quite severely disturbed children, in the presence of the child, about the child's problem. The interview was video-recorded without the parents' knowledge, so that we could analyze their behavior later on. Our measurements supplied both the amount of inconsistency between the parents' verbal-vocal and postural communications, and the total amount of liking that the parents communicated.

According to the double-bind theory, the parents of the more disturbed children should have behaved more inconsistently than the parents of the less disturbed children. This was not confirmed: there was no significant difference between the two groups. However, the *total amount* of positive feeling communicated by parents of the more disturbed children was less than that communicated by the other group.

This suggests that (1) negative communications toward disturbed children occur because the child is a problem and therefore elicits them, or (2) the negative attitude precedes the child's disturbance. It may also be that both factors operate together, in a vicious circle.

If so, one way to break the cycle is for the therapist to create situations in which the parent can have better feelings toward the child. A more positive attitude from the parent may make the child more responsive to his directives, and the spiral may begin to move up instead of down. In our own work with disturbed children, this kind of procedure has been used to good effect.

If one puts one's mind to it, one can think of a great many other applications for the findings I have described, though not all of them concern serious problems. Politicians, for example, are careful to maintain eye contact with the television camera when they speak, but they are not always careful about how they sit when they debate another candidate of, presumably, equal status.

Public relations men might find a use for some of the subtler signals of feeling. So might Don Juans. And so might ordinary people, who could try watching other people's signals and changing their own, for fun at a party or in a spirit of experimentation at home. I trust that does not strike you as a cold, manipulative suggestion, indicating dislike for the human race. I assure you that, if you had more than a transcription of words to judge from (seven per cent of total message), it would not.

For Discussion

1. Mehrabian says that the total impact of a message may be represented by the following equation: Total Impact = .07 Verbal + .38 Vocal + .55 Facial. Do you think this is an accurate account of the total impact of a message? an inaccurate one? Why? Would the percentages assigned to verbal, vocal, and facial communication differ on the basis of the type of message? the specific communicator? the audience? the purpose of the message? In what ways would such factors influence the relative importance placed on verbal, vocal, and facial information?

2. Mehrabian notes that sarcasm "can be defined as a message in which the information transmitted vocally contradicts the information transmitted verbally." Sarcasm, however, is also communicated in written form. How

might sarcasm in written communication be defined using this same notion of contradictory messages? In which form of communication (oral or written) is it easier to convey sarcasm? Why?

3. Analyze a recent communication breakdown which revolved around non-verbal messages. Describe, as specifically as possible, what went wrong. How might such a breakdown have been avoided?

4. Often we form an impression of a person without being aware of why we formed this impression and not another one. We might say, for example, "I don't know what it was but I just don't trust him" or "He seems very sincere" or "Although he didn't say so I'm sure he doesn't like me." In each of these cases it is possible that the impression formed was based on some nonverbal communication. Analyze a recent experience in which you formed an impression of someone and try to recreate the nonverbal communication exchange. Might this nonverbal communication account—at least in part—for the impression you formed? What nonverbal communications would you single out as particularly important for forming impressions? Why?

5. The way in which we communicate—verbally, vocally, and facially—is probably related in some way to our own individual personalities, to our needs and our motives, to our emotional state, to our desires and wants. And these, of course, are never the same in two different people; each of us is a unique personality and each of us communicates in a unique manner. Analyze your own way of communicating—verbally, vocally, and facially—in relation to your own personality. What psychological factors might be influencing your communications? How?

6. In his conclusion Mehrabian says: "Public relations men might find a use for some of the subtler signals of feeling. So might Don Juans." How?

Body
English

FRANK A. GELDARD

One of the most exciting aspects of communication study
is that there is always something new happening—always
new ideas, new theories, new inventions, new fields to be
explored. One of the most provocative of these new
developments is tactile communication or communication
by touch. Few of us have probably ever even considered
the possibility of communicating precise and detailed
information solely by touch. But such communication is
possible. Here Frank Geldard considers some of the latest
research and theory in this new and expanding field.

What kind of language can the skin understand? Well, most people would say, the skin can understand the "language" of texture—the rich, complex, unmistakable feels of silk, velvet, or tweed. Or the "language" of hot and cold, the "message" of the insect's sting, the language of warning, the affectionate touch on the shoulder, or the small number of pokes and jabs which can mean anything from, "Shhh—the boss is coming" to "Isn't that the most ridiculous thing you've ever heard?"

But what about language in a narrower sense—can skin receive and understand a complex impersonal system of symbols like Morse, semaphore, or even English?

And even if the skin can handle language in the communications sense, aren't the eyes and ears enough?

Eyes and ears were not enough during the early years of World War II, when fighter pilots were shot down too often because they could not hear their wing commanders, and they did not peel away fast enough when enemy planes closed in. Thus research was begun to find out if warning signals could be built into cushions so that pilots could "hear" by the seat of their pants.

Certainly it is painfully obvious that the eyes and ears are not enough if you are blind or deaf or both. Braille, for instance, is an arbitrary, very difficult language to learn, and most blind people do not read well in it. It is also obvious that there are a myriad of conditions in which even the nondefective eye or ear may be absorbed, or baffled, or in some way at a grave disadvantage—you can't hear when the water's running or bombs are falling or crowds are screaming. You can't see in the dark or in the fog. The human voice is wildly distorted by helium under deep-sea pressure, and so on.

Assuming then the practical need to explore all possible channels of communication, we can and should ask: What can the skin do? What kinds of signals can it handle? What kinds of discriminations can it make? How can these discriminations be used as the building blocks of a sophisticated, easily intelligible vehicle for hard information?

THE COMPROMISING SKIN

As a receiving instrument, the skin combines the best abilities of the eye and ear; it doesn't perform quite as well as the eye and ear do in their specialized fields, but it is the body's only receptor that can handle both fields fairly well.

By the ear's field, I don't mean sound—the blessed human voice, for instance, or the divine noise of the *Prelude* to *Parsifal*—I mean time. Within a continuous sound, the ear can detect a break or silence only two to four thousandths of a second long. The ear has a rather poor space-sensing ability, however; more often than not we speak of a sound coming from "somewhere." Space is the eye's province: the eye can be fooled, of course, but it can make extraordinarily fine discriminations— indeed the finest the human organism is capable of. On the other hand, the eye is a sluggish time organ; home movie screens which reflect only 24 discrete flashes of light per second are seen as a continuous picture or blaze of light.

The skin handles time almost as well as the ear. Under proper conditions, the skin can detect a break of about 10 thousandths of a second in a steady mechanical pressure or tactile buzz. For the eye, comparable time discriminations are much slower; eye discriminations are about 25–35 thousandths of a second. (Ball-park figures for the ear, for the eye, and for the skin are thus .003, .030, and .010 seconds, respectively.)

In terms of space, the skin can identify and distinguish between coded signals delivered from five to seven different locations within the chest area. The ear cannot identify the source of a sound (provided this sound is produced at some distance from the hearer) with anything like the same fineness, as anyone who has ever tried to "spot" a buzzing insect by ear can testify.

THE SKIN'S VOCABULARY

Given the skin's fairly accurate spatio-temporal perception, we can begin to talk about a language that uses discriminations in time and space as vocabulary items. The skin's time sense provides us with two vocabulary elements—duration and frequency.

When using duration in a system of signals, it is not worth considering vibratory pulses or buzzes shorter than 0.10 second (they are not felt as buzzes, and could easily be mistaken for an accidental poke or jab); at the other end, buzzes lasting more than two full seconds would slow any signaling system to a crawl. Between these limits, the skin can distinguish some 25 discrete, just-noticeable differences in length, at least four or five of which can be judged with absolute correctness. When presented in isolation, these four or five signals are felt to have a distinctive length—short, medium-short, medium, and long, for instance. These distinctive lengths can be coded and hence become meaningful elements in a language.

Frequency is a somewhat finer aspect of temporal discrimination, analogous to heard pitch. Such felt frequency depends primarily on the rate at which successive impacts are delivered to the skin. Usable or "hearable" frequency ranges for the skin are rates below 150 impacts per second, which is of course below the frequencies present in speech or the mid-musical range. But within this limited range, the skin does almost as well as the ear; for example, a frequency or pitch of 40 impacts per second can be distinguished from one of 39.5 or 40.5 impacts per second! Sixty impacts per second provides a good general carrier frequency or note upon which pitch variations can be played conveniently.

Another valuable vocabularly item or codable discrimination is that of intensity or "loudness." Sensitivity to loudness or softness varies from one location to another on the skin, so that figures have to be specified for particular body sites. But, in general, from the threshold below which nothing is felt, to a safe distance under the discomfort level, the average subject can detect some 15 just-noticeable differences in intensity. As with duration, some of these intensities can be recognized as having a unique value, like soft, medium, and loud, for instance, even when there is nothing to compare them with, and hence can be suitably coded to mean something.

The fourth useful dimension in cutaneous talk is location or space. There are a number of problems connected with the skin's space sense that are only now being investigated. (For example, when two chest vibrators are activated simultaneously, they are felt as one, but more about this later.) But so long as they are buzzed in sequence, with just a tiny time differential separating the signals, as many as seven vibrators may be placed on the chest and used as codable signal elements.

VIBRATESE—A WORKABLE SYSTEM

Vibratese was a language having 45 separate signals; three intensities (weak, medium, strong), and three durations (short, medium, long), were delivered to five different spots on the chest. (All steps could be combined with all others, $3 \times 3 \times 5$, giving 45 steps or signals.) Letters of the alphabet were each assigned a signal representing a unique combination of duration, intensity, and location. The times were kept short—0.1, 0.3, 0.5 seconds for short, medium, and long, respectively. The most frequently occurring language elements were assigned shorter durations, enabling the system to "fly" at a rapid pace. The code proved quite efficient, since the all-important vowels were assigned each to its own vibrator, and since letters followed each other promptly, with none of the wasteful silences that are built into International Morse.

The vibratese alphabet could be mastered in only a few hours, and it was not long before two- and three-letter words could be introduced, and then short sentences. Trainees found that, as with radio or telegraphic codes, they could "follow behind" and combine letters and words into larger patterns. When the training sessions were finally discontinued—not because the learning limit had been reached, but because the sending equipment could go no faster—one subject was receiving at a rate about twice that of proficient Morse reception.

The vibratese experiment taught some valuable lessons but, more importantly, it raised questions about the possibility of making far better use of the space dimension. Could vibrators be scattered all over the body? Could they be activated simultaneously? These questions had to remain open, given the purely technological limitations imposed by the equipment then available—the vibrators were extremely cumbersome, and the chest area was the only place to put them.

By the time the Cutaneous Communication Laboratory at Princeton University was established in 1962 (hitherto most work in this field was done at the University of Virginia), a major technological breakthrough had taken place. A small, compact, yet powerful vibrator somewhat like a hearing aid was developed in 1959 by R. C. Bice at the University of Virginia. Later, a more rugged and reliable vibrator of the same general type was developed at Princeton by Carl Sherrick. Both these instruments can be attached quite simply and firmly at any desired body site, and can be counted on to perform accurately over long periods.

It is possible that systems using only coded variations in spatial location can provide languages thoroughly adequate for many purposes—simple warning or tracking systems, for example.

In one experiment at Princeton we placed the vibrators on 10 different body sites (see illustration, page 120). These sites weren't arbitrarily selected, and many others were tried. It was surprising how far from each other vibrators had to be in order to act in relative independence of one another. It was also surprising how many potential sites had to be abandoned because they provided ready paths to the ear; subjects complained of hearing, rather than feeling, the vibratory bursts. Though

VIBRATOR SITES.
These sites, far enough
apart and devoid of bone,
form recognizable ele-
ments of language in
spatial terms.

we really don't know as yet whether exactly corresponding points on
the two sides of the body need to be avoided—as they are, intentionally,
in the illustration—general neurological principles seem to suggest this.

Subjects were exposed to patterns consisting of two vibratory bursts
one fifth of a second long, and separated by a half-second silence. Each
of these two bursts activated from one to nine sites at the same time. In
some of these patterns, both bursts were identical: exactly the same sites
were involved (see illustration, page 121). In other patterns, the two
bursts were different in varying degree. The same number of sites were
involved, but they weren't the same ones. Altogether, 1,000 patterns were
presented (more than half a million are possible); 500 were "sames" pairs
and 500 were "differents." The subject's task was merely to report which
were which.

The really important error-causing factor turned out to be not the
sheer number of sites involved, but rather the extent to which successive

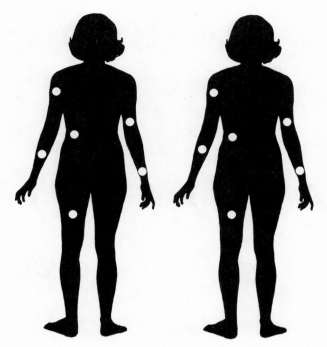

bursts had elements in common. That the number of sites alone was not primarily the culprit became evident when patterns utilizing no more than four vibrators were consistently misjudged to be the "same" because they had three sites in common (see illustration, page 122).

More elaborate patterns were discriminated perfectly, so long as they were different enough.

SPACE-TIME COOPERATION

It is clear now that tactile communication not only permits, but fairly demands, the coordination of both spatial and temporal variations. A peek into the future reveals at least one of the many possibilities to be explored.

At Princeton, we developed an instrument called the optohapt. The symbols supplied by a typewriter are transmuted into sequences and combinations of vibratory bursts distributed over the body surface. Nine of the locations (see illustration, page 120) are used.

A glance at the circular inset (see illustration, page 124) will reveal the essential mode of operation. In the case of an E passing steadily from right to left, the vertical backbone of the letter first activates in a

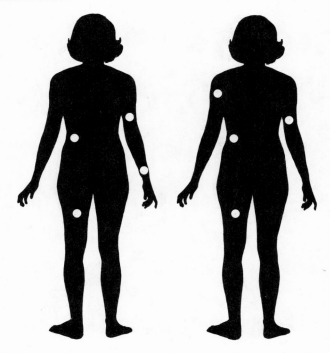

single burst the entire array of nine vibrators, then continues on with #1 (*top*), #5, and #9 (*bottom*). The middle one quits a little sooner than the top and bottom vibrators because of the shorter middle branch of the E. A distinctive spatio-temporal pattern is thus created, one which belongs exclusively to the E, though differing from an F only by the inclusion of a long burst on one vibrator (#9). Some of these time-space patterns are extremely attention-getting, to say the least; the letter W, for instance, sweeps vividly across the body, shoulder to ankle, shoulder to ankle, like a sort of tactile neon sign.

Actually, letters do not provide the best material. Punctuation signs and a variety of literary and business symbols are more distinctive and more readily learned.

In the exploratory stage, we examined a group of 180 symbols, searching for the most easily understandable signals. The final survivors for alphabetic coding are shown in the illustration below. These, if presented at the optimal speed—optimal means having suitable "zip" and vivid movement—are easy to learn and retain. They are also easy to combine into word-forming sequences.

The optohapt represents only one limited set of possibilities for presenting spatio-temporal patterns; typefaces arbitrarily dictate the patterns flashed to the skin, and the typewriter carriage moves only one

E	.	D	ıı	P	˙˙
T	⌣	U	ı	B	→
A	ıı	C	/	V	V
O	■	M	ɰ	K	˙˙
I	ı	F	−	X	Γ
N	▬	G	⑪	J	J
S	◊	W	\	Z	˥
R	⊓	Y	:	Q	ʏ
H	÷				
L	—				

→■ıı: . ▬⑪−I◊÷

BODY ENGLISH

THE OPTOHAPT ALPHABET. These symbols can be flashed to the skin rapidly and vividly; they are easy to learn and "read."

way, of course. The Cutaneous Communication Laboratory is just now putting into operation a tape system which tells a different story. The new device—speedy, accurate, and reliable—will provide what appears to be the ultimate challenge to the skin, a set of patterns containing far more elements than even the most rabid dermophile would ever claim to be within the skin's ability to conquer. Experiment will shortly decide if we shall ultimately arrive at a completely satisfactory "Body English."

A FRIENDLY LOOK BACKWARDS

In terms of research history, we have made a good deal of progress since 1762, when Jean-Jacques Rousseau proposed that the skin might serve as a channel of communication. In his revolutionary educational treatise, *Emile,* Rousseau drew attention to the common observation that the vibrations of the cello can be felt by the hand and fingers and that "one can distinguish without the use of eye or ear, merely by the way in which the wood vibrates and trembles, whether the sound given out is sharp or flat, whether it is drawn from the treble string or the bass." He asked whether "we might in time become so sensitive as to hear a whole tune by means of our fingers." Beyond that, he estimated

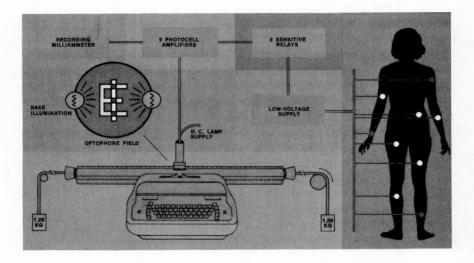

THE OPTOHAPT. It transforms photoelectric impulses from typewriter symbols into sequences and combinations of vibratory bursts which are played upon the skin as though upon a piano keyboard. The skin reads the bursts as a spacetime "tune."

that "tone and measure" might ultimately become "the elements of speech" for communication with the deaf.

The idea that the skin ought to be trainable to receive complex vibratory patterns never really was lost sight of in the more than two centuries since *Emile*. People continued to suggest that speech and music might be impressed on the skin much as it is delivered to the eardrums. Indeed the argument was an evolutionary one: the eardrum is basically a derivative from skin, and the tactile sense should therefore be able to learn to do, at least crudely, what the tympanic membrane does so superbly.

During the first third of this century there were elaborate and painstaking experiments, both in America and in Germany, aimed at teaching the skin to recognize complex chains of vibrations delivered to the fingertips. In the most extensive of these, words and sentences were spoken into a microphone which activated a small crystal speaker, an instrument known as the teletactor, which imparted its vibrations to the fingers. But the results were disappointing: only a series of poorly discriminated rhythmic accents could be learned, and not too effectively. In the mid-'30s the whole effort was abandoned, and it was many years before it was learned why these experiments had failed. Now we know that the frequencies important in speech are all but impossible for the skin to discriminate. The skin was being asked to do something at which it is quite inept.

The long course of research and speculation has led us to the knowledge that the skin can handle time and space discriminations fairly well. We have put this knowledge to the test, and have shown that the skin can receive rapid and sophisticated messages. There is every likelihood that skin languages of great subtlety and speed can be devised and used.

But the point is that we have much more in the way of basic fact than anyone has yet put to work. This fairly solid ground floor of data is available for a host of applications, and I have touched obliquely on a few of them—warning signal systems, supplementary directional systems, a sophisticated language for the blind or deaf, and, of course, all sorts of secret military or commercial uses. But I confess to a certain sympathy with the classic remark attributed to Michael Faraday on the occasion of his being asked what good his induction motor was: "Maybe you can tax it some day."

For Discussion

1. What emotions do you feel can be communicated solely by touching? How? Are there emotions which cannot be communicated in this way? Why?

2. What types of information do you feel the skin could not receive? Why?

3. In everyday communication we probably communicate a great deal more by touch than we at first realize. Keep a "communication log" for a period of one day and record all the instances of touch communication which you observe or engage in. What conclusions or generalizations based on this survey can you draw relevant to tactile communication? What is the relationship of tactile communication to vocal-auditory communication?

4. Some people find it extremely difficult to speak affectionately to others, to tell them that they are fond of them or that they want to be with them. Often it is easier to communicate such affection by touch. What reasons might you give which account for this?

5. Examine your own behavior in regard to communication by touch both as a sender and as a receiver. Do you often touch people in communicating? Do people touch you? Which type of people do you touch? Which type touch

you? Do you like it? Do you avoid it? What factors might account for these behavioral preferences?

6. What practical applications, other than those mentioned by Geldard, do you see for communication by touch?

The
Silent
Languages

DON FABUN

In this essay Don Fabun demonstrates that time, color, and space (and even silence itself), like words and gestures, communicate meaning. They can function to establish, maintain, and nourish a relationship as well as break it down. Because their communicative functions are learned without awareness their effects are subtle and often go unnoticed. Yet, clearly, they exert powerful influence on all human interaction and consequently deserve attention along with the more obvious forms of communication.

Although the fabric of our society is woven of spoken and visual symbols, we also communicate meaningfully in many non-verbal, non-symbolic ways. Consider, for instance, how silence itself is a way of communication. When someone says "Good morning," and we fail to respond, we communicate something.

When someone asks us a question and we fail to answer, we also communicate. We are social creatures and our society is made up of responses to each other. For one thing, we are in constant need of reassurance; not only that we are, indeed, alive (because we evoke responses from others) but also reassurance that those other creatures around us are friendly and not hostile. The stroked cat purrs; the petted dog wags his tail. We talk. When we fail to do so, a little bit of our world crumbles away. The world of silence may be a cold and bitter one; like the deep wastes of the Arctic regions, it is fit for neither man nor beast. Holding one's tongue may be prudent, but it is an act of rejection; silence builds walls—and walls are the symbols of failure.

THE LANGUAGE OF TIME

We may have a tendency to feel that time is experienced pretty much the same by everyone. After all, an hour is an hour, isn't it? What we sometimes fail to realize is that time, as we use and express it, is culturally determined and defined. Time for Americans, for instance, is experienced differently than for certain Indian tribes, who have no word for "waiting," because there is no established limit of time for an event to take place.

In our particular culture, we have "quantified" time by dividing it into years, seasons, months, weeks, days, hours, minutes, seconds, microseconds, milliseconds, and nanoseconds. Not all cultures do so, or, if they do, they assign different values to different segments. What is not always appreciated is that individuals have different time scales, too, and that failures to recognize this and to take it into account can lead to breakdowns in communication. Each carries his own "clock." It may or may not coincide with others.

The time of the president of the United States differs in important ways from that of the retired gentleman who is fishing off the pier. In the context of their social positions an hour—a minute—will be valued differently, both by society and themselves.

Let us look into the use of time in our culture a little more. If you were supposed to meet someone at 5 o'clock and showed up instead at 6 —or didn't show up at all—you would be communicating something. Like the language of silence, the language of time is most eloquent.

Being early, as to a lecture or a concert, can communicate something, too. It is a projection in time of eagerness, looking forward to; it says something.

Think about "awhile." It is a word we frequently use. "This will take awhile," says the man who repairs your car or watch. What does he mean? Minutes, hours, days? "I'll be through in awhile," is an expression we often use. "Awhile" is an important means of communication; it trembles on the edge of perceptivity; it is our personal expression of time as it relates to others.

What is important about "awhile" as far as communication is concerned is that the interpretation is contextual. "Awhile" means different things in different situations and with different people. It may be well to remember this; our concept of time, and our use of it, depends on our cultural and personal way of evaluating it.

When you are "ahead of time," "on time," or "behind time"; when you are "early" or "late," you express something in our culture. Failure to keep this in mind may lead you into situations in which communication becomes difficult, if not impossible. The mere fact of "being late" may create the sort of context in which you have to perform in an aura of hostility.

Another aspect of our expression of time, as it relates to communication, is the difference we make between points and duration.

Points are intersections on a four dimensional grid: "I'll meet you here at five," "class begins in Room 120 at eight," etc. The grid is an x,y,z matrix (longitude, latitude, height from ground) plus a specified point on an agreed-upon time track. Failure to match these up may result in a communications failure.

Duration, on the other hand, appears to have (for us) a beginning and an end and an unsegmented middle. It is a psychological area—unmapped—it is the time we spend in the doctor's waiting room, in the dentist's chair, waiting for a loved one, or just listening to someone else. Duration is differently experienced by different people—something to keep in mind when you are talking to someone else. Their area of duration may be different than your own—they are no longer at x,y,z^t, but at some indeterminate part of the spectrum of duration. It is as if you had agreed to meet at a certain place at a certain time, but only one of you showed up.

Differences in the individual experience of duration can cause communication to break down.

THE LANGUAGE OF COLOR

Just as time "speaks" and space "speaks," so does color, through our conscious and unconscious use of it.

What people mostly see of us is patterns of color; our choice of what colors and patterns to display in different situations is a silent language of its own. A girl who chooses to show up at a semi-formal afternoon party clad in brilliant red capri pants and a shawl with a psychedelic design is not only saying something about herself, but expressing an opinion about her hostess and the other guests as well. The businessman who shows up for work wearing a Beethoven sweatshirt and sandals is certainly communicating something, although he may not do so for long. The kind of communication that is likely to take place between one man in bathing trunks and another in formal dress is apt to be quite different than the communication that would take place if both were dressed alike.

Behavioralists claim it is probably not an exaggeration to say that a specific color situation is accompanied by a specific response pattern of the whole organism. The prevailing color in an environment may have important effects on the kind of communications that take place there. In general, it is felt that the "warm" colors—yellow, orange, red—stimulate creativity and make most people feel more "outgoing" and responsive to others. "Cool" colors—blue, green, gray—have a tendency to encourage meditation and deliberate thought processes, and may have a dampening effect on both the level and the quality of communication.

It has even been suggested that people should do creative thinking in a red room and then proceed to a green one to carry out the ideas.

THE LANGUAGE OF SPACE

The way in which we use space is another way that we communicate with one another. The distance between you and someone else may determine the nature of the communication. If you are a few inches away from someone's ear, chances are that you will whisper and the nature of the communication will be "secret." At a distance of several feet, the communication may still be private, but its tone and nature will have changed. The change is even greater if you are speaking to a large audience. Here the nature of the message may be determined in part by the distance between you and the most distant member of the audience.

Space "speaks" also in the way that we distribute ourselves in a classroom, bus, or lecture hall. As long as there is optional space, most people will tend to sit as far from strangers as possible. The distance they select to separate themselves from others in the audience—and from the speaker—is in itself a form of communication. In rigidized institutions, such as the military service, the distance to be maintained between persons of different ranks may even be a matter of regulation.

There is a cultural difference in the way we distribute ourselves in formal space—as in an office building. Thus Europeans are most likely to put their desks in the center of the room, and authority flows outward from the center. Proximity to the center is one way of saying, "That person is important." Americans, on the other hand, tend to distribute their working space around the edges of a room, leaving the center open for traffic and casual communication. Another way that Americans communicate through their use of space is in size and verticality. Most often, the size of an office will "say" something about the importance of the man who occupies it; the larger the space, the more important the man. Similarly, for many businesses and government departments and bureaus, the vertical distance between ground level and a person's office may act as an indication of his importance. Usually executive offices are located at or near the top of the building they occupy. Occupying a large room at the top of a building not only "says" a great deal about the person occupying it, but in part determines the kind of communication that can be carried on with him.

In addition to the cultural and social communications through the use of space, each of us has spaces we feel are our "own"—a favorite chair, a seat on the bus, a place at table, or even a favorite table in a restaurant. When someone (usually unknowingly) occupies one of these "private" spaces, we may become annoyed or upset. One is reminded of Goldilocks and the Three Bears: each successive violation of the bears' private space made communication more difficult.

The private space that each of us has is sometimes called "territoriality." It is as if we walked around with a plastic bubble hovering over us. When this space is violated—when someone gets "too close"—we may become tense or even hostile, and this will affect the nature of the communication that is possible. Most Americans and Englishmen prefer a certain distance for normal discourse. They feel more comfortable if a certain space between themselves and the other person is maintained. People of Latin descent apparently like a smaller distance. You can imagine a situation where a Latin talks to an American, and the American keeps retreating, trying to maintain his "proper" distance, all the way down a long hall.

In some situations—say riding on a crowded subway or bus—we are willing to sacrifice our personal territoriality and allow strangers to crowd up against us. We may feel uncomfortable about it, but in the interests of getting someplace we will temporarily allow our plastic "bubble" to shrink up about us. Such proximity in other situations would be intolerable. How close we allow others to get to us is one measure of our relationship to them, and helps establish the kind of communication that can take place. When we are face to face with another person, it is well to remember that he has his own plastic bubble surrounding him and that violating his territory by crowding too close may affect our ability to communicate with him.

Americans tend to see the edges of things and the intersection points of crossing lines, and to attach importance to them. Thus our streets are normally laid out in a grid pattern and we identify places by their proximity to intersections. Europeans and Orientals, however, are more inclined to attach importance to an area; thus a French street or avenue may change its name every few blocks; and houses in Japan may not have street numbers but be identified by name and area or the time at which they were built. As we travel more or are engaged in business with people from other cultures, it is well to remind onself that they see and attach importance to things that you might not see or attach significance to.

For Discussion

1. Don Fabun says: "The world of silence may be a cold and bitter one; like the deep wastes of the Arctic regions, it is fit for neither man nor beast.

Holding one's tongue may be prudent, but it is an act of rejection; silence builds walls—and walls are the symbols of failure." Yet, Karl Jaspers has observed that "the ultimate in thinking as in communication is silence." And Max Picard put it this way: "Silence is nothing merely negative; it is not the mere absence of speech. It is a positive, a complete world in itself." How would you characterize silence? Examine your own reactions to silence. Does it make you feel comfortable? uncomfortable? Why? Do your reactions depend on the persons you are with? In what way?

2. List some of the meanings silence may communicate. Do you agree that "silence builds walls"?

3. How does time speak about love? about aggression?

4. Fabun notes that "differences in the individual experience of duration can cause communication to break down." Can you cite any specific instances from your own experience when this has happened? How might such a breakdown have been avoided?

5. Examine the clothes you are wearing at the present time in terms of what the colors may be communicating to others. Then ask someone you do not know to comment on the colors' communications. Do the two views agree? disagree? How?

6. Recall a recent movie you saw and analyze the communicative function which color served. Was color used appropriately? inappropriately? Might other colors have been used to better effect? Explain.

7. The next time you are introduced to someone create an "abnormal" space between this person and yourself; stand extremely close or far away and carry on the conversation as you normally would. Observe how this person reacts to you. Does he try to change the space between you and him? Does the normal voice volume change? Does he seem uncomfortable? After a few minutes explain what you did and ask him to verbalize his feelings. Was he aware of the abnormal space? Did he resent it? Why? What were your feelings? Were you uncomfortable? Explain.

8. How does space speak about love? about aggression?

9. Edward T. Hall has observed that "the substance of a conversation can often demand special handling of space." Recall your own treatment of space when you ask, say in a department store, where is the rest room and where are the overcoats. Do you treat space differently in these two cases? Why?

A World of Smells

JOOST A. M. MEERLOO

Most writers on communication agree that information may be transmitted through any and all of our senses. Yet, extremely little has been written on our sense of smell despite its obvious importance—an importance which manufacturers of perfumes, colognes, and after-shave lotions have been quick to turn into multi-million dollar industries. Clearly these "olfactory messages" are in great demand; although those who use them may not think of them as messages they do communicate, often in very direct and explicit ways. As students of communication we need to be made aware of the entire "world of smells," as Joost Meerloo phrases it in this essay; we may be taking in a great deal more information with our noses than we realize.

In days long since gone by the streets never seemed to come to an end. Somewhere they went on and on for an indefinite distance, ending in a dreamy eternity that was filled with alluring fragrances.

Even now, having returned to my home town, the Hague in Holland, for a brief visit, I feel amazed that the familiar streets are as I remember them. But the old elusive feeling of infinity is gone. It comes to me that I am still looking for a special old tree or a fountain, for a landmark where the miracle of something far away first began.

And then, around the corner, a forgotten magic greets my nostrils—the old familiar sea breeze, the wind blowing in from the ocean and filled with salty delights. From that direction once came the stormwind we used to battle in late autumn, while making our way through the dunes and struggling against the driving rain.

As I walk along I pass my old school and another potpourri of smell memories washes over me . . . the scent of wooden floors intermingled with bathroom odors and children's moist clothes that seems to cling to all schools everywhere.

Further on I find again the little harbor with the pungent aromas of various mercantile products—coffee, cheese, and musty wheat flour, as well as the decaying flotsam floating in the water. Here in the park the flower buds open into blossoms after the rain and waft abroad their subtlest perfumes. There down a narrow street lives a wine merchant and always when passing I would try to sniff my fill of the intoxicating odors from his shop. The same thing happened when the baker brought his fresh bread out of the oven. It set my salivary juices flowing in great anticipation.

There I see the old fish market where women in quaint colorful garb sell their husbands' gleaming catches. There is no end to the glorious variety of smells. I breathe deeply and with the air I inhale the whole world.

"A World of Smells." From Joost A. M. Meerloo, Unobtrusive Communication: Essays in Psycholinguistics. Assen, Netherlands: Van Gorcum Ltd., 1964), pp. 166–69.

Often, when traveling through foreign lands, I have experienced this feeling of inhaling eternity. When a ship was taking me to some fertile forest-strewn coast, the peculiar scent of that green spot was in the air, like the shadow of Cyranno's nose, long before the vessel reached the shore. It never failed me—that welcoming cloud of smells, of tropical flowers and mouldering decay. It penetrated the salty sea air, giving sweet promise of the exotic experiences that awaited me in the jungle.

Now I head for the old flower market in the Hague with the sounds of the carillon ringing out an obligato for the feast of the senses. There under the acacias the man with the fruitstand always stood, and a little further on was "the *Waag*," the scales where the squirming pigs used to be weighed. Walking still further along there would come to me the smell of books, that dark smell that filled me with yearning as it invited one and all to read and dream and collect books.

Alas, the market is no longer there. Practical considerations forced the city council to do away with the ancient feast of smells and colors. I pass the little mews where the horses were once shod, the hoof burned before the shoe would fit, while the onlooker felt the thrill of riding far away over the distant plains. I walk through my home town. Yes, the smells have changed. The automobile with its exhaust has blotted out the delicate fragrances. Arriving at the ruins of the home where I lived before and during the war, I find there still lingers the smell of burning rubble and ashes. Strange that it should persist, so many years later.

Even the odors of the railway station are altered. Now the trains are electric. Time was when the engines belched forth mountains of steam and covered the cars in a sweet smelling shroud of smoke. When the locomotive started to pant and lurch forward it seemed as if an aroma from the distant horizon enveloped all those who bade goodbye to the travelers. Hot steam still has that magical effect on me—it stirs up my longing to travel.

There is a good explanation for all my olfactory nostalgia. After all, smell is related to our first loving contacts in the world. The newborn infant lives first in a world of pure smells, although the world soon teaches him to forego his nostril pleasures. For him mother is love at first smell. When he is older, he cannot sniff and smell keenly anymore because smelling has become taboo. Thanks to the enforced toilet taboos our innate perception of smell degenerates into chemical irritations by soaps and antiseptics. While sexual odors are taboo, man borrows these odors from flowers and plants. The sexual organs of plant and animal— musk, civet, and the rose—bring him what he has suppressed in his own life. Nevertheless, something of the instinctual passion for smells remains in man. It cannot be totally suppressed by the most pristine sanitary habits or by chlorophyl-minded merchants. Modern culture has made people feel ashamed of body odor. Whole industries thrive on that artificially induced self-consciousness. They create diseases such as halitosis just to make people feel inferior. Many a girl has become neurotic because she has completely suppressed the role and delights of perspiration.

Be that as it may, smell communication still exists. Every mood and emotion stimulates the organism to produce different hormones and different skin products, the smell of which is subliminally perceived by our fellows. I myself remain ultra-sensitive to smells. Every being communicates to me a different odor, whether pleasant or unpleasant, attractive or repelling. I often dream of familiar smells, of my father's pipe, of being back in the kitchen of my childhood, of pine woods in the rain. The odor of girls I have loved still takes me back in dreamy ecstasy to the days of my youth.

Clinical medicine has known for a long time that diseases have their special odor. I am convinced that different personalities can be differentiated by their smells. Curiously, it is not my nose that warns me that the smell of the room or person is bad. What happens is that I respond with a body reaction, with a headache—a defensive tension against any smell perceptions. My brain grows dull and I have to get away from the situation.

Friends have often asked me to tell them what my favorite smell experience is. Whereupon I always sing my paean of praise for the olfactory ecstasy of climbing mountains. All day long the sun burns down upon the trees. Gradually, as you work your way up, those woody smells give way to the grassy ones of the Alpine meadows, until you reach the higher regions where there is only stone and snow. You reach the top of the mountain and the high winds play upon your nostrils.

At that moment for the first time I feel free—free on top of the world, free from the compulsion to smell all those people below, each one wrapped in his own soulless deodorized mist.

For Discussion

1. What kinds of information can be communicated through our olfactory sense? What kinds of information do you think could not be communicated by smell? Why?

2. Try this familiar experiment on the role of smell in class. Have one student blindfolded and then have him close off his sense of smell. Be certain that the nasal passages are completely blocked. Then give the student a number of items to taste, for example, an onion, potato, apple, and turnip, or a piece of an orange, lemon, lime, and grapefruit. Be sure that the shape of

the food does not give any clues as to what it is. Is the student able to distinguish these items? On the basis of these results would you revise your view of taste? of smell?

3. Although we seldom talk about it, people each have their own peculiar odor. Select a few persons you like and a few whom you dislike and subtly but closely smell them. Do these two groups smell differently? Might smell have accounted—at least in part—for the attitudes you formed about them?

4. How might communication by smell relate to love? to aggression?

COMMUNICATION SOURCES AND RECEIVERS

How to Become
a Better
Premise Detective

HARRY E. MAYNARD

All of us hold beliefs and attitudes and are more than willing to argue in their behalf. Yet, we seldom—if ever—bother to question the assumptions and premises upon which these beliefs and attitudes are based. If we are to communicate effectively and efficiently, logically and sensibly, then these basic assumptions and premises need to be brought to consciousness, examined, and evaluated. In this brief article Harry E. Maynard gives us some clues and techniques for becoming better premise detectives.

Decision making is the essential role of an executive. But if decisions could be based on facts alone, executives would be perhaps unnecessary. We could feed information into computers and the best decisions would emerge. But precisely because we seldom have enough facts, the human executive is necessary. As Admiral Radford said, "A decision is the action an executive must take when he doesn't have enough facts to make the right answer self-evident."

For several years, I've been teaching a discipline called general semantics, which suggests that one can take a systematic, long-range and ordered approach to the decision making process. General semantics advises the man confronted with a problem to ask himself this question first: "What precisely is the problem?" And in the course of defining the problem, to re-examine the assumptions surrounding it. Too many people operate on beliefs. It isn't so much what we don't know that gets us in trouble; it's what we think we know that isn't so.

QUESTION AND LEARN

Here is how British philosopher Robin Skyner describes this general predicament: "Most people do not (consciously) operate on assumptions. They operate on beliefs. They do not treat the views they inherit tentatively, sceptically, as temporary pictures built up when less information was available. They treat them as established facts, self-evident truths, unquestionable dogmas, true everywhere and for all time. By doing this, they automatically prevent themselves, individually, from learning anything further. . . ." Thomas Fuller, British poet (1608–1661), put it well

"How to Become a Better Premise Detective." From Harry E. Maynard, "How to Become a Better Premise Detective," Public Relations Journal, *XIX (January 1963), 20–22. Reprinted by permission of the author and* Public Relations Journal.

—"He that nothing questioneth, nothing learneth." We must continually re-evaluate our own assumed beliefs.

In other words, every point of view or attitude has a built-in assumption or premise; so general semantics next suggests that we first need to learn and *recognize* the built-in premise and then constantly to question and re-examine it. To a greater or lesser degree, we all suffer from the tyranny of inaccurate assumptions (our unconscious metaphysics) and on the basis of these assumptions make inferences and judgments which many times fall wide of the mark.

We have all seen too many people spend too much of their time looking for the answers to problems and questions that were mis-stated and mis-defined from the beginning. Lexicographer Bergen Evans of Northwestern partly described this predicament when he said, "I think one of the most fruitful moments in my life came when my old zoology professor . . . told me that he would give any student an 'A' in his course who asked one intelligent question." Evans confessed that up to that time, he had *"assumed* that intelligence consisted in giving the answers"—the "right" answers.

General semantics as a discipline and study sets very careful criteria for the adequacy of premises and the procedure of reasoning from fact to inference to judgment. But the problem of discovering the adequate premise is not easy! If our major premise is inadequate or false, all our reasoning which proceeds from this premise is apt to be false.

Warren Weaver, Vice President, Alfred P. Sloan, New York, in an article in *Think* magazine (April 1961), raised these same issues when he said, "It is no good looking for hidden assumptions. They are not hidden. They are simply non-existent."

If I interpret Mr. Weaver correctly, he means many of us draw our conclusions from such inadequate data that we hardly have any intellectual right to reason from these flimsy premises. But regardless of the adequacy or inadequacy of our major premises, most logicians and mathematicians would agree that our thinking starts with our stated or unstated premise, consciously or unconsciously held. These premises can be tentatively or dogmatically held. And, as Mr. Weaver points out, they go from the most trivial decision to the most crucial decision.

A SEMANTIC OUTPUT

Where does semantics come into this problem? Studies show that a typical executive spends 80 per cent of his time listening to or reading someone else's symbolic packaging of the territory, not in first-hand observation of the territory. Imbedded in this semantic output are someone else's premises, explicitly or implicitly stated. If the listener, or reader, cannot spot the major premises in this spoken or written output, he, be he listener or reader, will be at a disadvantage in evaluating this second hand information as a basis for his decisions.

We all have beliefs and assumptions. We all have to make inferences and judgments. What the study of general semantics can do is to help people to become better premise detectives by constantly testing them on their awareness of hidden premises and invalid or inadequate premises. Here is a short example of the kind of test material I use to sensitize my students in this area.

Story I:

A man went for a walk one day and met a friend, whom he had not seen, or heard from, or heard of, in ten years. After an exchange of greetings, the man said, "Is this your little girl?" and the friend replied, "Yes, I got married about six years ago."

The man then asked the child, "What is your name?" and the little girl replied, "Same as my Mommy's." "Oh," said the man, "then it must be Margaret."

QUESTION:
If the man didn't know whom his friend had married, how could he know the child's name?

ANSWER:
See page 147

Here is another.

PROBLEM:
Can you, with one line, turn IX into the number 6?

ANSWER:
See page 147

Perhaps these seem like trick questions, but if you got the answers quickly, you would be atypical of many executives who generally don't do too well in answering a whole battery of similar story-question type tests.

After the executive has trained himself to spot premises, his next task is to judge what type of statement is wrapped around them.

We live in a world where we are literally inundated with the written and spoken word—whether we are talking face to face, talking over the telephone, listening to a radio, looking at television, reading the many magazines, newspapers, reports, etc., that we must digest in order to keep up with an ever changing world.

TRUE OR FALSE?

The statements we read or hear tend to fall into three main types: factual, inferential, and judgmental statements. When we are talking to another person or reading his written words, we must recognize when that other person is talking "facts"—making a statement that is true (or false), when he is making an inferential statement, i.e., going beyond the facts or making a judgmental statement. In general semantics, we try to train people to avoid making uncritical observations, because only sound observations can be turned into an adequate premise, a premise to proceed properly to a sound decision.

I've discovered in my teaching that for most of us it's very difficult in the rapid verbal ping pong games we play with each other to know where fact begins and ends and where inference and judgment start. Let me make it clear here that I'm not trying to denigrate inferential or judgmental statements. These have to be made. As Warren Weaver has pointed out, "the mathematics and logics our youngsters are often taught in our educational system, with rather rare exceptions, are based on the classical yes or no, right or wrong type of logic . . . the classical syllogistic 'if then' type of reasoning . . . the notion that any statement is either *correct or incorrect*. The youngsters are told, in effect, that if you want to reason logically, you *must* reason this way." This notion is dangerous if students don't discover how antiquated and limited the use of *just* two valued logic is and fail to go on and use some of the more modern logics. One of the most convenient logics for everyday problem solving is three-valued logic (symbolic logic). Here is what John Pfeiffer had to say in the *Scientific American* about this kind of logic:

> "Modern logicians, assisted by the powerful new technique (symbolic logic), have punched the Aristotelian system of logic full of holes. Of the 19 syllogisms stated by Aristotle and his medieval followers, four are now rejected and the rest can be reduced to five theorems. Modern logic has abandoned one of Aristotle's most basic principles: the law of the excluded middle, meaning that a statement must be either true or false. In the new system a statement may have three values: true, false, or indeterminate. A close analogy to this system in the legal field is the Scottish trial law, which allows three verdicts—guilty, not guilty or 'not proven.'"

This useful type of reasoning helps us sort out what we definitely know to be true, or what we definitely know to be false, or what is yet to be proven. It helps us recognize what is indeterminate. It helps us recognize where we must get more facts, in order to make an adequate decision. With this type of reasoning, we can perhaps avoid the necessity of using complex probability reasoning.

Here is a small part of a much larger test developed by William Haney, Ph.D., Associate Professor of business administration at Northwestern University, called "The Uncritical Inference Test." The part that follows is the shortest and easiest part of the test. I hope it gives the reader an insight into the difficulties involved.

INSTRUCTIONS:

1. You will read a brief story. Assume for purposes of the test that all of the information presented in the story is accurate and true. Read the story carefully. You may reread it and refer back to it whenever you wish.

2. You will then read statements about the story. *Answer them in the order in which they are asked.* Do not go back to fill in answers or to change answers.

STORY II

John Phillips, the research director of a midwestern food products firm, ordered a crash program of development on a new process. He gave three of his executives authority to spend up to $50,000 each without consulting him. He sent one of his best men, Harris, to the firm's west coast plant with orders to work on the new process independently. Within one week, Harris produced a highly promising new approach to the problem.

STATEMENTS ABOUT STORY II

1. Phillips sent one of his best men to the west coast.   *T   F   ?*

2. Phillips overestimated Harris's competence.   *T   F   ?*

3. Harris failed to produce anything new.   *T   F   ?*

4. Harris lacked authority to spend money without consulting him.   *T   F   ?*

5. Only three of Phillips' executives had authority to spend money without consulting him.   *T   F   ?*

6. The research director sent one of his best men to the firm's west coast plant. *T F ?*

7. Three men were given authority to spend up to $50,000 each without consulting Phillips. *T F ?*

8. Phillips had a high opinion of Harris. *T F ?*

9. Only four people are referred to in the story. *T F ?*

10. Phillips was research director of a food products firm. *T F ?*

11. While Phillips gave authority to three of his best men to spend up to $50,000 each, the story does not make clear whether Harris was one of these men. *T F ?*

ANSWERS

See page 148.

You may feel that some of these questions (after you've gotten the point of this test), are what I call "semantic lint picking." However, please remember that real life is much tougher than these tests. You and I, unless we carry a tape recorder around with us, cannot constantly refer back to a story and carefully recheck what people have said to us. The problem is doubly compounded when you consider that our auditory memory is the poorest memory we have. It takes much training (discipline) to quickly spot the verbal clues and know upon what level somebody is talking to us—or at what level we are talking.

I regard general semantics as an excellent aid in:

1. Developing a greater awareness on our part of our own and the other fellow's major premises;

2. Helping us to discover whether we are talking "facts" or going beyond the facts. It is necessary to have beliefs, but let's see these beliefs stand on as firm a foundation of fact as we can give them.

THE ANSWERS

ANSWER TO STORY I

Most people assume that the friend is a man. Not so in this case. It is the mother of the child. Then the problem is easy to solve.

ANSWER TO PROBLEM I

Most people assume this is a problem in Roman numerals. This is not so. If we avoided this erroneous assumption, the answer is simple—IX becomes SIX.

ANSWERS TO STORY II

1. T—that's what the story says.
2. ?—story doesn't say whether he did or not.
3. F—story says he did produce something new.
4. ?—story does not say whether or not Harris had authority to spend.
5. ?—story does not say whether others than the three mentioned had such authority.
6. T—that's what story says.
7. ?—not all executives are necessarily men.
8. ?—story suggests this but doesn't specify it.
9. ?—if Harris is one of the three given authority to spend $50,000, this would be true, but the story does not specify whether he was one of those three.
10. T—that's what story says.
11. ?—story does not specify whether Phillips gave such authority to his best men.

For Discussion

1. Examine your own attitudes on two or three controversial issues. What built-in assumptions or premises underlie these attitudes? Are these assumptions "logical"?

2. Read a recent editorial in the newspaper you normally read. Identify the unstated assumptions of the writer and evaluate them in terms of their adequacy-inadequacy. Does this procedure help you to better understand and evaluate a persuasive communication?

3. Cite an example from your own experience in which "two-valued logic" was illogically used. Under what conditions are people most prone to two-valued thinking?

4. Identify as many instances as you can of two-valued orientation which you see around you. Might a three-valued, a four-valued, or a multi-valued orientation be more advantageous? Why?

Serial Communication of Information in Organizations

WILLIAM V. HANEY

Here William V. Haney analyzes and illustrates some of the problems which beset effective and efficient communication and offers some suggestions and techniques for strengthening and improving serial transmission of information. Like most worthwhile suggestions those offered here are, as Haney puts it, "quite commonplace, common sense, but uncommonly used." Perhaps a good question to start with is, Why don't we use such "common sense" techniques?

An appreciable amount of the communication which occurs in business, industry, hospitals, military units, government agencies—in short, in chain-of-command organizations—consists of serial transmissions. A communicates a message to B; B then communicates A's message (or rather his *interpretation* of A's message) to C; C then communicates his interpretation of B's interpretation of A's message to D; and so on. The originator and the ultimate recipient of the message[1] are separated by "middle men."

"The message" may often be passed down (but not necessarily all the way down) the organization chain, as when in business the chairman acting on behalf of the board of directors may express a desire to the president. "The message" begins to fan out as the president, in turn, relays "it" to his vice presidents; they convey "it" to their respective subordinates; and so forth. Frequently "a message" goes up (but seldom all the way up) the chain. Sometimes "it" travels laterally. Sometimes, as with rumors, "it" disregards the formal organization and flows more closely along informal organizational lines.

Regardless of its direction, the number of "conveyors" involved, and the degree of its conformance with the formal structure, serial transmission is clearly an essential, inevitable form of communication in organizations. It is equally apparent that serial transmission is especially susceptible to distortion and disruption. Not only is it subject to the shortcomings and maladies of "simple" person-to-person communication

---

[1] "The message," as already suggested, is a misnomer in that what is being conveyed is not static, unchanging, and fixed. I shall retain the term for convenience, however, and use quotation marks to signify that its dynamic nature is subject to cumulative change.

"Serial Communication of Information in Organizations." From William V. Haney, "Serial Communication of Information in Organizations," in Sidney Mailick and Edward H. Van Ness, eds., Concepts and Issues in Administrative Behavior, © *1962, pp. 150–65. Reprinted by permission of Prentice-Hall, Inc., Englewood Cliffs, New Jersey.*

but, since it consists of a series of such communications, the anomalies are often *compounded*.

This is not to say, however, that serial transmissions in organizations should be abolished or even decreased. We wish to show that such communications *can be improved* if communicators are able (1) to recognize some of the patterns of miscommunication which occur in serial transmissions; (2) to understand some of the factors contributing to these patterns; (3) to take measures and practice techniques for preventing the recurrence of these patterns and for ameliorating their consequences.

I shall begin by cataloguing some of the factors which seemingly influence a serial transmission.[2]

MOTIVES OF THE COMMUNICATORS

When *B* conveys *A*'s message to *C* he may be influenced by at least three motives of which he may be largely unaware.

The Desire to Simplify the Message

We evidently dislike conveying detailed messages. The responsibility of passing along complex information is burdensome and taxing. Often, therefore, we unconsciously simplify the message before passing it along

---

[2] During the past three years I have conducted scores of informal experiments with groups of university undergraduate and graduate students, business and government executives, military officers, professionals, and so on. I would read the "message" (below) to the first "conveyor." He would then relay his interpretation to the second conveyor who, in turn, would pass along his interpretation to the third, etc. The sixth (and final member of the "team") would listen to "the message" and then write down his version of it. These final versions were collected and compared with the original.

> Every year at State University, the eagles in front of the Psi Gamma fraternity house were mysteriously sprayed during the night. Whenever this happened, it cost the Psi Gams from $75 to $100 to have the eagles cleaned. The Psi Gams complained to officials and were promised by the president that if ever any students were caught painting the eagles, they would be expelled from school.*

* Adapted from "Chuck Jackson" by Diana Conzett, which appears in Irving J. Lee's *Customs and Crises in Communication* (New York: Harper & Bros., 1954), p. 245. Reprinted by permission.

to the next person.[3] It is very probable that among the details most susceptible to omission are those we already knew or in some way presume our recipients will know without our telling them.

The Desire to Convey a "Sensible" Message

Apparently we are reluctant to relay a message that is somehow incoherent, illogical, or incomplete. It may be embarrassing to admit that one does not fully understand the message he is conveying. When he receives a message that does not quite make sense to him he is prone to "make sense out of it" before passing it along to the next person.[4]

The Desire to Make the Conveyance of the Message as Pleasant and/or Painless as Possible for the Conveyor

We evidently do not like to have to tell the boss unpleasant things. Even when not directly responsible, one does not relish the reaction of his superior to a disagreeable message. This motive probably accounts for a considerable share of the tendency for a "message" to lose its harshness as it moves up the organizational ladder. The first line supervisor may tell his foreman, "I'm telling you, Mike, the men say that if this pay cut goes through they'll strike—and they mean it!" By the time "this message" has been relayed through six or eight or more echelons (if indeed it goes that far) the executive vice president might express it to the

[3] On an arbitrary count basis the stimulus message used in the serial transmission demonstrations described in footnote 2 contained 24 "significant details." The final versions contained a mean count of approximately 8 "significant details"—a "detail loss" of 65%.

[4] The great majority (approximately 93%) of the final versions (from the serial transmission demonstrations) made "sense." Even those which were the most bizarre and bore the least resemblance to the original stimulus were in and of themselves internally consistent and coherent.

For example,

"At a State University there was an argument between two teams—the Eagles and the Fire Gems in which their clothing was torn."

"The Eagles in front of the university had parasites and were sprayed with insecticide."

"At State U. they have many birds which desecrate the buildings. To remedy the situation they expelled the students who fed the birds."

president as, "Well, sir, the men seem a little concerned over the projected wage reduction but I am confident that they will take it in stride."

One of the dangers plaguing some upper managements is that they are effectively shielded from incipient problems until they become serious and costly ones.

ASSUMPTIONS OF THE COMMUNICATORS

In addition to the serial transmitter's motives we must consider his assumptions—particularly those he makes about his communications. If some of these assumptions are fallacious and if one is unaware that he holds them, his communication can be adversely affected. The following are, in this writer's judgment, two of the most pervasive and dangerous of the current myths about communication:

The Assumption That Words Are Used in Only One Way

A study[5] indicates that for the 500 most commonly used words in our language there are 14,070 different dictionary definitions—over 28 usages per word, on the average. Take the word *run*, for example:

> Babe Ruth scored a *run*.
> Did you ever see Jesse Owens *run?*
> I have a *run* in my stocking.
> There is a fine *run* of salmon this year.
> Are you going to *run* this company or am I?
> You have the *run* of the place.
> Don't give me the *run* around.
> What headline do you want to *run?*
> There was a *run* on the bank today.
> Did he *run* the ship aground?
> I have to *run* (drive the car) downtown.
> Who will *run* for President this year?
> Joe flies the New York-Chicago *run* twice a week.
> You know the kind of people they *run* around with.
> The apples *run* large this year.
> Please *run* my bath water.

[5] Lydia Strong, "Do You Know How to Listen?" *Effective Communication on the Job,* Dooher and Marquis, eds. (New York: American Management Association, 1956), p. 28.

We could go on at some length—my small abridged dictionary gives eighty-seven distinct usages for *run*. I have chosen an extreme example, of course, but there must be relatively few words (excepting some technical terms) used in one and in only one sense.

Yet communicators often have a curious notion about words *when they are using them,* i.e., when they are speaking, writing, listening, or reading. It is immensely easy for a "sender" of a communication to assume that words are used in only one way—the way he intends them. It is just as enticing for the "receiver" to assume that the sender intended his words as he, the receiver, happens to interpret them at the moment. When communicators are unconsciously burdened by the assumption of the mono-usage of words they are prone to become involved in the pattern of miscommunication known as *bypassing.*

> A foreman told a machine operator he was passing: "Better clean up around here." It was ten minutes later when the foreman's assistant phoned: "Say, boss, isn't that bearing Sipert is working on due up in engineering pronto?"
>
> "You bet your sweet life it is. Why?"
>
> "He says you told him to drop it and sweep the place up. I thought I'd better make sure."
>
> "Listen," the foreman flared into the phone, "get him right back on that job. It's got to be ready in twenty minutes."
>
> . . . What the foreman had in mind was for Sipert to gather up the oily waste, which was a fire and accident hazard. This would not have taken more than a couple of minutes, and there would have been plenty of time to finish the bearing.[6]

Bypassing: Denotative and Connotative. Since we use words to express at least two kinds of meanings there can be two kinds of bypassings. Suppose you say to me, "Your neighbor's grass is certainly green and healthy looking, isn't it?" You could be intending your words merely to *denote,* i.e., to point to or to call my attention, to the appearance of my neighbor's lawn. On the other hand, you could have intended your words to *connote,* i.e., to imply something beyond or something other than what you were ostensibly denoting. You might have meant any number of things: that my own lawn needed more care; that my neighbor was inordinately meticulous about his lawn; that my neighbor's lawn is tended by a professional, a service you do not have and for which you envy or despise my neighbor; or even that his grass was not green at all but, on the contrary, parched and diseased; and so forth.

[6] Reprinted from *The Foreman's Letter* with permission of National Foremen's Institute, New London, Conn.

Taking these two kinds of meanings into account it is clear that by-passing occurs or can occur under any of four conditions:

1. *When the sender intends one denotation while the receiver interprets another.* (As in the case of Sipert and his foreman.)

2. *When the sender intends one connotation while the receiver interprets another.*

   A friend once told me of an experience she had had years ago when as a teenager she was spending the week with a maiden aunt. Joan had gone to the movies with a young man who brought her home at a respectable hour. However, the couple lingered on the front porch somewhat longer than Aunt Mildred thought necessary. The little old lady was rather proud of her ability to deal with younger people so she slipped out of bed, raised her bedroom window, and called down sweetly, "If you two knew how pleasant it is in bed, you wouldn't be standing out there in the cold."

3. *When the sender intends only a denotation while the receiver interprets a connotation.*

   For a brief period the following memorandum appeared on the bulletin boards of a government agency in Washington:

   > *Those department and sections heads who do not have secretaries assigned to them may take advantage of the stenographers in the secretarial pool.*

4. *When the sender intends a connotation while the receiver interprets a denotation only.*

   Before making his final decision on a proposal to move to new offices, the head of a large company called his top executives for a last discussion of the idea. All were enthusiastic except the company treasurer who insisted that he had not had time to calculate all the costs with accuracy sufficient to satisfy himself that the move was advantageous. Annoyed by his persistence, the chief finally burst out:

   "All right, Jim, all right! Figure it out to the last cent. A penny saved is a penny earned, right?"

   The intention was ironic. He meant not what the words denoted but the opposite—forget this and stop being petty. For him this was what his words connoted.

   For the treasurer "penny saved, penny earned" meant exactly what it said. He put several members on his staff to work on the problem and, to test the firmness of the price, had one of them interview the agent renting the proposed new quarters without explaining whom he represented. This indication of additional interest in the premises led the agent to raise the rent. Not until

the lease was signed, did the agency discover that one of its own em-
ployes had, in effect, bid up its price.[7]

The Assumption That Inferences Are Always
Distinguishable from Observations

It is incredibly difficult, at times, for a communicator (or anyone) to
discriminate between what he "knows" (i.e., what he has actually observed—seen, heard, read, etc.) and what he is only inferring or guessing.
One of the key reasons for this lies in the character of the language used
to express observations and inferences.

Suppose you look at a man and observe that he is wearing a white
shirt and then say, "That man is wearing a white shirt." Assuming your
vision and the illumination were "normal" you would have made a
statement of *observation*—a statement which directly corresponded to
and was corroborated by your observation. But suppose you now say,
"That man bought the white shirt he is wearing." Assuming you were
not present when and if the man bought the shirt that statement would
be *for you a statement of inference*. Your statement went *beyond* what
you observed. You inferred that the man bought the shirt; you did not
observe it. Of course, your inference may be correct (but it could be
false: perhaps he was given the shirt as a gift; perhaps he stole it or bor-
rowed it; etc.).

Nothing in the nature of our language (the grammar, spelling, pro-
nunciation, accentuation, syntax, inflection, etc.) prevents you from
speaking or writing (or thinking) a statement of inference *as if* you were
making a statement of observation. Our language permits you to say "Of
course, he bought the shirt" with certainty and finality, i.e., with as
much confidence as you would make a statement of observation. The
effect is that it becomes exceedingly easy to confuse the two kinds of
statements and also to confuse inference and observation on nonverbal
levels. The destructive consequences of acting upon inference as if acting
upon observation can range from mild embarrassment to tragedy. One
factual illustration may be sufficient to point up the dangers of such
behavior.

THE CASE OF JIM BLAKE[8]

Jim Blake, 41, had been with the Hasting Co. for ten years. For
the last seven years he had served as an "inside salesman," receiving

[7] Robert Froman, "Make Words Fit the Job," *Nation's Business* (July 1959),
p. 78. Reprinted by permission.
[8] The names have been changed.

phone calls from customers and writing out orders. "Salesman," in this case, was somewhat of a euphemism as the customer ordinarily knew what he wanted and was prepared to place an order. The "outside salesmen," on the other hand, visited industrial accounts and enjoyed considerably more status and income. Blake had aspired to an outside position for several years but no openings had occurred. He had, however, been assured by Russ Jenkins, sales manager, that as senior inside man he would be given first chance at the next available outside job.

Finally, it seemed as if Jim's chance had come. Harry Strom, 63, one of the outside men, had decided in January to retire on the first of June. It did not occur to Jenkins to reassure Blake that the new opening was to be his. Moreover, Blake did not question Jenkins because he felt his superior should take the initiative.

As the months went by Blake became increasingly uneasy. Finally, on May 15 he was astonished to see Strom escorting a young man into Jenkins' office. Although the door was closed Blake could hear considerable laughing inside. After an hour the three emerged from the office and Jenkins shook hands with the new man saying, "Joe, I'm certainly glad you're going to be with us. With Harry showing you around his territory you're going to get a good start at the business." Strom and the new man left and Jenkins returned to his office.

Blake was infuriated. He was convinced that the new man was being groomed for Strom's position. Now he understood why Jenkins had said nothing to him. He angrily cleaned out his desk, wrote a bitter letter of resignation and left it on his desk, and stomped out of the office.

Suspecting the worst for several months, Blake was quite unable to distinguish what he had inferred from what he had actually observed. The new man, it turned out, was being hired to work as an inside salesman—an opening which was to be occasioned by Blake's moving into the outside position. Jenkins had wanted the new man to get the "feel" of the clientele and thus had requested Strom to take him along for a few days as Strom made his calls.

TRENDS IN SERIAL TRANSMISSION

These assumptions,[9] the mono-usage of words, and the inference-observation confusion, as well as the aforementioned motives of the communicators, undoubtedly contribute a significant share of the difficul-

---

[9] For a more detailed analysis of these assumptions and for additional methods for preventing and correcting their consequences, see William V. Haney, *Communication: Patterns and Incidents* (Homewood, Ill.: Irwin, 1960), chs. III, IV, V.

ties and dangers which beset a serial transmission. Their effect tends to be manifested by three trends: omission, alteration, and addition.

Details Become Omitted

It requires less effort to convey a simpler, less complex message. With fewer details to transmit the fear of forgetting or of garbling the message is decreased. In the serial transmissions even those final versions which most closely approximated the original had omitted an appreciable number of details.

There are Eagles in front of the frat house at the State University. It cost $75 to $100 to remove paint each year from the eagles.

The essential question, perhaps, which details *will be retained?* Judging from interviewing the serial transmitters after the demonstrations these aspects will *not* be dropped out:

1. those details the transmitter wanted or expected to hear.

2. those details which "made sense" to the transmitter.

3. those details which seemed important *to the transmitter*.

4. those details which for various and inexplicable reasons seemed to stick with the transmitter—those aspects which seemed particularly unusual or bizarre; those which had special significance to him; etc.

Details Become Altered

When changes in detail occurred in the serial transmissions it was often possible to pinpoint the "changers." When asked to explain why they had changed the message most were unaware that they had done so. However, upon retrospection some admitted that they had changed the details in order to simplify the message, "clarify it," "straighten it out," "make it more sensible," and the like. It became evident, too, that among the details most susceptible to change were the qualifications, the indefinite. Inferential statements are prone to become definite and certain. What may start out as "The boss seemed angry this morning" may quickly progress to "The boss was angry."

A well-known psychologist once "planted" a rumor in an enlisted men's mess hall on a certain Air Force base. His statement was: "Is it true that they are building a tunnel big enough to trundle B-52's to—(the town two miles away)?" Twelve hours later the rumor came back to him as: "They are building a tunnel to trundle B-52's to—." The "Is-it-true" uncertainty had been dropped. So had the indefinite purpose ("big enough to").

It became obvious upon interviewing the serial transmitters that by-passing (denotative and connotative) had also played a role. For example, the "president" in the message about the "eagles" was occasionally by-passed as the "President of the U.S." and sometimes the rest of the message was constructed around this detail.

> The White House was in such a mess that they wanted to reno-vate it but found that the cost would be $100 to $75 to paint the eagle so they decided not to do it.

Details Become Added

Not infrequently details are added to the message to "fill in the gaps," "to make better sense," and "because I thought the fellow who told it to me left something out."

The psychologist was eventually told that not only were they building a tunnel for B-52's but that a mile-long underground runway was being constructed at the end of it! The runway was to have a ceiling slanting upward so that a plane could take off, fly up along the ceiling and emerge from an inconspicuous slit at the end of the cavern! This, he admitted, was a much more "sensible" rumor than the one he had started, for the town had no facilities for take-offs and thus there was nothing which could have been done wth the B-52's once they reached the end of the tunnel!

PICTORIAL TRANSMISSION

An interesting facet about serial transmission is that the three trends —omission, alteration, and addition—are also present when the "mes-sage" is pictorial as opposed to verbal. Our procedure was to permit the "transmitter" to view the stimulus picture (upper left corner of drawing below) for thirty seconds. He then proceeded to reproduce the picture as accurately as possible from memory. When he finished his drawing he showed it to transmitter$_2$ for thirty seconds, who then attempted to reproduce the first transmitter's drawing from memory, etc. Drawings 1 through 5 (p. 160) represented the work of a fairly typical "team" of five transmitters.

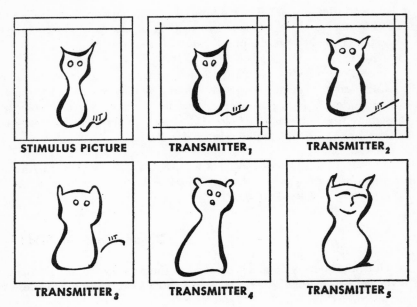

STIMULUS PICTURE   TRANSMITTER₁   TRANSMITTER₂

TRANSMITTER₃   TRANSMITTER₄   TRANSMITTER₅

Details Become Omitted. Note the progressive simplification of the configuration in the lower right and the eventual omission of it altogether. Note the omission of the border.

Details Become Altered. The border is an interesting example of alteration. The original border is quite irregular, difficult to remember.
Transmitter₁ when interviewed afterward said, "I remembered that
the frame was incomplete somehow but couldn't remember just
how it was incomplete." Note how indefinitely irregular his border
is. So subtle, in fact, that Transmitter₂ said he never recognized it
as purposefully asymetrical. "I thought he was just a little careless."
Transmitter₂ drew a completely regular border—easy to remember
but also easy to fail to notice. Transmitter₃ was surprised after-
wards to discover that the drawing he had tried to memorize had
had a border. It had apparently seemed so "natural," so much a
part of the background, that he had failed to attend to it.

Details Become Added. Transmitter₁ perceived the stimulus picture as a
cat and a cat it remained through the series. When shown that he
had added a nose Transmitter₄ admitted, "You know, I knew there
was something missing from that cat—I knew it had a body, a head,
ears, and eyes. I thought it was the mouth that was missing but
not the nose." Providing everything *except* a mouth was far too enticing for Transmitter₅. "I thought the other fellow made a mistake
so I corrected it!"

CORRECTIVES[10]

Even serial transmissions, as intricate and as relatively uncontrolled communications as they are, can be improved. The suggestions below are not sensational panaceas. In fact, they are quite commonplace, common sense, but uncommonly used techniques.

1. *Take notes*

Less than five percent of the serial transmitters took notes. Some said that they assumed they were not supposed to (no such restriction had been placed upon them) but most admitted that they rarely take notes as a matter of course. In the cases where all transmitters on a team were instructed to take notes the final versions were manifestly more complete and more accurate than those of the non-notetakers.

2. *Give details in order*

Organized information is easier to understand and to remember. Choose a sequence (chronological, spatial, deductive, inductive, etc.) appropriate to the content and be consistent with it. For example, it may suit your purpose best to begin with a proposal followed by supporting reasons or to start with the reasons and work toward the proposal. In either case take care to keep proposals and reasons clearly distinguished rather than mixing them together indiscriminately.

3. *Be wary of bypassing*

If you are the receiver, query (ask the sender what he meant) and paraphrase (put what you think he said or wrote into your own words and get the sender to check you). These simple techniques are effective yet infrequently practiced, perhaps because we are so positive we *know* what the other fellow means; perhaps because we hesitate to ask or rephrase for fear the other fellow (especially if he is the boss) will think less of us for not understanding the first time. The latter apprehension is usually unfounded, at least if we can accept the remarks of a hundred or more executives questioned on the matter during the last four years. "By all means," they have said almost to a man, "I *want* my people to check with me. The person who wants to be sure he's got it straight has a sense of responsibility and that's the kind of man (or woman) I want on my payroll."

Although executives, generally, may take this point of view quite sin-

---

[10] Most of these suggestions are offered by Irving J. and Laura L. Lee, *Handling Barriers in Communication* (New York: Harper & Bros., 1956), pp. 71–74.

cerely, obviously not all of them practice it. Querying and paraphrasing are *two-way* responsibilities and the sender must be truly approachable by his receivers if the techniques are to be successful.

This check-list may be helpful in avoiding bypassing:

> Could he be denoting something other than what I am?
> Could he be connoting something other than what I am?
> Could he be connoting whereas I am merely denoting?
> Could he be merely denoting whereas I am connoting?

4. *Distinguish between inference and observation*

Ask yourself sharply: Did I *really* see, hear, or read this—or am I guessing part of it? The essential characteristics of a statement of observation are these:

1. It can be made only by the observer.
   > (What someone tells you as observational is still inferential for you if you did not observe it.)

2. It can be made only *after* observation.

3. It stays with what has been observed; does not go beyond it.

This is not to say that inferential statements are not to be made—we could hardly avoid doing so. But it is important or even vital at times to know *when* we are making them.

5. *Slow down your oral transmissions*

By doing so, you give your listener a better opportunity to assimilate complex and detailed information. However, it is possible to speak *too* slowly so as to lose his attention. Since either extreme defeats your purpose, it is generally wise to watch the listener for clues as to the most suitable rate of speech.

6. *Simplify the message*

This suggestion is for the *originator* of the message. The "middlemen" often simplify without half trying! Most salesmen realize the inadvisability of attempting to sell too many features at a time. The customer is only confused and is unable to distinguish the key features from those less important. With particular respect to oral transmission, there is impressive evidence to indicate that beyond a point the addition of details leads to disproportionate omission. Evidently, you can add a straw to the camel's back without breaking it, but you run the decided risk of his dropping two straws.

7. *Use dual media when feasible*

A message often stands a better chance of getting through if it is reinforced by restatement in another communication medium. Detailed, complex, and unfamiliar information is often transmitted by such combinations as a memo follow-up on a telephone call; a sensory aid (slide, diagram, mockup, picture, etc.) accompanying a written or oral message, etc.

8. *Highlight the important*

Presumably the originator of a message knows (or should know) which are its important aspects. But this does not automatically insure that his serial transmitters will similarly recognize them. There are numerous devices for making salient points stand out as such; e.g., using underscoring, capitals, etc., in writing; using vocal emphasis, attention-drawing phrases ("this is the main point . . . ," "here's the crux . . . ," "be sure to note this . . ."), etc., in speaking.

9. *Reduce the number of links in the chain*

This suggestion has to be followed with discretion. Jumping the chain of command either upward or downward can sometimes have undesirable consequences. However, whenever it is possible to reduce or eliminate the "middle-men," "the message" generally becomes progressively less susceptible to aberrations. Of course, there are methods of skipping links which are commonly accepted and widely practiced. Communication downward can be reduced to person-to-person communication, in a sense, with general memos, letters, bulletins, group meetings, etc. Communication upward can accomplish the same purpose via suggestion boxes, opinion questionnaires, "talk-backs," etc.

10. *Preview and review*

A wise speech professor of mine used to say: "Giving a speech is basically very simple if you do it in three steps: First, you tell them what you're going to tell them; then you tell; then, finally, you tell them what you've told them." This three step sequence is often applicable whether the message is transmitted by letter, memo, written or oral report, public address, telephone call, etc.

SUMMARY

After the last suggestion I feel obliged to review this article briefly. We have been concerned with serial transmission—a widespread, essential, and yet susceptible form of communication. Among the factors which vitiate a serial transmission are certain of the communicator's motives and fallacious assumptions. When these and other factors are in play the three processes—omission, alteration, and addition—tend to occur. The suggestions offered for strengthening serial transmission will be more or less applicable, of course, depending upon the communication situation.

An important question remains: What can be done to encourage communicators to practice the techniques? They will probably use them largely to the extent that they think the techniques are needed. But *do* they think them necessary? Apparently many do not. When asked to explain how the final version came to differ so markedly from the original, many of the serial transmitters in my studies were genuinely puzzled. A frequent comment was "I really can't understand it. All I know is that I passed the message along the same as it came to me." If messages *were* passed along "the same as they came," of course, serial transmission would no longer be a problem. And so long as the illusion of fidelity is with the communicator it is unlikely that he will be prompted to apply some of these simple, prosaic, yet effective techniques to his communicating. Perhaps a first step would be to induce him to question his unwarranted assurance about his communication. The controlled serial transmission experience appears to accomplish this.

References

Allport, G. W., and L. Postman, "The Basic Psychology of Rumor," *Transactions of the New York Academy of Sciences,* Series II, 8 (1945), 61–81.

Allport, G. W., and L. Postman, *The Psychology of Rumor.* New York: Holt, Rinehart & Winston, 1947.

Asch, S., "Group Forces on the Modification and Distortion of Judgments," *Social Psychology.* Englewood Cliffs, N.J.: Prentice-Hall, 1952.

Back, K. W., "Influence through Social Communication," in *Readings in Social Psychology,* eds. Swanson, Newcomb, and Hartley. New York: Holt, Rinehart & Winston, 1952.

Back, K. W. and others, "A Method of Studying Rumor Transmission," in *Theory and Experiment in Social Communication,* Festinger and others. Ann Arbor, Mich.: Research Center for Group Dynamics, University of Michigan, 1950.

Borst, M., "Recherches experimentales sur l'éducabilité et la fidèlité du témoignage," *Archives de Psychologie,* 3 (1904), 204–314.

Bruner, J. S., "The Dimensions of Propaganda," *Journal of Abnormal and Social Psychology,* 36 (1941), 311–37.

Bruner, J. S., and L. Postman, "Emotional Selectivity in Perception and Reaction," *Personality,* 16 (1947), 69–77.

Cantril, H., H. Goudet, and H. Herzog, *The Invasion from Mars.* Princeton: Princeton University Press, 1940.

Carmichael, L., H. P. Hogan, and A. A. Walter, "An Experimental Study of the Effect of Language on the Reproduction of Visually Perceived Form," *Journal of Experimental Psychology,* 15 (1932), 73–86.

Carter, L. F., and K. Schooler, "Value, Need, and Other Factors in Perception," *Psychological Review,* 56 (1949), 200–207.

Claparède, E., "Expériences sur le témoignage: témoignage simple; appréciation; confrontation," *Archives de Psychologie,* 5 (1906), 344–87.

Communicating with Employees, Studies in Personnel Policy No. 129. New York: National Industrial Conference Board, 1952.

De Fleur, M. L., and O. N. Larsen, *The Flow of Information.* N.Y.: Harper & Bros., 1958.

Gardiner, Riley W., and Leander J. Lohrenz, "Leveling-Sharpening and Serial Reproduction of a Story," *Bulletin of the Menninger Clinic,* 24 (November, 1960).

Haney, W. V., *Measurement of the Ability to Discriminate Between Descriptive and Inferential Statements.* Unpublished doctoral dissertation, Northwestern University, 1953.

Higham, T. M., "The Experimental Study of the Transmission of Rumor," *British Journal of Psychology, General Section,* 42 (1951), 42–55.

Irving, J. A., "The Psychological Analysis of Wartime Rumor Patterns in Canada," *Bulletin of the Canadian Psychological Association,* 3 (1943), 40–44.

Jacobson, D. J., *The Affairs of Dame Rumor.* New York: Holt, Rinehart & Winston, 1948.

Katz, D., "Psychological Barriers to Communication," in *Mass Communications,* ed., Schramm. Urbana, Ill.: University of Illinois Press, 1949.

Katz, E., and P. Lazarsfeld, *Personal Influence: The Part Played by People in the Flow of Mass Communications.* Glencoe, Ill.: The Free Press, 1955.

Knapp, R. H., "A Psychology of Rumor," *Public Opinion Quarterly,* 8 (1944), 23–37.

Otto, M. C., "Testimony and Human Nature," *Journal of Criminal Law and Criminology,* 9 (1918), 98–104.

Postman, L., and J. S. Bruner, "Perception under Stress," *Psychological Review*, 55 (1948), 313–23.

Postman, L., J. S. Bruner, and E. McGinnies, "Personal Values as Selective Factors in Perception," *Journal of Abnormal and Social Psychology*, 43 (1948), 142–54.

Smith, G. H., "The Effects of Fact and Rumor Labels," *Journal of Abnormal and Social Psychology*, 42 (1947), 80–90.

Stefansson, V., *The Standardization of Error*. London: Routledge & Kegan Paul, 1928.

Whipple, G. M., "The Observer as Reporter: A Survey of the 'Psychology of Testimony,'" *Psychological Bulletin*, 6 (1909), 153–70.

For Discussion

1. Haney places quotation marks around the word "message" to call attention to its dynamic and changing nature. What types of messages appear most subject to change as they pass through the communication system? What types of messages seem least subject to change? Why?

2. In discussing "the desire to simplify the message" Haney says that "It is very probable that among the details most susceptible to omission are those we already knew or in some way presume our recipients will know without our telling them." What other kinds of details seem easily susceptible to omission? Why? What implications does this have for the communicator? for the receiver?

3. A message which moves up the organizational ladder tends to lose its harshness, according to Haney. How would you tell a fellow student that you hated a particular course and the instructor? How would you tell your instructor? What factors might account for the differences in these two messages?

4. Illustrate the pattern of miscommunication Haney calls "bypassing" by reference to a communication breakdown which you have witnessed or been involved in.

5. The humor of comic strips and cartoons frequently revolves around bypassing. Locate some examples and discuss them with particular reference to the four types of bypassing Haney considers.

6. The confusion between factual and inferential statements can lead to considerable problems in all forms of communication. Identify at least one instance from your own experience in which fact-inference confusion occasioned a breakdown in communication.

Psychological Barriers
to Communication

DANIEL KATZ

The great strides made in recent years in overcoming the physical problems of communication—satellite transmission being the most notable example—should not obscure the very real problems which still remain. In this paper Daniel Katz considers some of the psychological problems and obstacles which stand in the way of accurate and adequate communication. Although written more than twenty years ago this article is even more meaningful and relevant today than it was when written. The implications of the barriers Katz discusses for what we today call the "communication gap" and the "generation gap" are clear and to the point.

Accurate and adequate communication between groups and peoples will not in itself bring about the millennium, but it is a necessary condition for almost all forms of social progress. Physical barriers to communication are rapidly disappearing, but the psychological obstacles remain. These psychological difficulties are in part a function of the very nature of language; in part they are due to the emotional character and mental limitations of human beings.

THE NATURE OF LANGUAGE

Much of our communication in the great society must of necessity be by formal language rather than by visual presentation or by the explicit denotation or pointing possible in small face-to-face groups. Formal language is symbolic in that its verbal or mathematical terms stand for aspects of reality beyond themselves. Though onomatopoetic words are an exception, they constitute but a small fraction of any modern language. Because of its symbolic nature, language is a poor substitute for the realities which it attempts to represent. The real world is more complex, more colorful, more fluid, more multidimensional than the pale words or oversimplified signs used to convey meaning.

Nor is there any easy solution of the problem. A language too close to perceptual reality would be useless for generalization and would, moreover, ignore complex forms of experience. Language enables us to transcend the specificity of the single event and makes possible the analysis and comparison of experiences. But the abstraction and generalization through the use of symbols which has given man his control over

"Psychological Barriers to Communication." From Daniel Katz, "Psychological Barriers to Communication," Annals of the American Academy of Political and Social Science, *CCL (March 1947), pp. 17–25. Reprinted by permission of the author and The American Academy of Political and Social Science.*

the natural world also makes possible the greatest distortions of reality. Many language signs may in fact be completely lacking in objective reference. The semantic movement is the current effort to cope with the woeful inadequacies inherent in the symbolic nature of language. Thus far it has contributed more to exposing the inaccuracies and weaknesses in language than to developing a science of meaning.

The imperfection of language is not due solely to the weakness of its representational quality. Viewed realistically, language as a living process has other functions than accurate communication. It did not arise in the history of the race, any more than in the development of the child, solely in the interest of precise interchange of information. Language as it exists is not the product of scientists trying to perfect an exact set of symbols; it is the product of the arena of everyday life, in which people are concerned with manipulating and controlling their fellows and with expressing their emotional and psychological wants. The prototype of language as a functioning process can be seen in the child's acquisition of words and phrases to extend his control of his environment beyond his limited physical reach. Similarly, adults use language to obtain sympathy, bulldoze their fellows, placate or embarrass their enemies, warm and comfort their friends, deceive themselves, or express their own conflicts. Language in operation is often intended to conceal and obscure meaning. Hence as an instrument for accurate communication it suffers from emotional loadings, polar words, and fictitious concepts.

Even the will to interchange factual information, therefore, is embarrassed by the heritage of a language developed for other purposes. This is one of the reasons for the slow growth of social science compared with natural science. Once the physical and biological sciences had got under way, their data were so far removed from everyday observation that they were free to develop scientific terminology and concepts. But this initial step is much more difficult in the social realm because we already have a well-developed popular language applying to social events and relationships. For example, F. H. Allport demonstrated some twenty years ago the scientific inadequacy of the popular concepts of "group" and "institution" through which we personify the group and, in the manner of the cartoonist, speak of a paranoid Germany, a schizophrenic France, or a megalomaniacal Russia.[1] But his warning went unheeded because social scientists have been unable to shed the habitual modes of thought arising from their language and their culture.

These general considerations concerning the psychological nature of

[1] Floyd H. Allport, " 'Group' and 'Institution' as Concepts in a Natural Science of Social Phenomena," Publications of the American Sociological Society, Vol. XXII, pp. 83–99.

language are the background against which more specific difficulties in communication can be understood. The following specific obstacles merit special attention: (1) the failure to refer language to experience and reality, (2) the inability to transcend personal experience in intergroup communication, (3) stereotypes: the assimilation of material to familiar frames of reference, and (4) the confusion of percept and concept: reification and personification.

RELATION OF SYMBOL TO FACT

Psychological research abounds with illustrations of the principle that analytic thinking occurs not as the prevalent mode of human response but as a limited reaction under conditions of block or need. Men think critically and precisely only under specific conditions of motivation, and then only in reference to the particular pressing problem. Ordinarily they respond according to the law of least effort. In the field of language behavior, this appears at the most fundamental level in the tendency to confuse words with the things or processes they name. The word and its referent are fused as an unanalyzed whole in the mind of the individual. Among primitives, for example, it is not permitted to mention the name of a person recently deceased. Since there is deep fear of the spirit of the departed, it is dangerous to bring up his name, fundamentally because the name and the person named are psychologically confused. Even in our own society, many obscene and sacred words are taboo because the name is regarded as the equivalent of the object or process for which it stands.

This inability to grasp the difference between the symbol and its referent is one reason for the failure to check back constantly from language to experience and reality. Much has been said about the virtues of scientific method, but one unappreciated reason for the tremendous progress in natural science has been the constant referral of scientific language to the realities which it supposedly represents. Without such an interplay between symbol and experience, distortion in the symbol cannot be corrected.

Another difficulty is that the average man has little chance, even when motivated, to check language against the facts in the real world. In our huge, complex society the individual citizen often lacks the opportunity to test the language of the politicians, statesmen and other leaders by reference to the realities involved. Walter Lippmann has presented this problem brilliantly in the *Phantom Public,* in which he shows how little possibility exists for the man on the street to participate intelligently in the political process. But it is also true at the leadership level that the individual official or leader accepts reports of the working of his policies which are gross oversimplifications and even misrepresentations of the facts. The leader lives in a world of symbols, as do his followers, and he comes to rely upon what appears in newsprint for the facts instead of upon direct contact with reality.

In the world of social action the newspaper has been the most important single medium in our culture for relating symbol to fact. In theory, the newspaper has a staff of trained observers and fact finders who constantly make contact with the real world to give accuracy to the symbols presented in news columns. Though the newspaper has functioned surprisingly well, its limitations for fact finding and presentation are obvious. On many problems, research has shown that there is a wide discrepancy between the real world and the world of newsprint. Up until the action of Congress in undercutting the Office of Price Administration in July 1946, the history of price control is an interesting example of this point. The newspapers presented a story of public impatience with bureaucratic bungling during the very period when nation-wide polls, even those conducted by commercial agencies, indicated an overwhelming popular support for price controls and the OPA, and majority satisfaction with their actual functioning.

Polls and surveys have opened up new possibilities for leaders to refer words to the world of fact. During the war many governmental agencies discovered that they could learn more about the functioning of their policies through surveys using scientific samples and firsthand accounts than through press clippings or through the occasional visit of a high official to the field.

EXPERIENTIAL LIMITATION

The important psychological fact that men's modes of thinking—their beliefs, their attitudes—develop out of their ways of life is not commonly and fully appreciated. Their mental worlds derive from everyday experiences in their occupational callings, and they are not equipped to understand a language which represents a different way of life.

Because language is symbolic in nature, it can only evoke meaning in the recipient if the recipient has experiences corresponding to the symbol. It will not solve the problem of the basic difficulties in communication between the peoples of the world to have them all speak the same tongue if their experiential backgrounds differ. The individual lives in a private world of his own perception, emotion, and thought. To the extent that his perceptions, feelings, and thoughts arise from similar contacts with similar aspects of reality as experienced by others, the private world can be shared and lose something of its private character. But language itself, even if exact and precise, is a very limited device for producing common understanding when it has no basis in common experience. The linguists who argue for a world language neglect the fact that basic misunderstandings occur not at the linguistic but at the psychological level.

A dramatic example of the inability of verbal symbols to bridge the gap between different experiential worlds is the current lack of understanding between returned servicemen and civilians. Since foxhole existence has no real counterpart in unbombed America, American civilians are at a great disadvantage in understanding or communicating with returned combat servicemen.[2] In the same way the peoples of the world living under different conditions and undergoing different types of experience live in worlds of their own between which there is little communication. Even in our own society, different groups are unable to communicate. The farmer, whose way of life differs from that of the coal miner, the steel worker, or the banker, is as much at a loss to understand their point of view as they are to understand him or one another.

Labor-management controversies illustrate the gap between groups speaking different psychological languages as a result of following different ways of life. Granted that industrial disputes have as their bedrock real and immediate differences in economic interest, it is still true that these differences are augmented by the inability of each party to understand the opposing point of view. The employer, owner, or superintendent, through his executive function of making daily decisions and issuing orders and instructions, acquires a psychology of management. He can understand, though he may dislike, a union demand for more wages. But when the union requests, or even suggests, changes in the conditions of work or changes in personnel policy, he grows emotional and objects to being told by subordinates and outsiders how to run his own plant. For their part, the workers have little understanding of the competitive position of the employer. Since the employer enjoys a way of life luxurious in comparison with their own, they find his plea of inability to pay a higher wage laughable.

The role of imagination in bridging the gap is important. This, however, is largely the function of the artist, who has the sensitivity and the willingness to seek experience beyond his own original environment.

---

[2] The chasm between civilian and serviceman has been well described by the sociologist W. Waller in *The Veteran Comes Back* and by the novelist Z. Popkin in *Journey Home*.

By personalizing the experiences of people in plays, novels, and pictures, the artist often does more to develop mutual understanding between groups with divergent experiences than does the social scientist, the reformer, the politician, or the educator.

More and more, however, are psychologists and practitioners coming to realize the importance of common experience as the real basis of communication. Group workers and experimental educators are emphasizing the importance of role playing in true education. By assigning a person a new experiential role to play, it is possible to increase his understanding in a fashion which no amount of preaching or book learning could do. The modern trend in education, which emphasizes learning by doing, laboratory projects, and a mixture of work experience with book learning, is a recognition of the inadequacy of language divorced from experience to achieve much success in communication.

Surmounting the Difficulty

The difficulty of communication between people of different experiential backgrounds is augmented by the distinctive jargon which seems to develop in every calling and in every walk of life. Though groups may differ in their experiences, there is generally more of a common core of psychological reality between them than their language indicates. A neglected aspect of communication is the identification of these areas of common understanding and the translation of the problems of one group into the functional language of another. It is sometimes assumed that limitations of intelligence prevent the farmer or the worker from understanding the complexities of national and international affairs. Anyone, however, who has taken the trouble to discuss with the shipyard worker or the coal miner the economic and political factors operative in the worker's immediate environment will realize the fallacy of this assumption. Within his limited frame of reference, the coal miner, the steel worker, or the dirt farmer will talk sense. But he is unfamiliar with the language used by the professional economist or the expert on international affairs. He is capable of reacting intelligently to matters in this sphere if they are presented to him in terms of their specifics in his own experience. This translation is rarely made, because the expert or the national leader is as uninformed of the day-to-day world of the worker as the worker is of the field of the expert. And often the person most interested and active in talking to laymen in an understandable experiential language is the demagogue, whose purpose is to misinform.

STEREOTYPES

One aspect of the limitation imposed by one's own narrow experiences is the tendency to assimilate fictitiously various language symbols to one's own frame of reference. The mere fact we lack the experience or the imagination to understand another point of view does not mean that we realize our inadequacy and remain open-minded about it. Whether or not nature abhors a vacuum, the human mind abhors the sense of helplessness that would result if it were forced to admit its inability to understand and deal with people and situations beyond its comprehension. What people do is to fill the gap with their own preconceptions and to spread their own limited attitudes and ideas to cover all the world beyond their own knowledge.

In an older day it was popular to refer to this phenomenon through Herbart's concept of the *apperceptive mass;* later Lévy-Bruhl, in his anthropological interpretations, spoke of *collective* representations; twenty years ago psychologists embraced Walter Lippmann's notion of *stereotypes;* today we speak of assimilating material to our own frame of reference. Thus the farmer who knows little about Jews save from his limited contact with a single Jewish merchant in a nearby trading center will have an opinion of all Jews, and in fact of all foreigners, based on this extremely narrow frame of reference. In the same way he will feel great resentment at the high wages paid to the city worker, without any realization of the city worker's problems. The average citizen may assimilate all discussion of the Negro-white problem to the fractional experience he has had with Negroes forced to live in slum areas.

Nor need there be even a fragmentary basis in personal experience for the stereotype. The superstitions of the culture furnish the individual ready-made categories for his prejudgments in the absence of any experience. Research studies indicate that people in all parts of the United States feel that the least desirable ethnic and racial groups are the Japanese, the Negroes, and the Turks. When asked to characterize the Turk, they have no difficulty in speaking of him as bloodthirsty, cruel, and dirty; yet the great majority who make this judgment not only have never seen a Turk but do not know anyone who has. An Englishman, H. Nicolson, has written entertainingly of the stereotyped conception of his people held by the German, the Frenchman, and the American. He writes:

> Now when the average German thinks of the average Englishman he . . . visualizes a tall, spare man, immaculately dressed in top hat and frock coat, wearing spats and an eyeglass, and gripping a

short but aggressive pipe in an enormous jaw. . . . To him, the average Englishman is a clever and unscrupulous hypocrite; a man, who, with superhuman ingenuity and foresight, is able in some miraculous manner to be always on the winning side; a person whose incompetence in business and salesmanship is balanced by an uncanny and unfair mastery of diplomatic wiles; . . .

The French portrait of the Englishman . . . is the picture of an inelegant, stupid, arrogant, and inarticulate person with an extremely red face. The French seem to mind our national complexion more than other nations. They attribute it to the overconsumption of ill-cooked meat. They are apt, for this reason, to regard us as barbarian and gross. Only at one point does the French picture coincide with the German picture. The French share with the Germans a conviction of our hypocrisy. . . .

To the average American, the average Englishman seems affected, patronizing, humorless, impolite, and funny. To him also the Englishman wears spats and carries an eyeglass; to him also he is slim and neatly dressed; yet the American, unlike the German, is not impressed by these elegancies; he considers them ridiculous; . . .[3]

Though the oversimplified and distorted notions of racial and national groups are usually cited as examples of stereotypes, the process of assimilating material to narrow preformed frames of reference is characteristic of most of our thinking: of our judgment of social classes, occupational callings, artistic and moral values, and the characters and personalities of our acquaintances.

Motivation of the Stereotype

Stereotyping applies primarily to the cognitive weakness or limitation in our intellectual processes. But this stereotyped prejudgment has an emotional dimension as well. Many of our stereotyped labels or frames carry heavy emotional loading and so are the more resistant to fact and logic. Emotion attaches to them in many ways. Because they give the individual a crude and oversimplified chart in an otherwise confused universe, they afford him security. They tie in with his whole way of thinking and feeling and acting. To abandon them would be mental suicide. A famous British scholar, completely committed to spiritualism, enthusiastically witnessed a mind-reading performance by the magicians Houdini and Mulholland. When they tried to explain to him afterward that it was all a cleverly designed trick, he would have none of their

[3] From *Time*, July 15, 1935, p. 26.

explanation, and insisted that it was a clear instance of spiritualistic phenomena.

Emotion clings to words through association with emotional events which are never dissociated from the label itself. The feeling of dependence and affection that the child has for his mother saturates the words "mother" and "home" and related phrases. These conditioned words can then be used to call up the old emotions in logically irrelevant situations. In the same way the child acquires emotional content for the stereotypes of his group. If the hierarchy of social status is built on stereotypes about Negroes, foreigners, and the lower classes, then these stereotypes are not neutral but are invested with the emotional color associated with the superiority of the upper groups.

This last example suggests a further motivational basis of the stereotype. People cling to their prejudiced beliefs in labels because of the specific psychic income to be derived from the stereotype. If people the world over are to be judged solely on their merits as human personalities, there is little ego-enhancement in belonging to an in-group which bestows superiority upon its members merely through the act of belonging. The poor whites in the South are not going to abandon their notion of the Negro when this stereotyped belief itself makes them superior to every member of the despised group. The more frustrated the individual, the more emotionally inadequate and insecure, the easier it is to channelize his dissatisfaction and aggression against a stereotyped target.

REIFICATION AND PERSONIFICATION

The oversimplification of the stereotype is equaled by the extraordinary opportunities which language provides for reification and personification. We easily forget the distinction between words which refer to percepts, or aspects of perceived experience, and terms which designate concepts and abstractions. As a result, we take a concept like the state, which stands for many complexities of human interrelationships, and make that concept into a thing or person possessed of all the attributes of the object or person. Thus the state, like the individual, does things. It takes the life of a criminal, it glows with pride at the patriotic sacrifices of its citizens; it can grow old, become feeble, or wither away and die. When pressed, we readily admit that we do not mean to be taken literally, but are speaking metaphorically and analogically. Yet our thinking is so shot through with personification and analogy that the tendency is a serious impediment to our understanding and to our intelligent handling of important problems.

The problem of German war guilt is an interesting example. One school of thought made all German crimes the action of the German state; hence it was the state that should be punished, not individual Germans. The standard defense of high-ranking German generals, admirals, and officials was that they were mere servants of the state, who faithfully followed its orders. An opposed school of thought, likewise accepting the fallacy of a personified German nation, identified every German as a miniature of the German nation and so considered all Germans equally guilty. Our first treatment of the Germans was based on this logic. American troops, under the fraternization ban, were forbidden so much as to speak to any German man, woman, or child. This was mild treatment for leading Nazis, but relatively harsh treatment for German children.

In the same way, the original American information policy in Germany was to hammer away at German guilt and to make the German people feel guilty about concentration camp atrocities. But this blanket conception of German guilt took no account of the complex realities involved. It not only failed to take into account quantitative differences in guilt between high Nazis and lesser Nazis; *qualitative* differences between active leadership in atrocities and passive acceptance of or irresponsibility about them were also ignored. The type of guilt of the Nazi leaders who set up and ran the concentration camps was of one order. The social cowardice, political passivity, and irresponsibility of the German people who were afraid to voice objection or who were indifferent is guilt of another order.

Distorted Pictures

In place, then, of communication through accurate descriptions and conceptions, we reinforce and magnify for ourselves a distorted picture of the universe by our tendency to reify and personify. Perhaps the most effective account of this process is in the following by Stuart Chase:

> Let us glance at some of the queer creatures created by personifying abstractions in America. Here in the center is a vast figure called the Nation—majestic and wrapped in the Flag. When it sternly raises its arm we are ready to die for it. Close behind rears a sinister shape, the Government. Following it is one even more sinister, Bureaucracy. Both are festooned with the writhing serpents of Red Tape. High in the heavens is the Constitution, a kind of chalice like the Holy Grail, suffused with ethereal light. It must never be joggled. Below floats the Supreme Court, a black robed

priesthood tending the eternal fires. The Supreme Court must be addressed with respect or it will neglect the fire and the Constitution will go out. This is synonymous with the end of the world. Somewhere above the Rocky Mountains are lodged the vast stone tablets of the Law. We are governed not by men but by these tablets. Near them, in satin breeches and silver buckles, pose the stern figures of our Forefathers, contemplating glumly the Nation they brought to birth. The onion-shaped demon cowering behind the Constitution is Private Property. Higher than Court, Flag, or the Law, close to the sun itself and almost as bright, is Progress, the ultimate God of America.

Here are the Masses, thick black and squirming. This demon must be firmly sat upon; if it gets up, terrible things will happen, the Constitution may be joggled. . . .

Capital, her skirt above her knees, is preparing to leave the country at the drop of a hairpin, but never departs. Skulking from city to city goes Crime, a red loathsome beast, upon which the Law is forever trying to drop a monolith, but its Aim is poor. Crime continues rhythmically to rear its ugly head. Here is the dual shape of Labor—for some a vast, dirty, clutching hand, for others, a Galahad in armor. Pacing to and fro with remorseless tread are the Trusts and Utilities, bloated unclean monsters with enormous biceps. Here is Wall Street a crouching dragon ready to spring upon assets not already nailed down in any other section of the country. The Consumer, a pathetic figure in a gray shawl, goes wearily to market. Capital and Labor each give her a kick as she passes, while Commercial Advertising, a playful sprite, squirts perfume in her eye.[4]

The personified caricatures of popular thinking appeal not only because of their simplicity but also because they give a richness of imagery and of emotional tone lacking in a more exact, scientific description. Nor is the communication of emotional feeling to be proscribed. The problem is how to communicate emotional values without sacrificing adequacy and validity of description.

RESEARCH NEEDED

In brief, the psychological barriers to communication are of such strength and have such a deep foundation in human nature that the whole problem of social communication between individuals and groups needs to be re-examined in a new light. No simple formula will solve

[4] *Tyranny of Words,* p. 23.

the problems arising from the many complex causes and widely ramifying aspects of the limitations of the symbolic mechanism and other psychological processes. The older attempt at an easy solution was the study of the dictionary. One instance of this type of thinking was the college faculty committee which tried to discover the dividing line between legislative matters of policy and executive matters of administration by looking up the words involved in the dictionary. The newer approach of the semanticists, though more sophisticated and more promising, sometimes ignores the psychological difficulties and sometimes begs the question in an uncritical operationalism.

Perhaps the whole problem of communication is inseparable from the larger context of the over-all social problems of our time. There might well be possibilities of significant advance, however, if we were to employ the research methods of science in attacking the many specific obstacles to communication. Procedures are already being worked out on the basis of research evaluation for the alleviation of minority group prejudice. Studies now in contemplation would provide functional dictionaries to supplement the standard etymological works. The process of interpersonal communication has been the subject of some research in studies of rumor.

Though the importance to accurate communication of a maximum of objective reference in language symbols has experimental support, the fact remains that such complex and involved communication is much more feasible in science than in popular discussion. It is probable that precise scientific language, with its exact reference to the objective world and objective operation, will not solve the problem of communication in practical life, where short cuts in communication are essential. But it may be possible to determine the type of short-cut symbol which conveys meaning with minimum distortion. The problem invites research.

For Discussion

1. "Physical barriers to communication," says Daniel Katz, "are rapidly disappearing." What are some physical barriers to communication and how have they been disappearing? Compare, for example, the physical aspects of communication fifty years ago with those of today. What do you think the physical aspects of communication will be like fifty years from now? a thousand years from now?

2. In his discussion of the relation of symbol to fact, Katz says that "In the world of social action the newspaper has been the most important single

medium in our culture for relating symbol to fact." If this article were being written today it is likely that Katz would have called television the most important medium. Compare these two media with regard to their capacity for relating symbol to fact. What are the advantages and disadvantages of each medium?

3. Misunderstandings and breakdowns in communication, according to Katz, are due in large measure to the different experiences of the persons attempting to communicate. Even though the persons speak the same language, they often fail to communicate because the experiential worlds are different. Today there is much talk about the "generation gap"—the inability of one generation to communicate and relate meaningfully to another generation. Does Katz's discussion of "experiential limitation" shed any light on the possible causes of this generation gap? on the possible remedies? What specifically might be done to improve communication between children and parents? between students and teachers?

4. Examine your own stereotypes concerning some national, racial, religious, economic, social, or professional class. First, state, as concretely as possible, the assumptions about this class which are embodied in the stereotype. Second, examine the validity of each assumption. Is the assumption based on concrete evidence? on hearsay evidence? Is it a conclusion resulting from the examination of many individuals or just a few? Were the individuals examined representative of the class?

5. Political cartoons depend in great part on reification and personification. Examine a recent political cartoon in light of what Katz says about reification and personification. What are some of the possible dangers or communication barriers created by this tendency to reify or personify?

Communication: Its Blocking and Its Facilitation

CARL R. ROGERS

Communication is blocked when we evaluate a statement not from the speaker's or writer's point of view but rather from our own. Communication is facilitated when we listen with understanding. To listen with understanding, as Rogers defines it, is "to see the expressed idea and attitude from the other person's point of view, to sense how it feels to him, to achieve his frame of reference in regard to the thing he is talking about." To achieve this degree of empathy is extremely difficult but too important for us not to try.

It may seem curious that a person whose whole professional effort is devoted to psychotherapy should be interested in problems of communication. What relationship is there between providing therapeutic help to individuals with emotional maladjustments and the concern of this conference with obstacles to communication? Actually the relationship is very close indeed. The whole task of psychotherapy is the task of dealing with a failure in communication. The emotionally maladjusted person, the "neurotic," is in difficulty first because communication within himself has broken down, and second because as a result of this his communication with others has been damaged. If this sounds somewhat strange, then let me put it in other terms. In the "neurotic" individual, parts of himself which have been termed unconscious, or repressed, or denied to awareness, become blocked off so that they no longer communicate themselves to the conscious or managing part of himself. As long as this is true, there are distortions in the way he communicates himself to others, and so he suffers both within himself, and in his interpersonal relations. The task of psychotherapy is to help the person achieve, through a special relationship with a therapist, good communication within himself. Once this is achieved he can communicate more freely and more effectively with others. We may say then that psychotherapy is good communication, within and between men. We may also turn that statement around and it will still be true. Good communication, free communication, within or between men, is always therapeutic.

It is, then, from a background of experience with communication in counseling and psychotherapy that I want to present here two ideas. I wish to state what I believe is one of the major factors in blocking or

"Communication: Its Blocking and Its Facilitation." From Carl R. Rogers, "Communication: Its Blocking and Its Facilitation," ETC.: A Review of General Semantics, *IX, No. 2 (Winter 1952), 83–88. Copyright 1952, by the International Society for General Semantics. Reprinted by permission of the editor of* ETC. *and the International Society for General Semantics.*

182

impeding communication, and then I wish to present what in our experience has proven to be a very important way of improving or facilitating communication.

I would like to propose, as an hypothesis for consideration, that the major barrier to mutual interpersonal communication is our very natural tendency to judge, to evaluate, to approve or disapprove, the statement of the other person, or the other group. Let me illustrate my meaning with some very simple examples. As you leave the meeting tonight, one of the statements you are likely to hear is, "I didn't like that man's talk." Now what do you respond? Almost invariably your reply will be either approval or disapproval of the attitude expressed. Either you respond, "I didn't either. I thought it was terrible," or else you tend to reply, "Oh, I thought it was really good." In other words, your primary reaction is to evaluate what has just been said to you, to evaluate it from *your* point of view, your own frame of reference.

Or take another example. Suppose I say with some feeling, "I think the Republicans are behaving in ways that show a lot of good sound sense these days," what is the response that arises in your mind as you listen? The overwhelming likelihood is that it will be evaluative. You will find yourself agreeing, or disagreeing, or making some judgment about me such as "He must be a conservative," or "He seems solid in his thinking." Or let us take an illustration from the international scene. Russia says vehemently, "The treaty with Japan is a war plot on the part of the United States." We rise as one person to say "That's a lie!"

This last illustration brings in another element connected with my hypothesis. Although the tendency to make evaluations is common in almost all interchange of language, it is very much heightened in those situations where feelings and emotions are deeply involved. So the stronger our feelings, the more likely it is that there will be no mutual element in the communication. There will be just two ideas, two feelings, two judgments, missing each other in psychological space. I'm sure you recognize this from your own experience. When you have not been emotionally involved yourself, and have listened to a heated discussion, you often go away thinking, "Well, they actually weren't talking about the same thing." And they were not. Each was making a judgment, an evaluation, from his own frame of reference. There was really nothing which could be called communication in any genuine sense. This tendency to react to any emotionally meaningful statement by forming an evaluation of it from our own point of view, is, I repeat, the major barrier to interpersonal communication.

But is there any way of solving this problem, of avoiding this barrier? I feel that we are making exciting progress toward this goal and I would like to present it as simply as I can. Real communication occurs, and this evaluative tendency is avoided, when we listen with understanding. What does that mean? It means *to see the expressed idea and attitude from the other person's point of view, to sense how it feels to him, to achieve his frame of reference in regard to the thing he is talking about.*

Stated so briefly, this may sound absurdly simple, but it is not. It is an approach which we have found extremely potent in the field of psychotherapy. It is the most effective agent we know for altering the basic personality structure of an individual, and improving his relationships and his communications with others. If I can listen to what he can tell me, if I can understand how it seems to him, if I can see its personal meaning for him, if I can sense the emotional flavor which it has for him, then I will be releasing potent forces of change in him. If I can really understand how he hates his father, or hates the university, or hates communists—if I can catch the flavor of his fear of insanity, or his fear of atom bombs, or of Russia—it will be of the greatest help to him in altering those very hatreds and fears, and in establishing realistic and harmonious relationships with the very people and situations toward which he has felt hatred and fear. We know from our research that such empathic understanding—understanding *with* a person, not *about* him —is such an effective approach that it can bring about major changes in personality.

Some of you may be feeling that you listen well to people, and that you have never seen such results. The chances are very great indeed that your listening has not been of the type I have described. Fortunately I can suggest a little laboratory experiment which you can try to test the quality of your understanding. The next time you get into an argument with your wife, or your friend, or with a small group of friends, just stop the discussion for a moment and for an experiment, institute this rule: "Each person can speak up for himself only *after* he has first restated the ideas and feelings of the previous speaker accurately, and to that speaker's satisfaction." You see what this would mean. It would simply mean that before presenting your own point of view, it would be necessary for you to really achieve the other speaker's frame of reference—to understand his thoughts and feelings so well that you could summarize them for him. Sounds simple doesn't it? But if you try it you will discover it one of the most difficult things you have ever tried to do. However, once you have been able to see the other's point of view, your own comments will have to be drastically revised. You will also find the emotion going out of the discussion, the differences being reduced, and those differences which remain being of a rational and understandable sort.

Can you imagine what this kind of approach would mean if it were projected into larger areas? What would happen to a labor-management dispute if it was conducted in such a way that labor, without necessarily agreeing, could accurately state management's point of view in a way that management could accept; and management, without approving labor's stand, could state labor's case in a way that labor agreed was accurate? It would mean that real communication was established, and one could practically guarantee that some reasonable solution would be reached.

If then this way of approach is an effective avenue to good communication and good relationships, as I am quite sure you will agree if you try the experiment I have mentioned, why is it not more widely tried and used? I will try to list the difficulties which keep it from being utilized.

In the first place it takes courage, a quality which is not too widespread. I am indebted to Dr. S. I. Hayakawa, the semanticist, for pointing out that to carry on psychotherapy in this fashion is to take a very real risk, and that courage is required. If you really understand another person in this way, if you are willing to enter his private world and see the way life appears to him, without any attempt to make evaluative judgments, you run the risk of being changed yourself. You might see it his way, you might find yourself influenced in your attitudes or your personality. The risk of being changed is one of the most frightening prospects most of us can face. If I enter, as fully as I am able, into the private world of a neurotic or psychotic individual, isn't there a risk that I might become lost in that world? Most of us are afraid to take that risk. Or if we had a Russian communist speaker here tonight, or Senator Joe McCarthy, how many of us would dare to try to see the world from each of these points of view? The great majority of us could not *listen;* we would find ourselves compelled to *evaluate,* because listening would seem too dangerous. So the first requirement is courage, and we do not always have it.

But there is a second obstacle. It is just when emotions are strongest that it is most difficult to achieve the frame of reference of the other person or group. Yet it is the time the attitude is most needed, if communication is to be established. We have not found this to be an insuperable obstacle in our experience in psychotherapy. A third party, who is able to lay aside his own feelings and evaluations, can assist greatly by listening with understanding to each person or group and clarifying the views and attitudes each holds. We have found this very effective in small groups in which contradictory or antagonistic attitudes exist. When the parties to a dispute realize that they are being understood, that someone sees how the situation seems to them, the statements grow less exaggerated and less defensive, and it is no longer necessary to maintain the attitude, "I am 100% right and you are 100% wrong." The influence of such an understanding catalyst in the group permits the members to come closer and closer to the objective truth involved in the relationship. In this way mutual communication is established and some type of agreement becomes much more possible. So we may say that though heightened emotions make it much more difficult to understand *with* an opponent, our experience makes it clear that a neutral, understanding, catalyst type of leader or therapist can overcome this obstacle in a small group.

This last phrase, however, suggests another obstacle to utilizing the approach I have described. Thus far all our experience has been with small face-to-face groups—groups exhibiting industrial tensions, religious tensions, racial tensions, and therapy groups in which many personal tensions are present. In these small groups our experience, confirmed by a limited amount of research, shows that this basic approach leads to improved communication, to greater acceptance of others and by others, and to attitudes which are more positive and more problem-solving in nature. There is a decrease in defensiveness, in exaggerated statements, in evaluative and critical behavior. But these findings are from small groups. What about trying to achieve understanding between larger groups that are geographically remote? Or between face-to-face groups who are not speaking for themselves, but simply as representatives of others, like the delegates at Kaesong? Frankly we do not know the answers to these questions. I believe the situation might be put this way. As social scientists we have a tentative test-tube solution of the problem of breakdown in communication. But to confirm the validity of this test-tube solution, and to adapt it to the enormous problems of communication-breakdown between classes, groups, and nations, would involve additional funds, much more research, and creative thinking of a high order.

Even with our present limited knowledge we can see some steps which might be taken, even in large groups, to increase the amount of listening *with*, and to decrease the amount of evaluation *about*. To be imaginative for a moment, let us suppose that a therapeutically oriented international group went to the Russian leaders and said, "We want to achieve a genuine understanding of your views and even more important, of your attitudes and feelings, toward the United States. We will summarize and resummarize these views and feelings if necessary, until you agree that our description represents the situation as it seems to you." Then suppose they did the same thing with the leaders in our own country. If they then gave the widest possible distribution to these two views, with the feelings clearly described but not expressed in name-calling, might not the effect be very great? It would not guarantee the type of understanding I have been describing, but it would make it much more possible. We can understand the feelings of a person who hates us much more readily when his attitudes are accurately described to us by a neutral third party, than we can when he is shaking his fist at us.

But even to describe such a first step is to suggest another obstacle to this approach of understanding. Our civilization does not yet have enough faith in the social sciences to utilize their findings. The opposite is true of the physical sciences. During the war when a test-tube solution was found to the problem of synthetic rubber, millions of dollars and an army of talent was turned loose on the problem of using that finding. If synthetic rubber could be made in milligrams, it could and would be made in thousands of tons. And it was. But in the social science realm, if a way is found of facilitating communication and mutual understanding in small groups, there is no guarantee that the finding will be utilized. It may be a generation or more before the money and the brains will be turned loose to exploit that finding.

In closing, I would like to summarize this small-scale solution to the problem of barriers in communication, and to point out certain of its characteristics.

I have said that our research and experience to date would make it appear that breakdowns in communication, and the evaluative tendency which is the major barrier to communication, can be avoided. The solution is provided by creating a situation in which each of the different parties come to understand the other from the *other's* point of view. This has been achieved, in practice, even when feelings run high, by the influence of a person who is willing to understand each point of view empathically, and who thus acts as a catalyst to precipitate further understanding.

This procedure has important characteristics. It can be initiated by one party, without waiting for the other to be ready. It can even be initiated by a neutral third person, providing he can gain a minimum of cooperation from one of the parties.

This procedure can deal with the insincerities, the defensive exaggerations, the lies, the "false fronts" which characterize almost every failure in communication. These defensive distortions drop away with astonishing speed as people find that the only intent is to understand, not judge.

This approach leads steadily and rapidly toward the discovery of the truth, toward a realistic appraisal of the objective barriers to communication. The dropping of some defensiveness by one party leads to further dropping of defensiveness by the other party, and truth is thus approached.

This procedure gradually achieves mutual communication. Mutual communication tends to be pointed toward solving a problem rather than toward attacking a person or group. It leads to a situation in which I see how the problem appears to you, as well as to me, and you see how it appears to me, as well as to you. Thus accurately and realistically defined, the problem is almost certain to yield to intelligent attack, or if it is in part insoluble, it will be comfortably accepted as such.

This then appears to be a test-tube solution to the breakdown of communication as it occurs in small groups. Can we take this small scale answer, investigate it further, refine it, develop it, and apply it to the tragic and well-nigh fatal failures of communication which threaten the very existence of our modern world? It seems to me that this is a possibility and a challenge which we should explore.

For Discussion

1. Try the experiment suggested by Rogers where an individual, before speaking, must accurately restate the feelings and the ideas of the previous speaker. What are the advantages of such a procedure? What are the disadvantages?

2. Examine your own communication behavior in terms of what Rogers calls "our very natural tendency to judge, to evaluate, to approve or disapprove, the statement of the other person, or the other group." Do you tend to evaluate what another person says before making certain that you understand his point of view? To what factors would you attribute this tendency?

3. Recall a recent argument you had with a friend, parent, teacher, or employer. Can at least part of the disagreement or failure to communicate be explained in terms of Rogers' hypothesis that the major barrier to interpersonal communication is "this tendency to react to any emotionally meaningful statement by forming an evaluation of it from our own point of view"?

Clear
Only
If Known

EDGAR DALE

One of the most frequently made assumptions of speakers and writers is that the persons they are addressing know a great deal more than they in fact do. Consequently, they often omit significant information, utilize technical terms, and otherwise commit the COIK fallacy, the fallacy of communicating what is Clear Only If Known. Here Edgar Dale explains this COIK fallacy, its causes and its cures. In reading this article try to analyze your own communication habits, both as speaker and listener, writer and reader, for the COIK problem.

For years I have puzzled over the poor communication of simple directions, especially those given me when traveling by car. I ask such seemingly easy questions as: Where do I turn off Route 30 for the bypass around the business district? How do I get to the planetarium? Or, is this the way to the university? The individual whom I hail for directions either replies, "I'm a stranger here myself," or gives me in kindly fashion the directions I request. He finishes by saying pleasantly, "You can't miss it."

But about half the time you do miss it. You turn at High Street instead of Ohio Street. It was six blocks to the turn, not seven. Many persons tell you to turn right when they mean left. You carefully count the indicated five stoplights before the turn and discover that your guide meant that blinkers should be counted as stoplights. Some of the directions turn out to be inaccurate. Your guide himself didn't know how to get there.

Education is always a problem of getting our bearings, of developing orientation, of discovering in what direction to go and how to get there. An inquiry into the problem of giving and receiving directions may help us discover something important about the educational process itself. Why do people give directions poorly and sometimes follow excellent directions inadequately?

First of all, people who give directions do not always understand the complexity of what they are communicating. They think it a simple matter to get to the Hayden Planetarium because it is simple for them. When someone says, "You can't miss it," he really means, "I can't miss it." He is suffering from what has been called the COIK fallacy—Clear Only If Known. It's easy to get to the place you are inquiring about if you already know how to get there.

We all suffer from the COIK fallacy. For example, during a World

"Clear Only If Known." From Edgar Dale, "Clear Only If Known," The News Letter (*School of Education, Ohio State University*), *XXXI (April 1966), 1–4. Reprinted by permission of Edgar Dale, the author and editor of* The News Letter.

Series game a recording was made of a conversation between a rabid baseball fan and an Englishman seeing a baseball game for the first time.

The Englishman asked, "What is a pitcher?"

"He's the man down there pitching the ball to the catcher."

"But," said the Englishman, "all of the players pitch the ball and all of them catch the ball. There aren't just two persons who pitch and catch."

Later the Englishman asked, "How many strikes do you get before you are out?"

The baseball fan said, "Three."

"But," replied the Englishman, "that man struck at the ball five times before he was out."

These directions about baseball, when given to the uninitiated, are clear only if known. They are, in short, *COIK*.

Try the experiment sometime of handing a person a coat and asking him to explain how to put it on. He must assume that you have lived in the tropics, have never seen a coat worn or put on, and that he is to tell you verbally how to do it. For example, he may say, "Pick it up by the collar." This you cannot do, since you do not know what a *collar* is. He may tell you to put your arm in the sleeve or to button up the coat. But you can't follow these directions because you have no previous experience with either a sleeve or a button. He knows the subject-matter but he doesn't know how to teach it. He assumes that because it is clear to him it can easily be made clear to someone else.

The communication of teachers and pupils suffers from this COIK fallacy. An uninitiated person may think that the decimal system is easy to understand. It is—if you already know it. Some idea of the complexity of the decimal system can be gained by listening to an instructor explain the binary system—a system which many children now learn in addition to the decimal system. It is not easy to understand with just one verbal explanation. But when you understand it, you wonder why it seemed so hard.

A teacher once presented a group of parents of first-grade children with material from a first-grade reader which she had written out in shorthand, and asked them to read it. It was a frustrating experience. But these parents no longer thought it was such a simple matter to learn how to read. Reading, of course, is easy if you already know how to do it.

Sometimes our directions are overcomplex and introduce unnecessary elements. They do not follow the law of parsimony. Any unnecessary element mentioned when giving directions may prove to be a distraction. Think of the directions given for solving problems in arithmetic or for making a piece of furniture or for operating a camera. Have all unrelated and unnecessary items been eliminated? Every unnecessary step or statement is likely to increase the difficulty of reading and understanding the directions. There is no need to elaborate the obvious. Aristotle once said: "Don't go into more detail than the situation requires."

In giving directions it is easy to overestimate the experience of our questioner. It is hard indeed for a Philadelphian to understand that anyone doesn't know where the City Hall is. Certainly if you go down Broad Street, you can't miss it. We know where it is; why doesn't our questioner? Some major highways are poorly marked. In transferring to Route 128 in Massachusetts from Route 1 you must choose between signs marked "North Shore" and "South Shore." In short, you must be from Boston to understand them.

It is easy to overestimate the historical experience of a student. The college instructor may forget that college seniors were babies when Franklin D. Roosevelt died. Children in the ninth grade are not familiar with John L. Lewis, Henry Kaiser, Quisling, Tojo. Events that the instructor has personally experienced have only been read or heard about by the student. The immediate knowledge of the instructor is mediated knowledge to the student.

Another frequent reason for failure in the communication of directions is that explanations are more technical than necessary. Thus a plumber once wrote to a research bureau pointing out that he had used hydrochloric acid to clean out sewer pipes and inquired whether there was any possible harm. The first written reply was as follows: "The efficacy of hydrochloric acid is indisputable, but the corrosive residue is incompatible with metallic permanence." The plumber then thanked them for this information approving his procedure. The dismayed research bureau wrote again, saying, "We cannot assume responsibility for the production of toxic and noxious residue with hydrochloric acid and suggest you use an alternative procedure." Once more the plumber thanked them for their approval. Finally, the bureau, worried about the New York sewers, called in a third scientist who wrote: "Don't use hydrochloric acid. It eats hell out of the pipes."

We are surprised to discover that many college freshmen do not know such words as *accrue, acquiesce, enigma, epitome, harbinger, hierarchy, lucrative, pernicious, fallacious,* and *coerce.* The average college senior does not know such words as *ingenuous, indigenous, venal, venial, vitiate, adumbrate, interment, vapid, accouterments, desultory.* These words aren't hard—if you already know them.

Some words are not understood; others are misunderstood. For example, a woman said that the doctor told her that she had "very close veins." A patient was puzzled as to how she could take two pills three times a day. A parent objected to her boy being called a scurvy elephant. He was called a disturbing element. A little boy ended the Pledge of Allegiance calling for liver, tea, and just fish for all.

Another difficulty in communicating directions lies in the unwilling-ness of a person to say that he doesn't know. Someone drives up and asks you where Oxford Road is. You realize that Oxford Road is somewhere in the vicinity and feel a sense of guilt about not even knowing the streets in your own town. So you tend to give poor directions instead of admitting that you don't know.

Sometimes we use the wrong medium for communicating our direc-tions. We make them entirely verbal, and the person is thus required to hold them in mind until he has followed out each step in the directions. Think, for example, how hard it is to remember Hanford 6-7249 long enough to dial it after looking it up.

A crudely drawn map will often make our directions clear. Some indication of distance would also help, although many people give wrong estimates of distances in terms of miles. A chart or a graph can often give us at a glance an idea that is communicated verbally only with great difficulty.

But we must not put too much of the blame for inadequate direc-tions on those who give them. Sometimes the persons who ask for help are also at fault. Communication, we must remember, is a two-way process.

Sometimes an individual doesn't understand directions but thinks he does. Only when he has lost his way does he realize that he wasn't careful enough to make sure that he really did understand. How often we let a speaker or instructor get by with such terms as "cognitive dissonance," "viable economy," "parameter," without asking the questions which might clear them up for us. Even apparently simple terms like "needs," "individual instruction," or "interests" hide many confusions. Our desire not to appear dumb, to be presumed "in the know," prevents us from understanding what has been said. Sometimes, too, the user of the term may not know what he is talking about.

We are often in too much of a hurry when we ask for directions. Like many tourists, we want to get to our destination quickly so that we can hurry back home. We don't bother to savor the trip or the scenery. So we impatiently rush off before our informant has really had time to catch his breath and make sure that we understand.

Similarly, we hurry through school and college subjects, getting a bird's-eye view of everything and a close-up of nothing. We aim to cover the ground when we should be uncovering it, probing for what is under-neath the surface.

It is not easy to give directions for finding one's way around in a world whose values and directions are changing. Ancient landmarks have disappeared. What appears to be a lighthouse on the horizon turns out to be a mirage. But those who do have genuine expertness, those who possess tested, authoritative data, have an obligation to be clear in their explanations, in their presentation of ideas.

We must neither overestimate nor underestimate the knowledge of the inquiring traveler. We must avoid the COIK fallacy and realize that many of our communications are clear only if already known.

For Discussion

1. Identify a specific example from your own experience in which you committed what Dale calls the COIK fallacy. Identify an instance in which you have been the victim of the COIK fallacy. How could these have been avoided?

2. Dale notes that "the communication of teachers to pupils suffers from the COIK fallacy." Keep a record for one day of the COIK fallacies which occur in class. What do these examples tell you about your teachers? About yourself? About teacher-student relationships?

3. Dale mentions a number of words which teachers are surprised to learn that college students do not know. What words are in your active vocabulary that your teachers might not know? Make up a vocabulary test and quiz your instructor. What are some of the factors accounting for these different vocabularies?

Defensive
Communication

JACK R. GIBB

Communication is almost always ineffective when a
listener or reader perceives or anticipates a threat.
Regardless of how closely the message may adhere to the
standards of correctness or persuasiveness set down by the
experts, it will fail if it is seen as a threat and arouses
defensive behavior. Here Jack Gibb analyzes some of the
major types of defensive and supportive communication
climates and argues that the major influence on
communication effectiveness is interpersonal relationships.

One way to understand communication is to view it as a people process rather than as a language process. If one is to make fundamental improvement in communication, he must make changes in interpersonal relationships. One possible type of alteration—and the one with which this paper is concerned—is that of reducing the degree of defensiveness.

DEFINITION AND SIGNIFICANCE

Defensive behavior is defined as that behavior which occurs when an individual perceives threat or anticipates threat in the group. The person who behaves defensively, even though he also gives some attention to the common task, devotes an appreciable portion of his energy to defending himself. Besides talking about the topic, he thinks about how he appears to others, how he may be seen more favorably, how he may win, dominate, impress, or escape punishment, and/or how he may avoid or mitigate a perceived or an anticipated attack.

Such inner feelings and outward acts tend to create similarly defensive postures in others; and, if unchecked, the ensuing circular response becomes increasingly destructive. Defensive behavior, in short, engenders defensive listening, and this in turn produces postural, facial, and verbal cues which raise the defense level of the original communicator.

Defense arousal prevents the listener from concentrating upon the message. Not only do defensive communicators send off multiple value, motive, and affect cues, but also defensive recipients distort what they receive. As a person becomes more and more defensive, he becomes less and less able to perceive accurately the motives, the values, and the emotions of the sender. The writer's analyses of tape recorded discussions

"Defensive Communication." From Jack R. Gibb, "Defensive Communication," Journal of Communication, XI (1961), 141–48. *Reprinted by permission of the author and the International Communication Association.*

revealed that increases in defensive behavior were correlated positively with losses in efficiency in communication.[1] Specifically, distortions became greater when defensive states existed in the groups.

The converse, moreover, also is true. The more "supportive" or defense reductive the climate the less the receiver reads into the communication distorted loadings which arise from projections of his own anxieties, motives, and concerns. As defenses are reduced, the receivers become better able to concentrate upon the structure, the content, and the cognitive meanings of the message.

CATEGORIES OF DEFENSIVE AND SUPPORTIVE COMMUNICATION

In working over an eight-year period with recordings of discussions occurring in varied settings, the writer developed the six pairs of defensive and supportive categories presented in Table 1. Behavior which a listener perceives as possessing any of the characteristics listed in the left-hand column arouses defensiveness, whereas that which he interprets as having any of the qualities designated as supportive reduces defensive feelings. The degree to which these reactions occur depends upon the personal level of defensiveness and upon the general climate in the group at the time.[2]

Evaluation and Description

Speech or other behavior which appears evaluative increases defensiveness. If by expression, manner of speech, tone of voice, or verbal content the sender seems to be evaluating or judging the listener, then the receiver goes on guard. Of course, other factors may inhibit the reaction. If the listener thought that the speaker regarded him as an equal and was being open and spontaneous, for example, the evaluativeness in a message would be neutralized and perhaps not even perceived. This same principle applies equally to the other five categories of potentially defense-producing climates. The six sets are interactive.

[1] J. R. Gibb, "Defense Level and Influence Potential in Small Groups," in *Leadership and Interpersonal Behavior,* eds. L. Petrullo and B. M. Bass (New York: Holt, Rinehart and Winston, Inc., 1961), pp. 66–81.

[2] J. R. Gibb, "Sociopsychological Processes of Group Instruction," in *The Dynamics of Instructional Groups,* ed. N. B. Henry (Fifty-ninth Yearbook of the National Society for the Study of Education, Part II, 1960), pp. 115–35.

TABLE I

Categories of Behavior Characteristic of Supportive and Defensive Climates in Small Groups

Defensive Climates	Supportive Climates
1. Evaluation	1. Description
2. Control	2. Problem orientation
3. Strategy	3. Spontaneity
4. Neutrality	4. Empathy
5. Superiority	5. Equality
6. Certainty	6. Provisionalism

Because our attitudes toward other persons are frequently, and often necessarily, evaluative, expressions which the defensive person will regard as nonjudgmental are hard to frame. Even the simplest question usually conveys the answer that the sender wishes or implies the response that would fit into his value system. A mother, for example, immediately following an earth tremor that shook the house, sought for her small son with the question: "Bobby, where are you?" The timid and plaintive "Mommy, I didn't do it" indicated how Bobby's chronic mild defensiveness predisposed him to react with a projection of his own guilt and in the context of his chronic assumption that questions are full of accusation.

Anyone who has attempted to train professionals to use information-seeking speech with neutral affect appreciates how difficult it is to teach a person to say even the simple "who did that?" without being seen as accusing. Speech is so frequently judgmental that there is a reality base for the defensive interpretations which are so common.

When insecure, group members are particularly likely to place blame, to see others as fitting into categories of good or bad, to make moral judgments of their colleagues, and to question the value, motive, and affect loadings of the speech which they hear. Since value loadings imply a judgment of others, a belief that the standards of the speaker differ from his own causes the listener to become defensive.

Descriptive speech, in contrast to that which is evaluative, tends to arouse a minimum of uneasiness. Speech acts which the listener perceives as genuine requests for information or as material with neutral loadings is descriptive. Specifically, presentations of feelings, events, perceptions, or processes which do not ask or imply that the receiver change behavior or attitude are minimally defense producing. The difficulty in avoiding overtone is illustrated by the problems of news reporters in writing stories about unions, communists, Negroes, and religious activities without tipping off the "party" line of the newspaper. One can often tell from the opening words in a news article which side the newspaper's editorial policy favors.

Control and Problem Orientation

Speech which is used to control the listener evokes resistance. In most of our social intercourse someone is trying to do something to someone else—to change an attitude, to influence behavior, or to restrict the field of activity. The degree to which attempts to control produce defensiveness depends upon the openness of the effort, for a suspicion that hidden motives exist heightens resistance. For this reason attempts of nondirective therapists and progressive educators to refrain from imposing a set of values, a point of view, or a problem solution upon the receivers meet with many barriers. Since the norm is control, noncontrollers must earn the perceptions that their efforts have no hidden motives. A bombardment of persuasive "messages" in the fields of politics, education, special causes, advertising, religion, medicine, industrial relations, and guidance has bred cynical and paranoidal responses in listeners.

Implicit in all attempts to alter another person is the assumption by the change agent that the person to be altered is inadequate. That the speaker secretly views the listener as ignorant, unable to make his own decisions, uninformed, immature, unwise, or possessed of wrong or inadequate attitudes is a subconscious perception which gives the latter a valid base for defensive reactions.

Methods of control are many and varied. Legalistic insistence on detail, restrictive regulations and policies, conformity norms, and all laws are among the methods. Gestures, facial expressions, other forms of nonverbal communication, and even such simple acts as holding a door open in a particular manner are means of imposing one's will upon another and hence are potential sources of resistance.

Problem orientation, on the other hand, is the antithesis of persuasion. When the sender communicates a desire to collaborate in defining a mutual problem and in seeking its solution, he tends to create the same problem orientation in the listener; and, of greater importance, he implies that he has no predetermined solution, attitude, or method to impose. Such behavior is permissive in that it allows the receiver to set his own goals, make his own decisions, and evaluate his own progress—or to share with the sender in doing so. The exact methods of attaining permissiveness are not known, but they must involve a constellation of cues and they certainly go beyond mere verbal assurances that the communicator has no hidden desires to exercise control.

Strategy and Spontaneity

When the sender is perceived as engaged in a stratagem involving ambiguous and multiple motivations, the receiver becomes defensive. No one wishes to be a guinea pig, a role player, or an impressed actor, and no one likes to be the victim of some hidden motivation. That which is concealed, also, may appear larger than it really is with the degree of defensiveness of the listener determining the perceived size of the suppressed element. The intense reaction of the reading audience to the material in the *Hidden Persuaders* indicates the prevalence of defensive reactions to multiple motivations behind strategy. Group members who are seen as "taking a role," as feigning emotion, as toying with their colleagues, as withholding information, or as having special sources of data are especially resented. One participant once complained that another was "using a listening technique" on him!

A large part of the adverse reaction to much of the so-called human relations training is a feeling against what are perceived as gimmicks and tricks to fool or to "involve" people, to make a person think he is making his own decision, or to make the listener feel that the sender is genuinely interested in him as a person. Particularly violent reactions occur when it appears that someone is trying to make a stratagem appear spontaneous. One person has reported a boss who incurred resentment by habitually using the gimmick of "spontaneously" looking at his watch and saying, "My gosh, look at the time—I must run to an appointment." The belief was that the boss would create less irritation by honestly asking to be excused.

Similarly, the deliberate assumption of guilelessness and natural simplicity is especially resented. Monitoring the tapes of feedback and evaluation sessions in training groups indicates the surprising extent to which members perceive the strategies of their colleagues. This perceptual clarity may be quite shocking to the strategist, who usually feels that he has cleverly hidden the motivational aura around the "gimmick."

This aversion to deceit may account for one's resistance to politicians who are suspected of behind-the-scenes planning to get his vote, to psychologists whose listening apparently is motivated by more than the manifest or content-level interest in his behavior, or to the sophisticated, smooth, or clever person whose "oneupmanship" is marked with guile. In training groups the role-flexible person frequently is resented because his changes in behavior are perceived as strategic maneuvers.

In contrast, behavior which appears to be spontaneous and free of deception is defense reductive. If the communicator is seen as having a clean id, as having uncomplicated motivations, as being straightforward and honest, and as behaving spontaneously in response to the situation, he is likely to arouse minimal defense.

Neutrality and Empathy

When neutrality in speech appears to the listener to indicate a lack of concern for his welfare, he becomes defensive. Group members usually desire to be perceived as valued persons, as individuals of special worth, and as objects of concern and affection. The clinical, detached, person-is-an-object-of-study attitude on the part of many psychologist-trainers is resented by group members. Speech with low affect that communicates little warmth or caring is in such contrast with the affect-laden speech in social situations that it sometimes communicates rejection.

Communication that conveys empathy for the feelings and respect for the worth of the listener, however, is particularly supportive and defense reductive. Reassurance results when a message indicates that the speaker identifies himself with the listener's problems, shares his feelings, and accepts his emotional reactions at face value. Abortive efforts to deny the legitimacy of the receiver's emotions by assuring the receiver that he need not feel bad, that he should not feel rejected, or that he is overly anxious, though often intended as support giving, may impress the listener as lack of acceptance. The combination of understanding and empathizing with the other person's emotions with no accompanying effort to change him apparently is supportive at a high level.

The importance of gestural behavioral cues in communicating empathy should be mentioned. Apparently spontaneous facial and bodily evidences of concern are often interpreted as especially valid evidence of deep-level acceptance.

Superiority and Equality

When a person communicates to another that he feels superior in position, power, wealth, intellectual ability, physical characteristics, or other ways, he arouses defensiveness. Here, as with the other sources of disturbance, whatever arouses feelings of inadequacy causes the listener to center upon the affect loading of the statement rather than upon the cognitive elements. The receiver then reacts by not hearing the message, by forgetting it, by competing with the sender, or by becoming jealous of him.

The person who is perceived as feeling superior communicates that he is not willing to enter into a shared problem-solving relationship, that he probably does not desire feedback, that he does not require help, and/or that he will be likely to try to reduce the power, the status, or the worth of the receiver.

Many ways exist for creating the atmosphere that the sender feels himself equal to the listener. Defenses are reduced when one perceives the sender as being willing to enter into participative planning with mutual trust and respect. Differences in talent, ability, worth, appearance, status, and power often exist, but the low defense communicator seems to attach little importance to these distinctions.

Certainty and Provisionalism

The effects of dogmatism in producing defensiveness are well known. Those who seem to know the answers, to require no additional data, and to regard themselves as teachers rather than as co-workers tend to put others on guard. Moreover, in the writer's experiment, listeners often perceived manifest expressions of certainty as connoting inward feelings of inferiority. They saw the dogmatic individual as needing to be right, as wanting to win an argument rather than solve a problem, and as seeing his ideas as truths to be defended. This kind of behavior often was associated with acts which others regarded as attempts to exercise control. People who were right seemed to have low tolerance for members who were "wrong"—i.e., who did not agree with the sender.

One reduces the defensiveness of the listener when he communicates that he is willing to experiment with his own behavior, attitudes, and ideas. The person who appears to be taking provisional attitudes, to be investigating issues rather than taking sides on them, to be problem solving rather than debating, and to be willing to experiment and explore tends to communicate that the listener may have some control over the shared quest or the investigation of the ideas. If a person is genuinely searching for information and data, he does not resent help or company along the way.

CONCLUSION

The implications of the above material for the parent, the teacher, the manager, the administrator, or the therapist are fairly obvious. Arousing defensiveness interferes with communication and thus makes it difficult—and sometimes impossible—for anyone to convey ideas clearly and to move effectively toward the solution of therapeutic, educational, or managerial problems.

For Discussion

1. In listening or reading we often become defensive or resentful of the speaker or writer without being able to pinpoint the specific source of this defensive attitude. Examine your own recent listening and/or reading behavior for defensive reactions in terms of the six categories of behavior defined by Gibb. Can these categories effectively explain your defensive reactions? What other categories might be significant in explaining defensive communications?

2. Write two paragraphs or speeches on a real or fictional incident. Write one so that it is primarily or wholly defensive and one so that it is primarily or wholly supportive. First, describe the way in which the language used conveys the defensive and supportive climates. Second, ask one or more listeners to react to these communications. Do their reactions support Gibb's conclusions regarding defensive versus supportive listening?

3. Compare and contrast two persons (for example, teachers, friends, employers) who seem to represent extremes in terms of their tendency to arouse defensive and supportive climates. Specify, as concretely as possible, the communication behaviors of these persons which produce these different climates and relate these behaviors to Gibb's six categories. What specific advice would you give to the communicator prone to create a defensive climate? What factors do you think might account for his tendency toward defensive communication?

4. Draw up a list of "suggestions for persuasive communication" which might be derived from Gibb's discussion of defensive communication. Are these suggestions in agreement or in disagreement with those found in a representative text on persuasion or rhetoric?

Do We Know How to Listen?
Practical Helps
in a Modern Age

RALPH G. NICHOLS

Listening is a most peculiar subject. We have all been listening since we were born and consequently most of us feel that we therefore know how to listen. But listening is a skill which can be developed and which can be improved. Considering the number of hours we spend in listening every day, a little energy directed toward the improvement of our listening abilities seems an extremely worthwhile investment.

In 1940 Dr. Harry Goldstein completed a very important research project at Columbia University. It was underwritten by one of our educational foundations, was very carefully drawn, and two very important observations emerged from it. One, he discovered that it is perfectly possible for us to listen to speech at a rate more than three times that at which we normally hear it, without significant loss of comprehension of what we hear. Two, he suggested that America may have overlooked a very important element in her educational system, that of teaching youngsters how to listen.

Shortly after that Richard Hubbell, an important figure in the television industry, produced a new book. In it, he declared without equivocation that 98 per cent of all a man learns in his lifetime he learns through his eyes or through his ears. His book tended to throw a spotlight upon a long-neglected organ we own, our ears.

Together, the declarations of Goldstein and Hubbell put into perspective the highly significant studies of Paul Rankin, of Ohio State University. Rankin was determined to find out what proportion of our waking day we spend in verbal communication. He kept careful log on 65 white-collar folk, much like you and me, at 15-minute intervals for two months on end. Here is what he found: seven out of every ten minutes that you and I are conscious, alive, and awake we are communicating verbally in one of its forms; and our communication time is devoted 9 per cent to writing, 16 per cent to reading, 30 per cent to speaking, and 45 per cent to listening.

OUR UPSIDE-DOWN SCHOOLS

Quantitatively speaking, America has built her school system upside down. Throughout the twelve years a youngster normally spends in

"Do We Know How to Listen? Practical Helps in a Modern Age." From Ralph G. Nichols, "Do We Know How to Listen? Practical Helps in a Modern Age," The Speech Teacher, X (1961), 118–24. Reprinted by permission of the author and the Speech Communication Association.

school, some teacher is continually trying to teach him how to write a sentence, in the hope that sometime he will be able to write a full paragraph, and then a complete report. Countless tax dollars and teacher hours of energy go into improving the *least used* channel of communication.

For some reason inexplicable to me, we usually chop off all reading improvement training at the end of the eighth grade, and from that time on the reading done is of an extensive, voluntary, and general character. Then we decry, sometimes, the fact that America is a nation of sixth-grade reading ability. We should not be shocked at that fact, in view of the maximum training received. However, a lot of tax dollars are devoted to improving this *second least-used* channel of communication.

Then we come to something important—speech itself. Thirty per cent of our communication time is devoted to it; yet speech training in America is largely an extracurricular activity. In a typical school you will find an all-school play once or twice a year. There may be a debating team with a couple of lawyer's sons on it. There may be an orator, along with an extempore speaker, and that is about the size of it. You will find it very difficult to discover a single high school in America where even one semester of speech training is required of the youngsters going through. Actually, much of the speech taught in America today is provided by Dale Carnegie and his cohorts in night classes at a cost of about $125 per student for enrollment. Too expensive, and too late in life, to do many of us much good!

Then we come to listening. Forty-five per cent of our communication time is spent in it. In 1948, when I first became concerned about this field, you could hardly find anyone really concerned about refining his listening ability. I asked my University for a sabbatical leave that year, and spent twelve months doing research related to the characteristics of good and bad listeners. First, I learned that nobody knew much about effective listening. Only three researches which you could call experimental and scientific had been published in 1948 in the field of listening comprehension. By comparison, over 3,000 scientific studies had been published in the parallel learning medium, that of reading comprehension.

TEN YEARS MAKES A DIFFERENCE

Between 1950 and 1960 a very dramatic page has been turned. Many of our leading universities are now teaching listening, under that label. Today these schools are not only teaching listening—they are doing, at long last, graduate-level research in the field. Today, also, scores of businesses and industries have instituted their own listening training programs for selected management personnel. Three departments of the Federal Government and a number of units of our military service have followed suit.

Very important to the growing interest in listening training in the public schools has been the steady support given by the National Council of Teachers of English and the Speech Association of America. Under their guidance and help new "language arts guides" are being widely adopted. Typically, these guides give equal emphasis to the four communication skills of reading, writing, speaking, and listening.

TWO CENTRAL QUESTIONS

In view of this rather sudden surge of interest in effective listening, I should like to raise two questions, and very closely pursue answers to them.

Question number one: Is efficient listening a problem? For insight on this issue, let us revert to the classroom for a moment, for the first person to produce important evidence on it was H. E. Jones, a professor at Columbia University. One year he was in charge of the beginning psychology classes there, and frequently lectured to a population of some 476 freshmen.

It seemed to him, when he gave comprehension tests over his lecture content, that the students were not getting very much of what he was trying to say. He hit upon a very novel idea for an experiment. He talked 50 of his colleagues on the faculty at Columbia into cooperating with him. Each professor agreed to prepare and deliver to Jones' students a ten-minute lecture from his own subject-matter area. Each one submitted his lecture excerpt to Jones ahead of time, and Jones painstakingly built an objective test over the contents. Half of the questions in each quiz demanded a recalling of facts, and the other half required the understanding of a principle or two imbedded in the lecture excerpt.

EFFICIENCY LEVEL—25 PER CENT

Professor Number 1 came in, gave his little ten-minute lecture, disappeared, and the group was questioned on its content. Number 2 followed. At the end of the fiftieth presentation and the fiftieth quiz, Jones scored the papers and found that freshmen were able to respond correctly to about half the items in each test. Then came the shock. Two months later he reassembled the 476 freshmen and gave them the battery of tests a second time. This time they were able to respond correctly to only 25 per cent of the items in the quizzes. Jones was forced to conclude, reluctantly, that without direct training, university freshmen appear to operate at a 25 per cent level of efficiency when they listen.

I could not believe it could be that bad. I decided to repeat the experiment at the University of Minnesota, and did so. I did not let two months go by before the retest, for I was pretty certain that the curve of forgetting takes a downward swoop long before two months have passed. Yet I got exactly the same statistics: fifty per cent response in the immediate test situation; 25 per cent after two weeks had passed.

Several other universities have run off essentially the same experiment, and all tend to report approximately the same statistics. I think it is accurate and conservative to say that we operate at almost precisely a 25 per cent level of efficiency when listening to a ten-minute talk.

WHAT CAN BE DONE?

Let us turn to a second major question: Is there anything that can be done about the problem? After all, if you and I listen badly, only 25 per cent efficiently, and can do nothing about it, the future holds a pretty dismal outlook. Fortunately, if we want to become better listeners, or to make our students or employees better listeners, it is a goal perfectly possible to attain.

A few years ago we screened out the 100 worst listeners and the 100 best listeners we could identify in the freshman population on my campus. Standardized listening tests and lecture-comprehension tests were used, and we soon had two widely contrasting groups. These poor suffering 200 freshmen were then subjected to about 20 different kinds of objective tests and measures.

We got scores on their reading, writing, speaking, listening; mechanical aptitude, mathematics aptitude, science aptitude, six different types of personality inventories; each one filled out a lengthy questionnaire, and I had a long personal interview with each of the 200.

TEN GUIDES TO EFFECTIVE LISTENING

At the end of nine months of rather close and inductive study of these 200 freshmen, it seemed to us that ten factors emerged, clearly differentiating good and bad listeners. We reported in a number of articles what we called "the ten worst listening habits of the American people." In recent years the elimination of these bad habits, and the replacement of them with their counterpart skills, seems to have become the central concern of most listening training programs. Thus, we have ten significant guides to effective listening.

1. *Find areas of interest*

All studies point to the advantage in being interested in the topic under discussion. Bad listeners usually declare the subject dry after the first few sentences. Once this decision is made, it serves to rationalize any and all inattention.

Good listeners follow different tactics. True, their first thought may be that the subject sounds dry. But a second one immediately follows, based on the realization that to get up and leave might prove a bit awkward.

The final reflection is that, being trapped anyhow, perhaps it might be well to learn if anything is being said that can be put to use.

The key to the whole matter of interest in a topic is the word *use*. Whenever we wish to listen efficiently, we ought to say to ourselves: "What's he saying that I can use? What worthwhile ideas has he? Is he reporting any workable procedures? Anything that I can cash in, or with which I can make myself happier?" Such questions lead us to screen what we are hearing in a continual effort to sort out the elements of personal value. G. K. Chesterton spoke wisely indeed when he said, "There is no such thing as an uninteresting subject; there are only uninterested people."

2. *Judge content, not delivery*

Many listeners alibi inattention to a speaker by thinking to themselves: "Who could listen to such a character? What an awful voice! Will he ever stop reading from his notes?"

The good listener reacts differently. He may well look at the speaker and think, "This man is inept. Seems like almost anyone ought to be able to talk better than that." But from this initial similarity he moves on to a different conclusion, thinking "But wait a minute . . . I'm not interested in his personality or delivery. I want to find out what he knows. Does this man know some things that I need to know?"

Essentially we "listen with our own experience." Is the conveyor to be held responsible because we are poorly equipped to decode his message? We cannot understand everything we hear, but one sure way to raise the level of our understanding is to assume the responsibility which is inherently ours.

3. *Hold your fire*

Overstimulation is almost as bad as understimulation, and the two together constitute the twin evils of inefficient listening. The overstimulated listener gets too excited, or excited too soon, by the speaker. Some of us are greatly addicted to this weakness. For us, a speaker can seldom talk for more than a few minutes without touching upon a pet bias or conviction. Occasionally we are roused in support of the speaker's point; usually it is the reverse. In either case overstimulation reflects the desire of the listener to enter, somehow, immediately into the argument.

The aroused person usually becomes preoccupied by trying to do three things simultaneously: calculate what hurt is being done to his own pet ideas; plot an embarrassing question to ask the speaker; enjoy mentally all the discomfiture visualized for the speaker once the devastating reply to him is launched. With these things going on, subsequent passages go unheard.

We must learn not to get too excited about a speaker's point until we are certain we thoroughly understand it. The secret is contained in the principle that we must always withhold evaluation until our comprehension is complete.

4. *Listen for ideas*

Good listeners focus on central ideas; they tend to recognize the characteristic language in which central ideas are usually stated, and they are able to discriminate between fact and principle, idea and example, evidence and argument. Poor listeners are inclined to listen for the facts in every presentation.

To understand the fault, let us assume that a man is giving us instructions made up of facts A to Z. The man begins to talk. We hear fact A and think: "We've got to remember it!" So we begin a memory exercise by repeating "Fact A, fact A, fact A. . . ."

Meanwhile, the fellow is telling us fact B. Now we have two facts to memorize. We're so busy doing it that we miss fact C completely. And so it goes up to fact Z. We catch a few facts, garble several others and completely miss the rest.

It is a significant fact that only about 25 per cent of persons listening to a formal talk are able to grasp the speaker's central idea. To develop this skill requires an ability to recognize conventional organizational patterns, transitional language, and the speaker's use of recapitulation. Fortunately, all of these items can be readily mastered with a bit of effort.

5. *Be flexible*

Our research has shown that our 100 worst listeners thought that note-taking and outlining were synonyms. They believed there was but one way to take notes—by making an outline.

Actually, no damage would be done if all talks followed some definite plan of organization. Unfortunately, less than half of even formal speeches are carefully organized. There are few things more frustrating than to try to outline an unoutlinable speech.

Note-taking may help or may become a distraction. Some persons try to take down everything in shorthand; the vast majority of us are far too voluminous even in longhand. While studies are not too clear on the point, there is some evidence to indicate that the volume of notes taken and their value to the taker are inversely related. In any case, the real issue is one of interpretation. Few of us have memories good enough to remember even the salient points we hear. If we can obtain brief, meaningful records of them for later review, we definitely improve our ability to learn and to remember.

The 100 best listeners had apparently learned early in life that if they wanted to be efficient note-takers they had to have more than one system of taking notes. They equipped themselves with four or five systems, and learned to adjust their system to the organizational pattern, or the absence of one, in each talk they heard. If we want to be good listeners, we must be flexible and adaptable note-takers.

6. *Work at listening*

One of the most striking characteristics of poor listeners is their disinclination to spend any energy in a listening situation. College students, by their own testimony, frequently enter classes all worn out physically; assume postures which only seem to give attention to the speaker; and then proceed to catch up on needed rest or to reflect upon purely personal matters. This faking of attention is one of the worst habits afflicting us as a people.

Listening is hard work. It is characterized by faster heart action, quicker circulation of the blood, a small rise in bodily temperature. The overrelaxed listener is merely appearing to tune in, and then feeling conscience-free to pursue any of a thousand mental tangents.

For selfish reasons alone one of the best investments we can make is to give each speaker our conscious attention. We ought to establish eye contact and maintain it; to indicate by posture and facial expression that the occasion and the speaker's efforts are a matter of real concern to us. When we do these things we help the speaker to express himself more clearly, and we in turn profit by better understanding of the improved communication we have helped him to achieve. None of this necessarily implies acceptance of his point of view or favorable action upon his appeals. It is, rather, an expression of interest.

7. *Resist distractions*

The good listeners tend to adjust quickly to any kind of abnormal situation; poor listeners tend to tolerate bad conditions and, in some instances, even to create distractions themselves.

We live in a noisy age. We are distracted not only by what we hear, but by what we see. Poor listeners tend to be readily influenced by all manner of distractions, even in an intimate face-to-face situation.

A good listener instinctively fights distraction. Sometimes the fight is easily won—by closing a door, shutting off the radio, moving closer to the person talking, or asking him to speak louder. If the distractions cannot be met that easily, then it becomes a matter of concentration.

8. *Exercise your mind*

Poor listeners are inexperienced in hearing difficult, expository material. Good listeners apparently develop an appetite for hearing a variety of presentations difficult enough to challenge their mental capacities.

Perhaps the one word that best describes the bad listener is "inexperienced." Although he spends 45 per cent of his communication day listening to something, he is inexperienced in hearing anything tough, technical, or expository. He has for years painstakingly sought light, recreational material. The problem he creates is deeply significant, because such a person is a poor producer in factory, office, or classroom.

Inexperience is not easily or quickly overcome. However, knowledge of our own weakness may lead us to repair it. We need never become too old to meet new challenges.

9. *Keep your mind open*

Parallel to the blind spots which afflict human beings are certain psychological deaf spots which impair our ability to perceive and understand. These deaf spots are the dwelling place of our most cherished notions, convictions, and complexes. Often, when a speaker invades one of these areas with a word or phrase, we turn our mind to retraveling familiar mental pathways crisscrossing our invaded area of sensitivity.

It is hard to believe in moments of cold detachment that just a word or phrase can cause such emotional eruption. Yet with poor listeners it is frequently the case; and even with very good listeners it is occasionally the case. When such emotional deafness transpires, communicative efficiency drops rapidly to zero.

Among the words known thus to serve as red flags to some listeners are: mother-in-law, landlord, redneck, sharecropper, sissy, pervert, automation, clerk, income tax, hack, dumb farmer, pink, "Greetings," antivivisectionist, evolution, square, punk, welsher.

Effective listeners try to identify and to rationalize the words or phrases most upsetting emotionally. Often the emotional impact of such words can be decreased through a free and open discussion of them with friends or associates.

10. *Capitalize on thought speed*

Most persons talk at a speed of about 125 words a minute. There is good evidence that if thought were measured in words per minute, most of us could think easily at about four times that rate. It is difficult—almost painful—to try to slow down our thinking speed. Thus we normally have about 400 words of thinking time to spare during every minute a person talks to us.

What do we do with our excess thinking time while someone is speaking? If we are poor listeners, we soon become impatient with the slow progress the speaker seems to be making. So our thoughts turn to something else for a moment, then dart back to the speaker. These brief side excursions of thought continue until our mind tarries too long on some enticing but irrelevant subject. Then, when our thoughts return to the person talking, we find he's far ahead of us. Now it's harder to follow him and increasingly easy to take off on side excursions. Finally we give up; the person is still talking, but our mind is in another world.

The good listener uses his thought speed to advantage; he constantly applies his spare thinking time to what is being said. It is not difficult once one has a definite pattern of thought to follow. To develop such a pattern we should:

1. Try to anticipate what a person is going to talk about. On the basis of what he's already said, ask ourself: "What's he trying to get at? What point is he going to make?"

2. Mentally summarize what the person has been saying. What point has he made already, if any?

3. Weigh the speaker's evidence by mentally questioning it. As he presents facts, illustrative stories and statistics, continually ask ourself: "Are they accurate? Do they come from an unprejudiced source? Am I getting the full picture, or is he telling me only what will prove his point?"

4. Listen between the lines. The speaker doesn't always put everything that's important into words. The changing tones and volume of his voice may have a meaning. So may his facial expressions, the gestures he makes with his hands, the movement of his body.

Not capitalizing on thought speed is our greatest single handicap. The differential between thought speed and speech speed breeds false feelings of security and mental tangents. Yet, through listening training, this same differential can be readily converted into our greatest single asset.

For Discussion

1. Nichols raises an important and pervasive problem when he notes that "Quantitatively speaking, America has built her school system upside down."

The least used skills are given the most emphasis and the most used skills are given the least emphasis. Examine your own college catalog with particular reference to required courses. Is what Nichols says true of your college's required curriculum? What changes do you feel should be made?

2. Examine your own listening habits in relation to the ten guides to effective listening. Which of these do you follow regularly? Which do you fail to follow? Why?

3. Most textbooks devoted to effective speaking assert that it is the responsibility of the speaker to make the listeners listen. Nichols, however, argues that it is the listener's responsibility to listen attentively. Whom do you feel bears the primary responsibility, speaker or listener? Is there any advantage to both the speaker and the listener feeling that the major responsibility is their own?

4. Experiment with different systems of note-taking while listening to speeches or lectures (for example, outlining the entire talk, jotting down key words and phrases, noting main ideas). Which system works best for you? In what ways does the effectiveness of the system of note-taking depend upon the type of a speech given?

5. Nichols notes some words which he says serve as "red flags," words which arouse emotional reactions and prevent efficient listening. Of course, those words which are emotion-arousing to one person may not be to another person. And certainly the effects which certain words have change with time. Make a list of those words which are particularly emotion-arousing for you. Why do they have the effects they do? Compare your list with those of other students. What factors might account for the similarities and differences in these lists? Of what value is it for the listener to be aware of the possible causes and effects of these words? Of what value is such awareness to the speaker?

6. It appears that one of the greatest obstacles to improving our listening skills is that we feel that we are efficient listeners—when we want to be—and that listening ability really cannot be improved significantly anyway. Examine your own attitudes and beliefs concerning listening and listening training. What factors do you suppose contributed to the formation of these attitudes and beliefs? Are these attitudes and beliefs the products of rational decision-making or, at the other extreme, are they merely "conveniences" we use to avoid the hard work involved in listening and in its improvement?

Retortmanship:
How to Avoid
Answering Questions

CHANDLER WASHBURNE

In this satirical and humorous essay Chandler Washburne
tells us how to "avoid" answering questions. In so doing
he supplies us with a clearly developed picture of the too
frequently observed speaker who does everything but come
to grips with the issues. Here is the teacher who, afraid to
say "I don't know," attacks our questions as being poorly
phrased or ill-timed. Here is the politician who, afraid to
offend some voters, lets go with a mountain of words but
never gets around to answering our questions. You will
have no difficulty in locating specific instances of the
retortmanship techniques Washburne discusses.

At the risk of being considered somewhat Machiavellian, I would like to deal with some practical methods in use today to defend man from the omnipresent question. Our age, in addition to being atomic, contains further dangers to the individual—in that he is continually bombarded with questions. Atomic bombardment is viewed as evil, whereas we have come to accept the deluge of questions, prying into every aspect of our lives, as a natural event. In a democracy this trend is particularly strong. The idea of equality allows anyone, as an equal, to presume to question you and makes you feel compelled to answer. A clear demonstration of this is seen in politics. Even the President is continually subjected to questioning by newsmen. He cannot revert to a position of superiority, from which he could resist being questioned or not feel the need to give answers, as a dictator might.

All this means that various defenses must be built against the question: methods must be developed by which we can keep the questioner from feeling that his question has not been answered. In other words, we appear to cooperate in answering the question; yet somehow he fails to secure the information which we do not wish revealed—without his being fully aware of it, as this would only lead to another question. (Washington, D.C. would be the world's greatest laboratory.) We leave him (1) satisfied or (2) in a position where he is restrained by politeness from further imposition or (3) in a state of confusion, which prevents him from formulating another query.

A further limitation which has been placed on the methods used here is that the reply should be within the limits of truth. The outright lie is not dealt with here. Distraction and misunderstandings may be exploited, but using the methods that follow should prevent one from

"Retortmanship: How to Avoid Answering Questions." From Chandler Washburne, "Retortmanship: How to Avoid Answering Questions," ETC.: A Review of General Semantics, XXVI, No. 1 (1969), 69–75. Copyright 1969, by the International Society for General Semantics. Reprinted by permission of the editor of ETC. and the International Society for General Semantics.

being faced later with contradictory "facts." This is because these methods are really ways of not responding to what the question is asking about—primarily by throwing roadblocks in the questioner's way, which hinder his progress or get him off on other roads.

There are two aspects of the subject of questions which we have to look at before we begin to think about the answer that is not an answer.

First, we must determine as closely as possible what meaning the question has for the questioner. This is where people frequently make their first mistake. In psychological terms, they project their own meaning into the question, rather than holding it to the meaning of the person who asked it. "What did you do last night?" is not an attempt to find out about the crime you committed then. The answer can very well be a statement about the delightful supper which preceded the act. We do not have to avoid answering, in many cases, if we interpret the question properly.

The second principle in regard to the question grows out of the first. It is limitation of the question to certain restricted meanings—associated with the intent of the questioner. We often lead others just to the area we don't want them to investigate by responding as if their questions were directed to this area. The neurotic person may feel that all questions are focused on his guilty secret and then is constantly on the defensive. Heavily defended areas are likely to draw fire. We thus do not let our opponent—if I may call him that—know what area we are defending; or, even better, we do not let him know that we are defending any area and that he is our opponent.

If we look at the questioner's meaning and limit the question to this, we may find it harmless to answer. If not, we must then proceed in one of several ways to avoid answering the question.

There are three basic methods of solving the problem of not answering: (1) not answering at all; (2) managing the question; (3) managing the questioner. There is a certain amount of interrelationship among them; but, for the purposes of study, let us look at them separately.

Perhaps it should be pointed out that the methods don't have to be used in a particular order. Feel free to work them in any combination, depending upon circumstances and inclination. Remember that retortmanship is an art; to perfect it, practice the ones that are not familiar.

Not Answering at All

Some questions can get along in life very well without a mate. Let us not suppose that every question demands an answer. Many people have burned themselves by picking up a hot question which they might well have left lying. Even if the question seems to demand an answer, there are ways of avoiding making any response at all. The simplest is to ignore or apparently not hear the question. This can be done in some circumstances without impoliteness. Sometimes it is best to wait and see if your interrogator is going to force the question into your awareness.

Or you may cope with the question by means of *distraction*. The commonest tactic is related to the use of cigarettes. You may let time lapse—and the more time, the better—by lighting a cigarette, inhaling, removing ashes, coughing, and choking. If the situation has still not changed, at least you have had time to plan a defense. Pipe smokers have excellent props for delaying action for several minutes. Occasionally one can try things along the line of spilling a glass of water (preferably over the questioner), or the smoker may drop his cigarette into the depths of the sofa. But what if we get beyond all this, into the dangerous quicksands of the evasive answer?

Managing the Question

A method that can be used occasionally is *misunderstanding* the question. Although we have carried out the first step of probing the meaning of the question, we lead the questioner to think that we have misunderstood it. If he asks about Tuesday night, start in by saying: "Well, Monday we had gone. . . ." He waits, thinking you will go to Tuesday, but you never do. It helps if the misunderstanding is not immediately detected and therefore subject to correction. The example starts as if laying background, so you are not stopped. If the questioner asks you to go back to Tuesday after you finish, he seems to be imposing. One can generally count on a question not being repeated, but if it is, additional techniques can be used.

Limitation is closely connected with misunderstandings. Limitation does not call for confirming the question to the interrogator's intent; it requires artfully constructing it to the desired meaning. "How did you like my play?" is answered with, "I particularly noticed the storekeeper's role; it must be extremely difficult." Or, "What did you do Tuesday night?" can be answered with, "We started off with a wonderful dinner. The soup, you can't imagine! It was made of. . . ." Then you discuss foods for half an hour. You have limited the field twice, first to the dinner situation, then to the foods, and you have moved the question into neutral territory.

Another method related to misunderstanding is the *non sequitur*. The politician, when asked about food prices, may end up talking about red-blooded Americans, motherhood, and the Fourth of July. The answer is not logically related to the question. Some when asked a question they can make neither head nor tail of—or do not care to answer—give a five-minute history of aviation or some such thing. In this case, you should usually start in by saying, "As I understand that, it would include . . ." or "I think I can best answer by drawing a parallel example," or "This whole thing seems closely related to. . . ."

In using the non sequitur, it often is advisable to respond with things that have emotional appeal to the questioner. The politician refers to motherhood, and we are drawn up in the associated emotions and forget the question. It helps if the answer is fairly long and wide-ranging, so that the questioner can read his own answer into the material you present.

Another method most useful to the professor, politician, or lecturer, but well adapted to everyday usage, is *restatement*. One takes the question and then, apparently in the interests of clarity, restates it before starting to answer. This is the opportunity to convert the question into one that is easy to answer. The politician may be asked, "Are we going into a depression?" He says, "As I understand your question, you are really asking about the present state of the business cycle. Business income is the highest in history. . . ." He has restated the question and thus secured permission in advance to answer his own version of the question. The questioner is seldom alert enough to notice the skirting of his question when we use restatement and begin by saying, "What you are really asking is. . . ."

A method similar to restatement is that of the *more fundamental question*. When asked, "Are you a socialist?" you can respond that we must first consider a more fundamental question: "What is socialism?" This gives you the opportunity not to answer until you resolve the fundamental issue, and you can avoid this by arguing over the definition. Don't think that what you claim as more fundamental must be so; almost any sort of question can be thrown in as a roadblock, just so you make it seem necessary to deal with the second point before answering the original question.

The *hypothetical answer* or the use of *objectivity* is a method widely used by intellectuals. When asked a question, you answer, "Well, now, I would like to respond to that. Supposing you were in this position, then you might feel this; or again, in another position, you might feel that." A senator might be asked, "Should Red China be admitted to the U.N.?" An answer might be, "Let us look at this objectively. There are a number of courses open to the United States. . . . And, of course, is the United States in a position to prevent Red China from entering?" The essence of the method lies in presenting various alternatives without committing yourself to any specific position.

One of the most interesting operations is the approach I call: *Is this really a question?* Using this method, you proceed to destroy the question. You show that it really consists of three or four questions, or that it sets up a false situation or uses false premises, or that the terms have no fixed meaning. On the question about admitting Red China to the U.N., one answers, "That is really several questions: What is the purpose of the U.N.? What government represents China? What do U.N. members feel?" Take the question, "Do you believe in evolution?" You answer, "It is not really a question of belief, but of the meaning of certain pieces of evidence. . . ." After you break the question down into three or four others, from the various parts you select one you want to expand upon, and you keep from having the question put back together again.

A somewhat similar method is the *moot* question approach. Whether the question is answerable or not, you assert that it is really a point that can't be answered. Taking the Red China question, we answer: "One should not really speculate upon a question of that type, because of the imponderable elements. We cannot know what the future will bring or what position we will be in, and crossing bridges before we come to them is foolhardy."

The *assertion-of-nothing* is often most satisfactory in answering. The proud mother asks what you think of her ugly baby, and you answer, "That *is* a baby!" (But not: *"That* is a baby?") A display of strong feeling and emphasis is necessary to carry this method off, as you seem to be saying something so strongly the questioner feels you must be answering.

Managing the Questioner

This is the counterattack approach. Not recommended generally is putting the original questioner on the defensive, so that he becomes engaged in defending himself. You can point out what profound ignorance such a question reveals, or you can say you feel sorry for anyone who does not understand these things. This is likely to silence him in regard to further questions, but it will also make him angry and vengeful. This technique can be most effective when a friendly manner is used—for example, "You probably didn't mean to ask that, what you would really like to know is. . . ."

Another typical form of counterattack is to answer with *another question*. Question: "What do you think of the Republicans?" Answer: "First we should look at political parties; what do you think of them?" Question: "What did you do Tuesday night?" Answer: "I never do much. You probably had a much more interesting time; what did you do?" Any good evasive technique should always end with a question. As long as you are talking, you are safe. When stopping, pick the topic for the other person in safe territory.

Already in the preceding example we are moving on to an excellent and very subtle counterattack. This is the method of *compliment*. Question: "What do you feel about Marie?" Answer: "How penetrating that you should ask such a question. You seem to have a wonderful understanding of what people are feeling. How did you ever develop this ability?" (Or: "I have long wanted your opinion of her.") Praise is one of the most disarming of methods. That is why the questioner, unless he is particularly alert, is likely to be so absorbed in feelings of gratification that it will be difficult for him to recognize a smokescreen for operations of another kind.

You are now on your own. You will discover many subtle variations and combinations as you work on this. The future of this much-needed science is in your hands.

For Discussion

1. One of the most difficult sentences to learn to say is "I don't know," though clearly there are many times when we simply do not know. What psychological and sociological factors might be responsible for our tendency to avoid confessing ignorance or lack of knowledge?

2. Evaluate the effectiveness of the satire in Washburne's article. Would his argument have been more or less effective if he had simply stated his position and defended it and had avoided the satire? Why?

3. Listen to a question and answer session (for example, press conferences, debates, class lectures) with particular reference to Washburne's techniques of retortmanship. Does the speaker utilize any of these techniques? Are the listeners aware of this retortmanship or do they feel that the questions have been answered satisfactorily?

4. What are some of the factors which might motivate people to avoid answering questions and to employ the techniques of retortmanship?

5. What responsibilities or obligations does a communicator have when, after stating his position, he is confronted with questions? Put differently, what ethical standards should govern answering questions?

6. Does the questioner have any responsibilities concerning the questions he asks or the way in which he asks them? That is, what are the ethical considerations which should apply to the questioner and to the questions?

For
Further
Reading

Here you should find works particularly appropriate for pursuing your study of communication. I have tried to include works emphasizing different aspects of and approaches to communication. Thus, there are included here works by researchers in anthropology, business, engineering, psychology, sociology, and speech. These works, of course, constitute only a small portion of the available literature. Additional references may be found in the articles included in this collection as well as in each of the books listed here. In the annotations I have tried to give some idea of the nature and scope of the work and of the level for which the book seems most appropriate. Those books marked with an asterisk (*) are currently available in paperback.

* Aranguren, J. L., *Human Communication,* trans. Frances Partridge. New York: McGraw-Hill, World University Library, 1967. 251 pp.

Addressed to the general reader this work surveys the field of communication primarily from the point of view of the sociologist. Its numerous photographs illustrating the varied forms and aspects of communication are particularly helpful. The style of the work is extremely awkward, however, and this makes for difficult reading. The book is valuable for its broad coverage and for providing a communication perspective for viewing topics not normally included in the study of this field, for example, art, religion, science, and the like.

Barnlund, Dean C., ed., *Interpersonal Communication: Survey and Studies.* Boston, Massachusetts: Houghton Mifflin, 1968. 727 pp.

Contains thirty-seven articles organized into seven sections: Theories and Models of Interpersonal Communication, Communicator Choice, Social Context of Communication, Channels of Communication, Perspectives on Verbal Interaction, Nonverbal Interaction, and Therapeutic Communication. Each section is prefaced by a thorough and excellent review article which summarizes the research findings to date. Most of the articles are reports of experiments rather than theoretical expositions. Suitable for advanced undergraduates and graduates.

Berlo, David, *The Process of Communication.* New York: Holt, 1960. 318 pp.

This is a nontechnical introduction to the behavioral approach to human communication. Particularly important are the discussions of learning, interaction, and meaning. The Source-Message-Channel-Receiver model developed here has been particularly influential in speech-communication theory and research. This work will provide an excellent starting point for the student interested in communication and communication theory and will provide a suitable companion volume for the more technical works of Cherry and Pierce.

Borden, George A., Richard B. Gregg, and Theodore G. Grove, *Speech Behavior and Human Interaction.* Englewood Cliffs, New Jersey: Prentice-Hall, 1969. 260 pp.

Addressed to the beginning student this book is divided into three sections: The Individual's Communication System, Interpersonal Communication, and Public Communication. Drawing on research and theory from numerous and diverse disciplines this work is particularly valuable as a summary and synthesis of contemporary thinking about communication.

* Cherry, Colin, *On Human Communication: A Review, a Survey, and a Criticism,* rev. ed. Cambridge, Massachusetts: M.I.T. Press, 1968. 333 pp.

Originally published in 1957 and not substantially changed in the revised edition, this work is a particularly perceptive analysis of communication theory. Especially valuable is Cherry's discussion of information theory and of the relationships among the sciences concerned with speech, language, and communication. Although presented as an introduction, this work will be difficult reading for most beginning students. It is well worth the required effort, however.

Dance, Frank E. X., ed., *Human Communication Theory: Original Essays.* New York: Holt, 1967. 332 pp.

A collection of ten essays exploring communication from the viewpoint of different disciplines, for example, anthropology, psychiatry, psycholinguistics, psychology, sociology, and speech. In addition to these this work contains a synthesis article by the editor, "Toward a Theory of Human Communication," and an annotated bibliography of works on symbolic analysis. Many of the readings require prior knowledge of the particular field and of communication and are most suitable for graduate students.

Haney, William V., *Communication and Organizational Behavior: Text and Cases,* rev. ed. Homewood, Illinois: Richard D. Irwin, 1967. 533 pp.

After providing a general introduction to communication and organizational behavior and to the behavioral basis of communication, the author devotes the major portion of the book to explaining and illustrating nine patterns of miscommunication. Although designed primarily for students of business this work is of considerable value to anyone concerned with effective and meaningful communication and with avoiding and overcoming the barriers to communication.

*Huseman, Richard C., Cal M. Logue, and Dwight L. Freshley, eds., *Readings in Interpersonal and Organizational Communication.* Boston, Massachusetts: Holbrook Press, 1969. 496 pp.

Contains forty-five introductory articles concerned with such topics as "The Process of Communication," "Communication and Motivation," "Communication Through Written-Oral Methods," and "Communication through Listening." Although concerned primarily with business and industrial communication, the readings are valuable for persons concerned with any aspect of communication.

Hymes, Dell, ed., *Language in Culture and Society: A Reader in Linguistics and Anthropology*. New York: Harper, 1964. 764 pp.

Contains sixty-nine carefully chosen articles dealing with various aspects of communication from a linguistic-anthropological viewpoint. Of special interest are the articles dealing with expressive speech, speech play and verbal art, and processes and problems of change. Extensive bibliographies are included for each topic covered. Suitable for the advanced undergraduate and graduate student with some background in linguistics and/or anthropology.

Keltner, John W., *Interpersonal Speech-Communication: Elements and Structures*. Belmont, California: Wadsworth, 1970. 422 pp.

This book is divided into two parts. In the first part, "Elements," are considered such topics as messages and meanings, feedback, nonverbal communication, attention and listening, barriers to communication, persuasion, and conflict. In the second, "Structures," are considered interviewing, group discussion, public speaking, oral reading, and theatre. Although a textbook designed for the beginning student, this work has much to recommend it for all students of human communication. Each chapter is prefaced by behavioral objectives and followed by excellent suggestions for further reading and exercises.

*Kibler, Robert J., and Larry L. Barker, eds., *Conceptual Frontiers in Speech-Communication: Report on the New Orleans Conference on Research and Instructional Development*. New York: Speech Communication Association, 1969. 226 pp.

Contains the recommendations of the conference participants concerning issues and responsibilities, research priorities, and graduate instruction in speech-communication. Also included are four conference papers and responses to them. This is essential reading for the student majoring in speech-communication.

Matson, Floyd W., and Ashley Montagu, eds., *The Human Dialogue: Perspectives on Communication*. New York: Free Press, 1967. 595 pp.

A collection of fifty articles concerned with "communication as the path to communion and the ground of self-discovery" organized into eight sections: Communication as Science, Communication as Dialogue, Person to Person: Psychological Approaches, Democratic Dialogue, The

Modern Persuasion, Symbolic Interaction, Culture as Communication, and The Philosophy of Communication. There is something here for everyone.

*Miller, George A., *Language and Communication,* rev. ed. New York: McGraw-Hill, 1963. 298 pp.

This work, originally published in 1951 and only modified slightly for the revised edition, is one of the major contributions to the literature on communication. Of particular interest are the discussions of speech perception, the role of learning, and the statistical and social approaches to communication. This book should be read in conjunction with one which was written more recently in order to obtain a more comprehensive and contemporary view of communication. Particularly recommended for this purpose are Parry's *The Psychology of Human Communication* or Pierce's *Symbols, Signals and Noise.* Miller writes extremely well and makes even the most difficult concepts easily understandable.

Parry, John, *The Psychology of Human Communication.* London, England: University of London Press, 1967. 248 pp.

Divided into four parts (Types of Information, Barriers to Human Communication, Communication Problems in Complex Activities, and Communication as an Area of Psychological Research) this book surveys the implications of information theory for psychology and various other areas, for example, medicine, art, education, literary criticism, and the like. The book requires some familiarity with psychological terminology.

*Pierce, J. R., *Symbols, Signals and Noise: The Nature and Process of Communication.* New York: Harper, 1961. 305 pp.

This is an excellent introduction to the basics of information theory and of its numerous applications. The mathematics are at times difficult but much can be gained even without a complete understanding of the mathematical foundations of this theory. A glossary of information theory terminology and an appendix on mathematical notation are particularly helpful.

Schramm, Wilbur, ed., *The Science of Human Communication.* New York: Basic Books, 1963. 158 pp.

Addressed to the general reader this volume begins with a history of communication research by Wilbur Schramm. This is followed by ten papers each of which considers an important recent development in communication. Particularly appropriate are the contributions by Joseph Klapper on the effects of mass communication, Leon Festinger on cognitive dissonance theory, Charles Osgood on semantic space, and Nathan Maccoby on the new rhetorics.

Smith, Alfred G., ed., *Communication and Culture: Readings in the Codes of Human Interaction.* New York: Holt, 1966. 626 pp.

This collection of fifty-five readings is one of the best single sources of articles on communication. The readings are organized around Charles Morris's concepts of syntactics, semantics, and pragmatics. An introductory section on the mathematical, social psychological, and linguistic theories of human communication provides a broad view of the ways in which communication may be approached. The articles range from relatively easy to extremely difficult and include both theoretical discussions and reports of experimental research.

Smith, Raymond G., *Speech-Communication: Theory and Models.* New York: Harper, 1970. 230 pp.

Provides the groundwork for "a unified and comprehensive theoretical framework for the study of spoken communication" and "a theoretical point of departure for investigating speech as behavioral science." This book is particularly valuable for its review of research strategies and options available to the speech-communication researcher. It is most appropriate for the advanced undergraduate or graduate student.

Sondel, Bess, *The Humanity of Words: A Primer of Semantics.* Cleveland, Ohio: World Publishing Co., 1958. 245 pp.

After an introduction to the communication process, Sondel treats the theories of C. K. Ogden and I. A. Richards, Alfred Korzybski, and Charles Morris. On the basis of these insights the author develops a "field theory of communication." Addressed to the beginning student this book is easy and pleasant reading.

Watzlawick, Paul, Janet Helmick Beavin, and Don D. Jackson, *Pragmatics of Human Communication: A Study of Interactional Patterns, Pathologies, and Paradoxes.* New York: W. W. Norton, 1967. 296 pp.

Concentrating on the behavioral (pragmatic) effects of communication, the authors attempt to build the foundations of a theory of the relations existing between communication and behavior. Although emphasis is given to pathological communication in the examples and cases cited, the theory and its implications are applicable to all forms of interaction. The author's discussion of why one cannot not communicate and their communication analysis of the play "Who's Afraid of Virginia Woolf" are particularly thought-provoking.

Index

1981